MOON HANDBOOKS®

MONTEREY & CARMEL

SECOND EDITION

KIM WEIR

© JUSTIN MARLER

AVALON TRAVEL

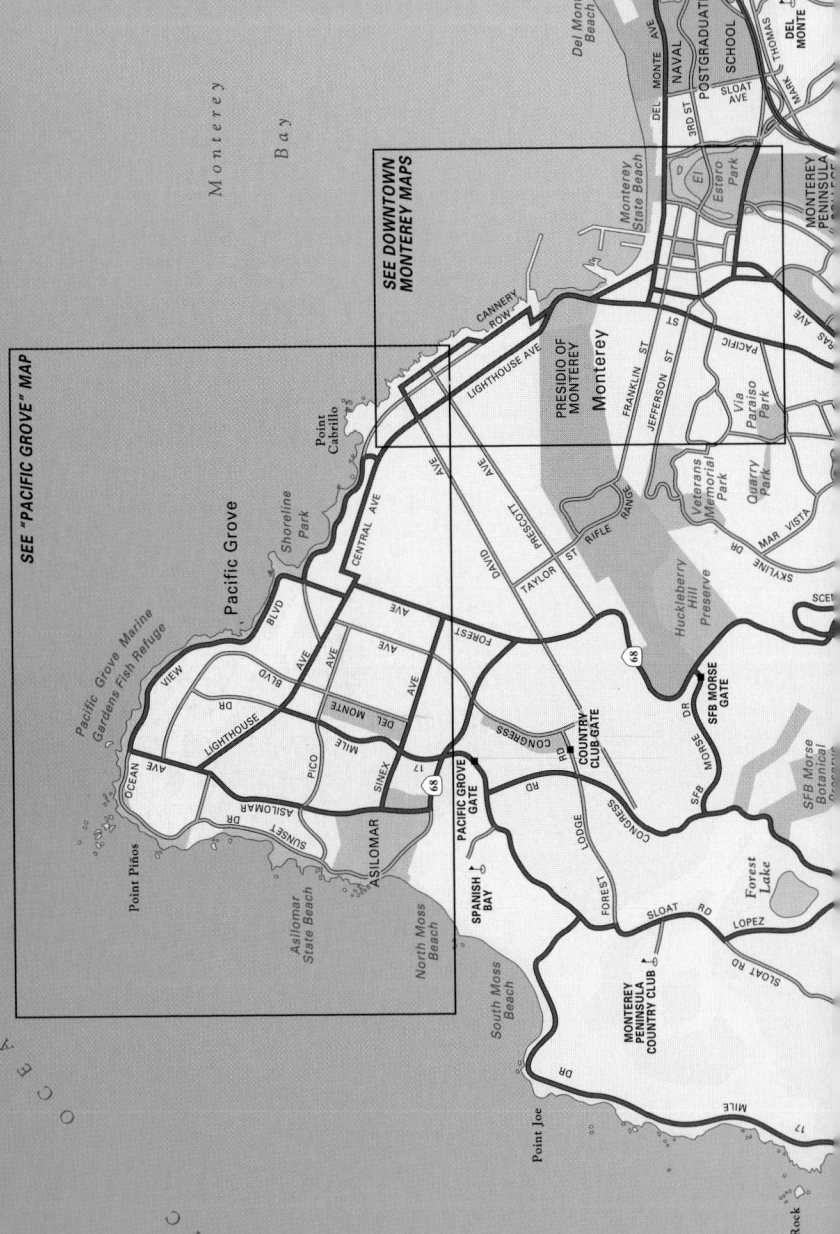

MONTEREY PENINSULA

SEE "PACIFIC GROVE" MAP

SEE DOWNTOWN MONTEREY MAPS

Monterey Bay

Del Monte Beach

Monterey State Beach

El Estero Park

POSTGRADUATE SCHOOL

NAVAL

DEL MONTE AVE

DEL MONTE AVE

SLOAT AVE

3RD ST

MARK THOMAS DR

DEL MONTE

MONTEREY PENINSULA

CANNERY ROW

LIGHTHOUSE AVE

PRESIDIO OF MONTEREY

Monterey

Point Cabrillo

Shoreline Park

Pacific Grove

Pacific Grove Marine Gardens Fish Refuge

CENTRAL AVE

CENTRAL AVE

PRESCOTT

DAVID

FOREST AVE

TAYLOR ST

RIFLE RANGE ST

PACIFIC ST

PACIFIC

RAS AVE

FRANKLIN ST

JEFFERSON ST

Via Paraiso Park

Veterans Memorial Park

Quarry Park

MAR VISTA

SKYLINE DR

SCE

Huckleberry Hill Preserve

BLVD

VIEW

LIGHTHOUSE

OCEAN AVE

SUNSET DR

ASILOMAR

PICO

DEL MONTE

MILE

SINEX

AVE

AVE

AVE

AVE

BLVD

DR

FOREST

CONGRESS

17

68

PACIFIC GROVE GATE

COUNTRY CLUB GATE

SFB MORSE GATE

SFB MORSE DR

SFB Morse Botanical

Point Piños

Asilomar State Beach

North Moss Beach

SPANISH BAY

South Moss Beach

LODGE RD

RD

CONGRESS

FOREST

SLOAT RD

Forest Lake

LOPEZ

SLOAT RD

MILE

17

MONTEREY PENINSULA COUNTRY CLUB

Point Joe

Bird Rock

PACIFIC OCEAN

DR

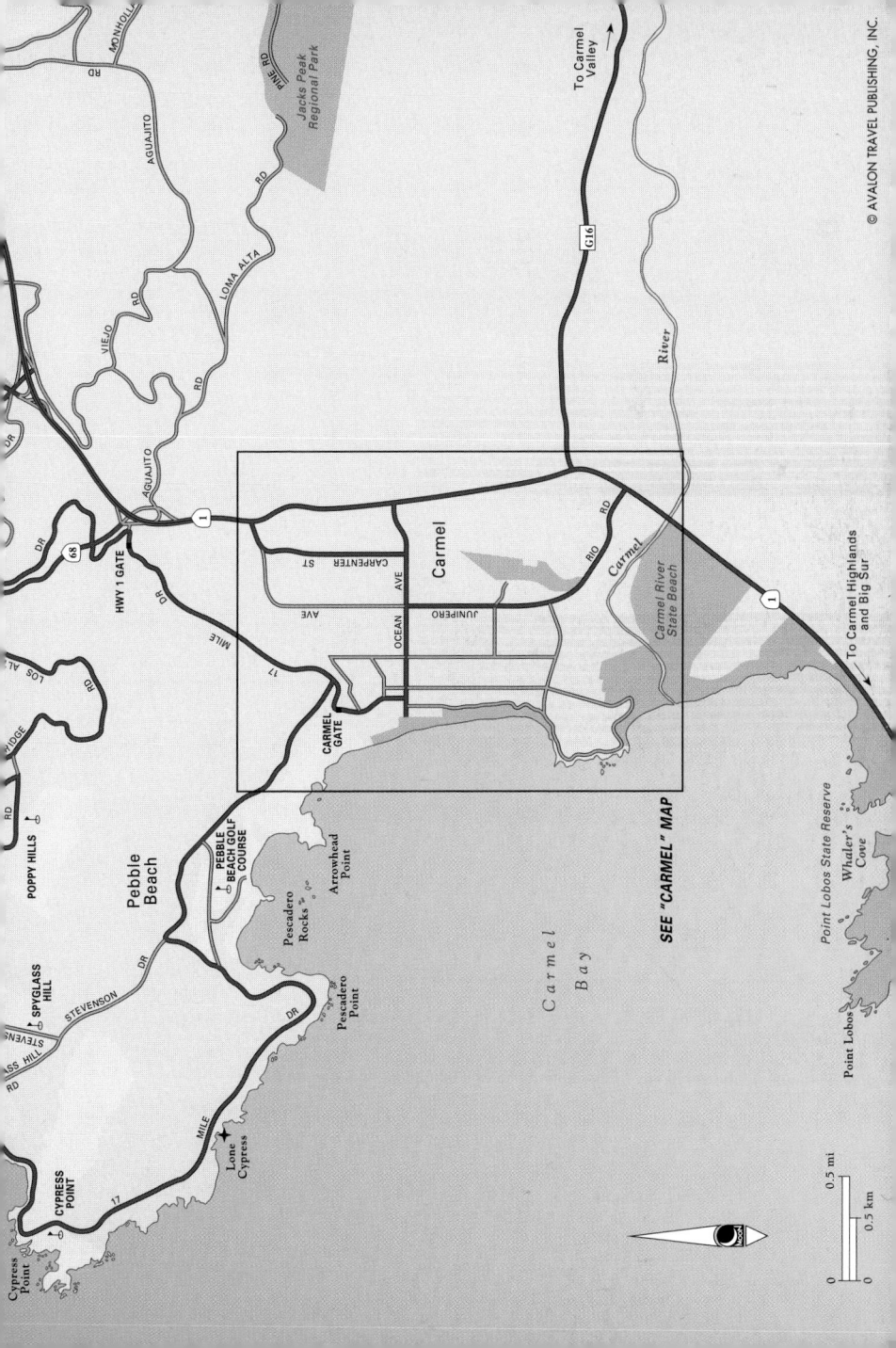

© AVALON TRAVEL PUBLISHING, INC.

CONTENTS

Discover Monterey & Carmel

Explore Monterey & Carmel

Monterey

MAPS

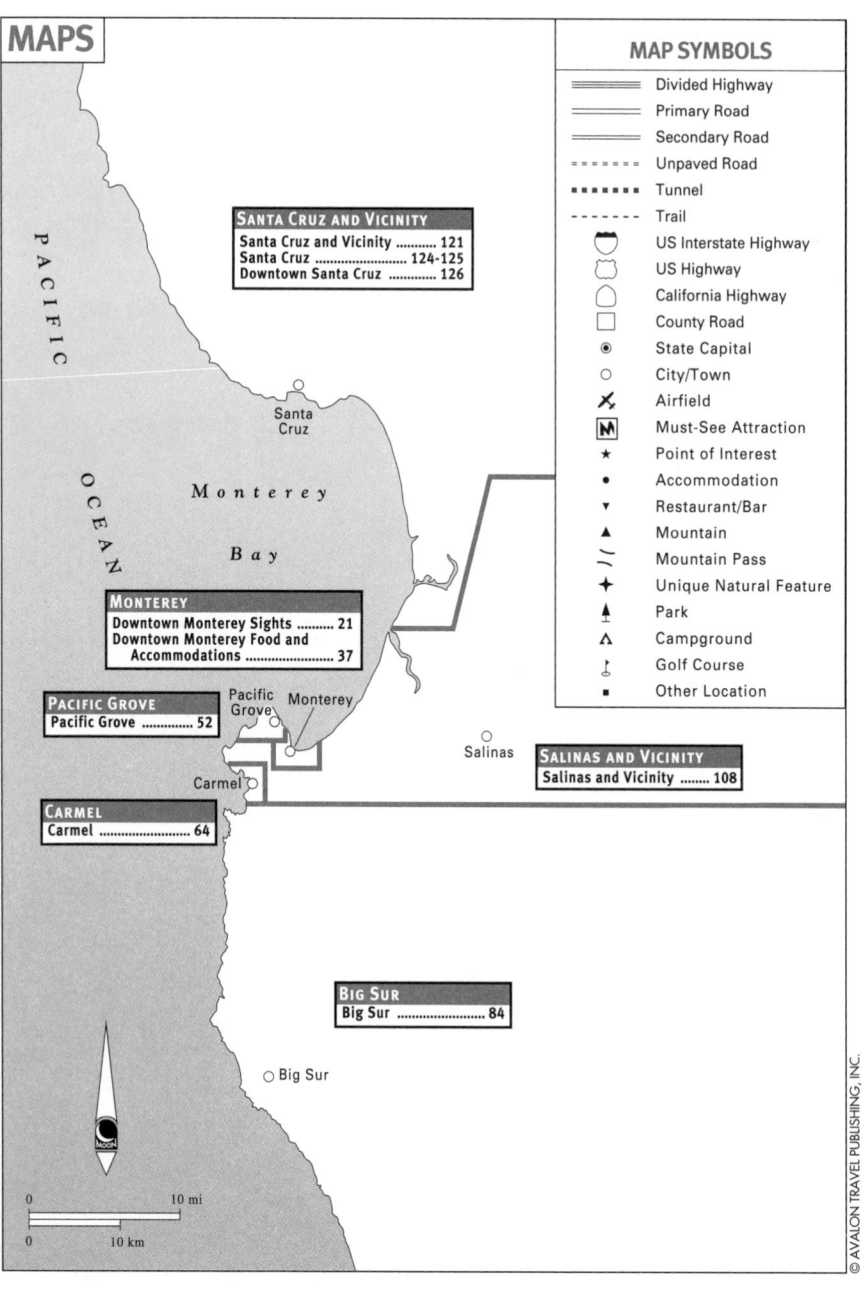

MAP SYMBOLS

═══════	Divided Highway
─────	Primary Road
────	Secondary Road
-------	Unpaved Road
■■■■■■	Tunnel
- - - - -	Trail
⬡	US Interstate Highway
⬡	US Highway
⬠	California Highway
▢	County Road
◉	State Capital
○	City/Town
✗	Airfield
Ⓜ	Must-See Attraction
★	Point of Interest
•	Accommodation
▼	Restaurant/Bar
▲	Mountain
≍	Mountain Pass
✛	Unique Natural Feature
⬧	Park
⋀	Campground
⌶	Golf Course
▪	Other Location

PACIFIC OCEAN

Santa Cruz

Monterey Bay

Pacific Grove   Monterey

Salinas

Carmel

○ Big Sur

0	10 mi
0	10 km

Discover Monterey & Carmel

The only remembered line of the long-lost Ohlone people's song of world renewal, "dancing on the brink of the world," has a particularly haunting resonance around Monterey Bay. Here, in the unfriendly fog and ghostly cypress along the untamed coast, the native "coast people" once danced. Like the area's vanished dancers, Monterey Bay is a mystery: Everything seen, heard, tasted, and touched only hints at what remains hidden.

The first mystery is magnificent Monterey Bay itself, almost 60 miles long and 13 miles wide. Its offshore canyons, grander than Arizona's Grand Canyon, are the area's most impressive (if unseen) feature: The bay's largest submarine valley dips to 10,000 feet, and the adjacent tidal mudflats teem with life.

A second mystery is how cities as different as Carmel, Monterey, and Santa Cruz could all take root and thrive near Monterey Bay.

The moneyed Monterey Peninsula is fringed by shifting sand dunes and some of the state's most ruggedly wild coastline. Carmel, or Carmel-by-the-Sea, is where Clint Eastwood once made everybody's day as mayor. (Inland is Carmel Valley, a tennis pro playground complete with shopping centers. The

Carmel Highlands hug the coast on the way south to Big Sur.) Noted for its storybook cottages and spectacular crescent beach, Carmel was first populated by artists, writers, and other assorted bohemians who were shaken out of San Francisco following the 1906 earthquake. Yet the founding of Carmel must be credited to Father Junípero Serra and the Carmelite friars of the Carmel Mission, built here in 1771, the second Spanish mission in California.

The original version of the Carmel mission was built the previous year, however, near the Spanish presidio in what is now Monterey. The cultured community of Monterey would later boast California's first capital, first government building, first federal court, first newspaper, and—though other towns also claim the honor—first theater. Between Carmel and Monterey is peaceful Pacific Grove, where alcohol has been legal only since the 1960s, and where the annual monarch butterfly migration is big news.

Just inland from the Monterey Peninsula is the agriculturally rich Salinas Valley, boyhood stomping grounds of John Steinbeck. Steinbeck's focus on Depression-era farm workers unleashed great local wrath—all but forgotten and almost forgiven, since his fame has subsequently benefited area tourism. South of Salinas and east of Soledad is Pinnacles National Monument, a fascinating volcanic jumble and almost "the peak" for experienced rock climbers. Not far north, right on the San Andreas Fault, is Mission San Juan Bautista, where Jimmy Stewart and Kim Novak conquered Stewart's fear of heights in Alfred Hitchcock's *Vertigo*. Nearby are the headwaters of San Benito Creek, where lucky rockhounds might stumble upon some gem-quality, clear or sapphire-blue samples of the state's official gemstone, benitoite, found only here. Also in the neighborhood is Gilroy, self-proclaimed garlic capital of the world.

Once working-class Santa Cruz has a slightly seedy board-walk, sandy beaches, good swimming, surfers, and—helped along by the presence of UC Santa Cruz—an intelligent and open-minded social scene. Nearby are the redwoods, waterfalls, and mountain-to-sea hiking trails of Big Basin, California's first state park, plus the Año Nuevo coastal area, until recently the world's only mainland mating ground for the two-ton northern elephant seal.

Like the rest of California, much of the Monterey Bay area is crowded—both with people trying to live the California dream on a permanent basis and with those who come to visit, to re-create themselves on the standard two-week vacation plan. Summer, when school's out, is generally when the area is most crowded, though this pattern is changing rapidly now that year-round schools and off-season travel are becoming common. Another trend: "mini-vacations," with workaholic Californians and other Westerners opting for one- to several-day respites spread throughout the year rather than traditional once-a-year holidays. It was once a truism that great bargains, in accommodations and transport particularly, were widely available during California's nonsummer travel season. Given changing travel patterns, this is no longer entirely true. Early spring and autumn are among the best times to tour the coastline, for example.

Official holidays, especially during the warm-weather travel season and the Thanksgiving–Christmas–New Year holiday season, are often the most congested and popular (read: more expensive) times to travel or stay in the Monterey Bay area. Yet this is not always true; great holiday-season bargains in accommodations are sometimes available at swank hotels that primarily cater to businesspeople. Though most tourist destinations are usually jumping, banks and many businesses close on the following major holidays: New Year's Day (January 1); Martin Luther King Jr. Day (the third Monday in January); Presidents' Day (the third Monday in February); Memorial Day (the last Monday in May); Independence Day (July 4); Labor Day (the first Monday in September); Veterans Day (November 11); Thanksgiving (the fourth Thursday in November); and Christmas (December 25). California's newest state holiday is César E. Chávez Day, in honor of the late leader of the United Farm Workers (UFW), signed into law in August 2000 and celebrated each year on the Friday or Monday closest to March 31, Chávez's birthday. In honor of the nation's most famous Latino civil rights leader, all state offices close but banks and other businesses may not.

How best to combine those notable earthy assets of the greater Santa Cruz–Monterey area, fine wines and rare coast redwoods, without endangering banana slugs and other living things? Drinking, then driving (or hiking) is out of the question. But visiting area wineries to purchase primo fruit of the vine—the bottled edition—is certainly a valid warm-up for an all-day hike, followed by a fine picnic and your own private tasting.

SANTA CRUZ MOUNTAINS WINERIES

Since the late 1800s, these coastal mountains have been as well known for vineyards as redwoods. Regional winemaking got a big boost in 1981, with official recognition of the Santa Cruz Mountains appellation, for wine grapes grown from Half Moon Bay in the north to Mount Madonna in the south. More than 40 wineries now produce Santa Cruz Mountains wines, including eclectic Bonny Doon Vineyard, historic Hallcrest Vineyards, and Sarah's Vineyard, near Gilroy.

For a more personal introduction, attend events sponsored by the Santa Cruz Mountains Winegrowers Association (831/479-9463, www.wines.com /santa_cruz_mountains). The association's Passport quarterly tasting-and-tour events are held at participating wineries on the third Saturday of January, April, July, and November. On a Tuesday evening in February comes the Ultimate Winemakers' Dinner at the Shadowbrook Restaurant in Capitola, a grand meal and showcase for more than 40 winemakers. Come the first weekend in May for the Santa Cruz Mountains Wine Auction benefit, which includes a fine meal and auction on a Friday night—plus the Sunday afternoon grand tasting and auction, which offer the year's only chance to sample virtually all area wines in one place. The Vintner's Festival, held the first two weekends in June, offers "tastes" of special wines, food, music, and art, as well as barrel tastings and winery tours. Come to the Santa Cruz County Fair in Watsonville on the second Saturday in September for the Wine Competition & Tasting at the Fair then return to the fairgrounds in November for the gala Evening of Wine and Roses. Mid-September also brings Capitola's annual Art & Wine Festival.

MONTEREY AREA WINERIES

Vineyards also do quite well near Monterey and Carmel, particularly with chardonnay and pinot noir, but also with cabernet sauvignon, merlot, syrah, and sauvignon blanc. The area supports eight distinct appellations. The region's winning wineries include much-lauded Ventana Vineyards/Meador Estate, just outside Monterey; tiny Chateau Julien Winery; organic Heller Estate Vineyards; and the posh foodie destination, Bernardus Winery, in Carmel Valley.

To plan visits to these and other fine wineries, pick up the free *Monterey Wine Country* brochure and map at area visitors centers, or contact the Monterey County Vintners & Growers Association (831/375-9400, www.montereywines.org). Local winery events well worth showing up for include the mid-February Passport Weekend Valentine's gala and auction, the annual Winemakers' Celebration in Au-

Fortino Winery vineyard

gust, and the Great Wine Escape Weekend in November. If you're short on touring time, many Monterey County wines are available for tasting at A Taste of Monterey on Cannery Row; or show up in April for the Monterey Wine Festival, featuring more than 200 California wineries.

HIKING IN THE REDWOODS

You've packed up some good wine, along with great local picnic fixings or weekend campout supplies. Where to?

Some 20 miles up-canyon from Santa Cruz via Highway 9 is Big Basin Redwoods State Park. Hiking is sublime—especially in autumn, when the days are sunny and the crowds have scattered. There are 80-plus miles of trails here. Shorter, easy trails lead through historic groves of giants and to the onetime site of the Tom Maddock cabin. Moderately challenging trail loops are perfect for nature picnics, or revel in this spectacular place by staying the night. If you're too old to sleep on the cold, hard ground, or just don't carry camping gear, sign up for one of Big Basin's grand tent cabins, which come complete with beds. Such a deal. If you take a more ambitious hike, such as the Skyline-to-the-Sea trail, you can sleep trailside (reservations required for trail camps). Backpackers' camps and equestrian camps are available at Rancho Del Oso.

The Redwood Grove in the dark San Lorenzo Canyon at Henry Cowell Redwoods State Park is one of the most impressive redwood groves anywhere along the central coast. The Neckbreaker, Giant, and Fremont Trees are all standouts. The park's northern Fall Creek section takes in most of the creek's watershed. Since the summer of 1999, the U-Con Trail has connected Henry Cowell to Wilder Ranch State Park on the coast—making it possible to hike, bike, or horseback ride from the redwoods here to the ocean. The campground at Henry Cowell is one of the best anywhere.

Good for rugged hiking and solitude is Forest of Nisene Marks State Park in Aptos, comprising some 10,000 acres of hefty second-growth redwoods on the steep southern slopes of the Santa Cruz Mountains. There are six creeks and more rugged trails than anyone can hike in a day. Bring your own water and food.

In the Monterey Bay Area, it's easy to tour nature—or, more accurately, to participate vicariously—in nature's grand, ongoing tours of California. Due to the bay's deep submarine canyon and the upwelling of nutrient-rich waters, life here is abundant. Monterey Bay serves either as migration corridor or permanent home for 26 species of marine mammals, 94 seabird species, and 345 specific types of fish, plus sea turtles, invertebrates, and marine algae.

Get into the spirit of Monterey migrations at Natural Bridges State Beach in February for the Migration Festival. A perfect place to study Monterey Bay's wildlife is the Monterey Bay Aquarium. When it opens, the new Pacific Migrations visitors center at New Brighton State Beach can also help orient you to this topic.

GRAY WHALES

Most famous of the year's whale migrations is the annual sojourn of the gray whale. Once endangered by whaling, the grays are now swimming steadily along the comeback trail. Early in October, the fat and sassy gray whales—with an extra 6–12 inches of blubber on board, following months of dining in rich arctic seas—start south, taking a 6,000-mile journey to winter in the warmer waters of Baja, Mexico. Pregnant females leave first, traveling alone or in small groups. Larger groups make up the rear guard, with the older males and nonpregnant females engaging in highly competitive courtship and mating rituals along the way. Males, newly pregnant females, and young gray whales head north from February to June, followed by cows and calves between March and July.

To watch migrating whales from land, there are prime "whale vistas" all along the Santa Cruz, Monterey, and Big Sur coastlines, starting near Año Nuevo and continuing south to Point Lobos and Big Sur. Oceangoing commercial whale-watching tours are also offered in various locales.

NORTHERN ELEPHANT SEALS

The migration of northern elephant seals is almost as famous as that of the gray whale. Also hunted to the edge of extinction, northern elephant seals numbered only 20 to 100 at the turn of the 20th century. All these survivors lived off the west coast of Baja California. Their descendants eventually began migrating north to California in winter, and now show up in vast numbers every year along the San Mateo coast, just north of Santa Cruz.

Male northern elephant seals start arriving at the Año Nuevo State Reserve in December, followed in January by the females, ready to bear offspring conceived the previous year. The males battle over status, with the successful alpha bulls fighting to protect harems of 50 or so females from marauders. (Because these are wild, aggressive animals, keeping a 20-foot minimum distance between you and the seals is important.) Public access to the reserve is technically allowed only on guided tours. Yet the first males begin to arrive before the official docent-led tours begin, so it is possible to tour the area unsupervised. Visit the dunes without a tour guide in spring and summer also, when many elephant seals return here to molt.

Another significant "e-seal" colony can be observed just south of Piedras Blancas, about 4.5 miles north of Hearst Castle. Docent-guided tours are available there, too.

MONARCH BUTTERFLIES

Pacific Grove is the best known of the 20 or so places where monarch butterflies winter—no wonder the town is nicknamed Butterfly City, U.S.A. Here, there's a big fine and/or a sentence of six months in jail for "molesting" monarch butterflies. Stop by the Pacific Grove Museum of Natural History to see the facsimile butterfly tree, and come in October for Pacific Grove's delightful Butterfly Parade, part of Welcome Back Monarch Day. From October to February the most popular destination in town is the Monarch Grove Sanctuary, where docent-led tours are offered.

Here and elsewhere up and down the coast, adult monarch butterflies arrive in late October and early November, their orange-and-black wings sometimes tattered and torn after migrating thousands of miles. Yet they still have that urge to merge, first alighting on low shrubs, then meeting at certain local "butterfly trees" to socialize, sun themselves, and mate. Their offspring—actually, their offspring's grandchildren—make their way back to the California coast, without ever having been here.

MONTEREY BAY BIRDS

Winter is prime time for appreciating the grand brown pelican, a fish-eating species known for its spectacular, 60-foot dives into coastal waters. Once endangered by DDT, the brown pelican has made a dramatic comeback in recent decades. More than 90 species of seabirds—nearshore, offshore, and migrants—have been observed here. The best places for bird-watching include Elkhorn Slough, a protected federal and state estuarine sanctuary, where you can also observe the California clapper rail and the California least tern; and Carmel River State Beach, a bird sanctuary for hawks, kingfishers, cormorants, herons, pelicans, sandpipers, snowy egrets, and sometimes migrating ducks and geese.

A few moments standing on the shores of Monterey Bay, a first glance off the edge of the world from Highway 1 in Big Sur—that's all it takes to understand why writers would be drawn to this area.

MONTEREY

Robert Louis Stevenson was among the first to discover Monterey. Stevenson was in town a very short time, waiting for his love, Fanny Osbourne, to disentangle herself from an unhappy marriage so they could marry and return to Scotland, where the writer would pen the works that later brought him fame. In Monterey, the writer lived for several months in 1879 at the French Hotel adobe boardinghouse on Houston Street, now included in Monterey State Historic Park. Stevenson did some writing in Monterey, but most significantly, he collected material—including grand landscapes, real and imagined, which would later appear in *Treasure Island*. Point Lobos inspired *Treasure*'s Spyglass Hill, for example, according to local lore.

More famous in Monterey and vicinity is Pulitzer and Nobel Prize–winner John Steinbeck, author of *The Grapes of Wrath* and *Of Mice and Men*. He was born and raised in nearby Salinas, though his depictions of Cannery Row and adjacent Pacific Grove resonate just as powerfully. Steinbeck was reviled in his hometown during his lifetime, but today, two must-see destinations—the National Steinbeck Center and the Steinbeck Home—pay suitable homage. Also in Salinas is the one-room 1897 Old Lagunita School House featured in Steinbeck's story "The Red Pony."

The Steinbeck family also had a summer cottage in Pacific Grove, where the prodigal son started his life as a writer. A number of area sights are associated with Steinbeck, including El Carmelo Cemetery, Point Piños Lighthouse, and Holman's Department Store on Lighthouse Avenue, where the writer bought supplies. Then there's Cannery Row. In Steinbeck's day, Cannery Row was home to Monterey's sardine industry. In his novel

COURTESY HAWAII STATE ARCHIVES

Robert Louis Stevenson

by the same name, Steinbeck described the Row as "a poem, a stink, a grating noise, a quality of light, a tune, a habit, a nostalgia, a dream," though most would have recognized it as a corrugated collection of sardine canneries, honky-tonks, whorehouses, and waterfront laboratories. The then-American Can Company produced cans for local packing houses, and its original location is now home to the American Tin Cannery Factory Outlets. The former Hovden Food Products/Portola Packing Co. is now the famed Monterey Bay Aquarium.

CARMEL

Carmel also boasts a dazzling literary past, especially given the "Carmel bohemians" who once called this community home: Mary Austin, Sinclair Lewis, and Upton Sinclair among them. The poet Robinson Jeffers was also a local bohemian, though he stood apart from the beginning, making his home outside the city limits. Jeffers and his wife, Una, built their grand, medieval-looking granite home, Tor House (open on weekends for tours), to overlook the ocean, with Jeffers assisting the stonemasons and horse teams in dragging the boulders up from the ocean. Working single-handedly for four years, Jeffers later completed adjacent Hawk Tower, a retreat for his wife and sons.

BIG SUR

Much later, Big Sur attracted its own bohemians—the beat variety. Lawrence Ferlinghetti, who published Allen Ginsberg's poetic anthem *Howl* and later founded San Francisco's City Lights Books, owned a cabin beneath the Bixby Bridge—the focus of the 1962 novel *Big Sur,* by Jack Kerouac. Ferlinghetti encouraged Kerouac to retreat to the cabin to regroup.

Even more famous as a Big Sur literary icon was Henry Miller, author of *Tropic of Cancer* and *Tropic of Capricorn,* who made his home there from 1944 to 1963. Today, visitors can stop by the Henry Miller Memorial Library, a friendly array of Miller memorabilia and writings collected by his good friend Emil White, now also a community cultural arts center operated by the Big Sur Land Trust.

Big Sur's Nepenthe restaurant pays at least indirect homage to another great American writer—and actor and director and producer—Orson Welles, of *Citizen Kane* fame. Welles bought a cabin for actress Rita Hayworth that stood on almost the exact spot now occupied by Nepenthe.

The phrase may be more common farther down the coast near San Luis Obispo, home pasture for all those aspiring agriculture and ag business majors at SLO's California Polytechnic State University. Yet the agricultural heritage of the Monterey Bay area is rich.

SANTA CRUZ

Just north of Santa Cruz is **Wilder Ranch State Park,** a historic dairy farm open on weekends for docent-guided tours. The Victorian ranch house, completely refurbished, boasts period furnishings and serves as a museum. Other restored farm buildings can be explored, including an 1890s-vintage dairy, an elaborate stable, and a bunkhouse/workshop featuring water-powered machinery. Vintage vehicles and farm equipment are scattered throughout. Also study up on local ag history in Watsonville at the **Agricultural History Project,** at the Santa Cruz County Fairgrounds, where exhibits and demonstrations are open to the public from Thursday through Sunday afternoons.

To taste contemporary agriculture, plan your trip around local certified farmers markets, and pick up a copy of the County Crossroads farm trails and wineries map. Outstanding in the field of foodie tourism is **Outstanding in the Field,** a program of events in which local organic farmers and noted winemakers pair up with visiting chefs to offer organic farm tours and unique regional multicourse meals—on well-laden tables that do, in fact, stand out in the farmer's field. **Ag Venture Tours** specializes in winery tours and vineyard picnics in the Santa Cruz Mountains, Salinas Valley, Monterey, and Carmel Valley.

The **University of California at Santa Cruz** also has an agricultural presence. As part of the Swords to Plowshares program, developed in conjunction with UCSC's Center for Agroecology and Sustainable Food Systems, employee-owned **Dynasty Farms** is cultivating a large-scale organic farm on former Fort Ord land just north of Monterey.

CARMEL

In **Carmel Valley,** is another outpost of organic produce: Earthbound Farm, whose 60-acre showcase includes just-picked local produce, as well as veggies, fruits, herbs, and flowers from other locales. The farm's Organic Kitchen can pack a picnic basket with gourmet goodies, or come for low-key adventure in the Kids' Garden, the Cut-Your-Own Herb Garden, and the Aromatherapy Labyrinth.

SALINAS AND VICINITY

You can also tour on your own. **Castroville,** the "Artichoke Center of the

World," grows 75 percent of California's 'chokes—the real kind, the globe variety—though you'll find the tasty thistle growing throughout Santa Cruz and Monterey Counties. Come for the annual Artichoke Festival and parade every May. Watsonville is the mushroom capital of the United States, though its berries are a better reason to stop. An almost mandatory stop is Gizdich Ranch, famous from late summer through fall for its fresh

Get your deep-fried artichokes in Watsonville.

MELISSA SHEROWSKI

apples, homemade apple pies, and fresh-squeezed natural apple juices—but beloved earlier in the year as a "Pik-Yor-Self" berry farm, with raspberries, olallieberries, and strawberries. Another fine pick-your-own bet for berries is Emile Agaccio Farms. Come to Watsonville in early August for the annual Monterey Bay Strawberry Festival, in mid-September for the Santa Cruz County Fair.

Or party hearty just northeast of Watsonville in Gilroy, home of the world famous Gilroy Garlic Festival, held on the last full weekend in July. Garlic ice cream, anyone?

Worth the trip southeast of Watsonville is the charming mission town of San Juan Bautista, also a state historic park. A significant artistic and cultural outgrowth of the farm workers' role in California agriculture is also here: El Teatro Campesino ("Theatre of the Farm Worker"), founded by Chicano playwright Luis Valdez on the United Farm Workers' picket lines as a guerrilla theater troupe.

Big in Salinas, since 1911, is the four-day California Rodeo, held on the third weekend in July—one of the world's largest. Some of the local homage to the West is quite artistic, including the triptych sculpture by Claes Oldenburg titled *Hat in Three Stages of Landing,* and the colossal cutout John Cerney agriculture-related art—some of it associated with The Farm, on Highway 68, just west of town. The National Steinbeck Center honors writer John Steinbeck, as well as the region's agricultural roots in regular exhibits and the special Valley of the World Gallery agriculture showcase. Nearby Steinbeck House does its part to recognize area agriculture as well, now that the Salinas Valley Guild serves up gourmet lunches there, featuring Salinas Valley produce and Monterey County wines and beer. Agriculture has also influenced area architecture. In the nearby town of Spreckels, for example, a company town founded by sugar mogul Claus Spreckels in the late 1890s, sugar-beet motifs still decorate the roof gables of many historic homes.

There are intriguing events here, too, including Vino, Vittles and Verse, a Cowboy Poetry Wine Supper staged in July in Old Town Salinas. In September comes Taste of the Valley, a food and wine festival serving as the centerpiece of the annual local Salute to Agriculture.

Why not start at the top? Of best places for kids, to both amaze and amuse them, the Monterey Bay Aquarium tops the list. The fact that grownups love it here, too, is a bonus. This world-class cluster of fish tanks is the brainchild of marine biologist Nancy Packard and her sister, aquarium director Julie Packard, a nonprofit public-education project launched with the financial and technical help of their parents, Hewlett-Packard computer magnate David Packard and his wife, Lucille Packard. The aquarium's philosophy, "endorsing human interaction" with the natural world, means visitors get a fish-eye view of kelp forests, octopus gardens, drifting sea nettles, galloping seahorses, anchovies going off to "school," and sharks. Kids can "pet" velvety bat rays and starfish, watch sea otters feed and frolic, and begin to understand the powerful kinship they share with all life on earth. In summer, the aquarium offers two-hour guided Fishing for History Walking Tours in conjunction with the Maritime Museum of Monterey.

Discover other kid's stuff along Monterey's Cannery Row, where the Monterey Bay Aquarium is anchored. The Monterey County Youth Museum on Wave Street offers hands-on adventure—interactive exhibits on science, art, and more—of greatest appeal to younger children. These days, older kids will be drawn like so many techno zombies to the nearby Edgewater Packing Company Family Fun Center, packed to the gills with classic and high-tech amusements, from the NASCAR simulator and the virtual-reality batting cage to the Dance Revolution Extreme video game.

©1997 MONTEREY AQUARIUM, RANDY WILDER

Monterey Bay Aquarium

Special-effects amazements come and go, but it's still true that if the kids need to let off some steam, nothing beats fresh air and exercise. Try a long walk or bike ride on the **Monterey Bay Recreation Trail,** or hit the playground. Locally loved, but lesser known among visitors, is the colorful **Dennis the Menace Playground** at El Estero, designed by cartoonist Hank Ketcham and first opened to the public in 1955. Recently renovated, the park is a wonder—from the hedge maze and new giant roller slide to the unique climbing wall.

Looking for an attraction with still more giddy-up? Hightail it to **Molera Horseback Tours** at Andrew Molera State Park in Big Sur, where you can sign on for one- to three-hour naturalist-guided rides along the beach and through the redwoods.

Also fun for family play is Gilroy's fantastic, $100 million **Bonfante Gardens** theme park. The 40 rides and other diversions here are great, from the cool antique car ride and 1927 carousel to the roller coaster, yet what's truly impressive is the way all attractions here are artfully woven into the landscape—a relaxed atmosphere and an inspired horticultural feat.

The three-ring circus of California theme parks presides over the northern shores of Monterey Bay: the **Santa Cruz Beach Boardwalk,** the West Coast's answer to Atlantic City. Open daily in summer and on weekends the rest of the year, the boardwalk is an authentic amusement park, with dozens of great carnival rides, good-time arcades, and other cheap thrills, plus quirky shops and eateries. And if your kids' primary relation to reality is virtual, bring them back to reality with one of the best roller coasters in the nation, the historic 1924 **Giant Dipper,** a gleaming white wooden rocker 'n' roller—truly impressive when lit up at night. Also impressive and a National Historic Landmark is the 1911 **Charles Looff carousel,** one of a handful of Looff creations still operating in the United States. This one has 70 handcrafted horses, two chariots, and a circa-1894 Ruth Band pipe organ, all lovingly restored to their original glory. Tell the kids not to worry. There are plenty of virtual thrills at the Boardwalk. For more actual reality—before it all disappears—take them bowling at **Boardwalk Bowl,** across the street.

Wherever you started your kid-sized Monterey Bay adventure, a great place to end it is with some family camping at **Big Basin Redwoods State Park,** near Santa Cruz. Big Basin is a marvelous place to introduce youngsters to the amazing natural history of coastal redwoods and associated forest life. Every bit as fun, though, is the camping—that roaring campfire, s'mores, the hoot of an owl, and spooky stories. For those who can't imagine laying their tired bones down on the cold, hard ground, Big Basin offers rustic but quite adequate **tent cabins,** complete with beds. Nearby **Henry Cowell Redwoods State Park** offers an exceptional family campground.

Monterey was prominent in the early days of California settlement. Cabrillo spotted Point Piños and Monterey Bay in 1542. Sixty years later, Vizcaíno sailed into the bay and named it for the viceroy of Mexico, the count of Monte-Rey. A century further along came Portolá and Father Crespi, who later, together with Father Junípero Serra, founded both Monterey's presidio and mission. The latter soon relocated to Carmel. Monterey became the first capital of Alta California in 1775 and remained California's capital until 1845, when Los Angeles temporarily wrested the title away. In July 1846, the area was claimed as American, though some of the town's Spanish tranquility survived even the arrival of Yankee farmers, fishing fleets, fish canneries, and whalers. California's first constitution was drawn up in Monterey, at Colton Hall, in 1849, during the state's Constitutional Convention.

Beautifully restored remnants of Monterey history remain at **Monterey State Historic Park.** Excellent examples of the distinctive "Monterey colonial" architectural style—a marriage of Yankee woodwork and Mexican adobe—can be seen here, including at **Larkin House,** a two-story redwood frame with adobe walls, low shingled roof, and second-floor wooden balconies, and the **Cooper-Molera Adobe.**

Other notable Monterey homes include the showcase **Casa Serrano,** once home to Monterey's second *alcade* (mayor) under American rule, now the shelter for a wealth of early California art and antiques. Exquisite **La Mirada,** the onetime Castro Adobe and Frank Work Estate overlooking El Estero, is now home to the local art museum's Asian art and artifacts collection. Nearby is the only surviving building from Monterey's Royal Presidio. The **San Carlos Chapel** on Church Street (near Figueroa), a national historic landmark, is now a parish church and a National Historic Landmark. The chapel's interior walls are decorated with Native American and Mexican folk art.

The 1771 **Carmel Mission** is California's second, onetime headquarters and favorite foreign home of Father Junípero Serra. The stunning Baroque stone church, with its four-bell Moorish tower and arched roof, was completed in 1797. Most of the buildings are reconstructions, nowhere near the size and complexity of the original mission compound. The mission gardens are evocative and inviting, featuring some rare and old-fashioned plants.

The Santa Cruz mission was destroyed long ago, but there is another, very evocative mission town nearby. **Mission San Juan Bautista** and adjacent **San Juan Bautista State Historic Park,** just north of Salinas via Highway 101, evoke the spirit of Spanish California. Come in June to experience mid-1800s mission days at **Early Days in San Juan Bautista,** a traditional celebration complete with horse-drawn carriages, period dress, music, and fandango. Movie fans may remember Jimmy Stewart and Kim Novak in the mission scenes from Alfred Hitchcock's *Vertigo,* filmed here.

Spanish Renaissance architectural styles are understandably strong in California, and just south of Big Sur in San Simeon is one of the world's most remarkable examples: the spectacular **Hearst San Simeon State Historic Monument,** built for media magnate William Randolph Hearst. Designed by Berkeley architect Julia Morgan, the buildings are handsome and huge. The centerpiece La Casa Grande features 100 rooms—including a movie theater, billiards room, two libraries, and 31 bathrooms—and is adorned with furnishings and art Hearst collected from around the world. A number of different guided tours are offered year-round (advance reservations advised).

Explore Monterey & Carmel

Monterey

In his novel by the same name, local boy John Steinbeck described Monterey's Cannery Row as "a poem, a stink, a grating noise, a quality of light, a tune, a habit, a nostalgia, a dream," and also as a corrugated collection of sardine canneries, restaurants, honky-tonks, whorehouses, and waterfront laboratories. The street, he said, groaned under the weight of "silver rivers of fish." People here liked his description so much that they eventually put it on a plaque and planted it in today's touristy Cannery Row, among the few Steinbeck-era buildings still standing.

Local promoters claim that the legendary writer would be proud of what the tourist dollar has wrought here, but this seems unlikely. When Steinbeck returned in 1961 from his self-imposed exile, he noted the clean beaches, "where once they festered with fish guts and flies. The canneries that once put up a sickening stench are gone, their places filled with restaurants, antique shops, and the like. They fish for tourists now, not pilchards, and that species they are not likely to wipe out."

An early port for California immigrants—California's first pier was built here—and now a bustling tourist mecca, Monterey (literally, "the King's Wood") is trying hard to hang onto its once cloistered charm. The justifiably popular Monterey Bay Aquarium is often blamed for the hopeless summer traffic snarls, though tourism throughout the Monterey Peninsula is the actual culprit. *Creative States Quarterly* editor Raymond Mungo once described Monterey as a city "under siege," asking rhetorically: "How do you describe the difference a tornado makes in a small town, or the arrival of sudden prosperity in a sleepy backwater?" How, indeed?

During peak summer months, you can avoid feeling under siege yourself—and worrying that you're contributing unduly to the city's siege state—by using Monterey's public WAVE trolleys whenever possible.

Must-Sees

Monterey Bay Aquarium

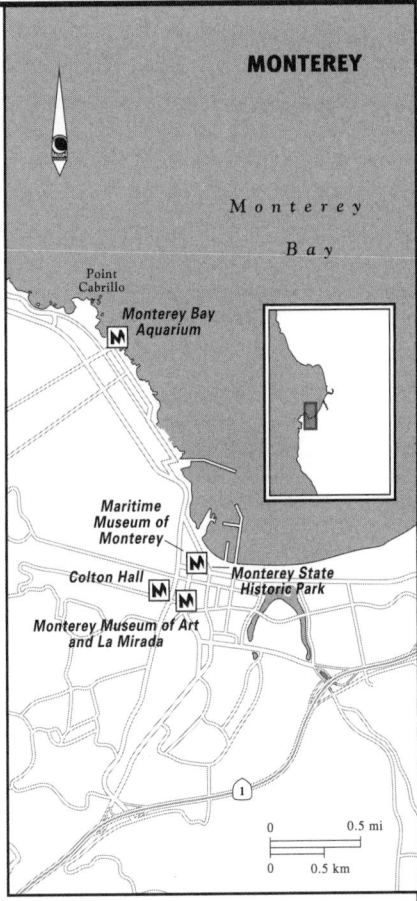

⋈ **Monterey Bay Aquarium:** The fish are back on Cannery Row. This world-class cluster of fish tanks, built into the Row's converted Hovden Cannery, is now the number one aquarium in the United States (page 20).

⋈ **Maritime Museum of Monterey:** Here you'll find the bells and whistles of Monterey history, along with compasses, fabulous photography, ship models, a scrimshaw collection, and the original Fresnel lens from the Point Sur lighthouse (page 26).

⋈ **Monterey State Historic Park:** This "pathway of history" in California's first capital city protects and preserves a variety of fine historic adobes, many of which exemplify the Monterey colonial style (page 26).

⋈ **Colton Hall:** California's Constitutional Convention took place here, at what is now a city museum, during September and October 1849, and the state constitution was drafted upstairs (page 29).

⋈ **Monterey Museum of Art and La Mirada:** Enjoy this excellent collection of regional, California, and Western art before adjourning to the exquisite Monterey-style adobe La Mirada, home to the museum's Asian art and artifacts collection (page 30).

Sights

MONTEREY BAY AQUARIUM

The fish are back on Cannery Row, at least at the west end. Doc's Western Biological Laboratory and the canneries immortalized by Steinbeck may be long gone, but Monterey now has an aquarium that the bohemian biologist would love.

Just down the street from Doc's legendary marine lab, the Monterey Bay Aquarium on Cannery Row is a world-class cluster of fish tanks built into the converted Hovden Cannery. Luring 2.35 million visitors in 1984, its first year, Monterey's best attraction is the brainchild of marine biologist Nancy Packard and her sister, aquarium director Julie Packard. Much help came from Hewlett-Packard computer magnate David Packard and wife, Lucile, who supported this nonprofit, public-education endeavor with a $55 million donation to their daughters' cause. Not coincidentally, Packard also personally designed many of the unique technological features of the major exhibits here. Through the aquarium's foundation, the facility also conducts its own research and environmental education and wildlife rescue programs. The aquarium's trustees, for example, have allocated $10 million for a five-year unmanned underwater exploration and research project in the bay's Monterey Canyon.

The philosophy of the folks at the Monterey Bay Aquarium, most simply summarized as "endorsing human interaction" with the natural world, is apparent throughout the facility. From a multilevel view of kelp forests in perpetual motion to face-to-face encounters with sharks and wolf eels, from petting velvety bat rays and starfish in "touch pools" to watching sea otters feed and frolic, the exhibits enable visitors to observe the native marine plants and wildlife of Monterey Bay up close and personal. More than 300,000 animals and plants representing 571 species—including fish, invertebrates, mammals, reptiles, birds, and plant life—can be seen here in environments closely approximating their natural communities. Volunteer guides, dressed in

Sea otters are one of the Monterey Bay Aquarium's most popular exhibits

rust-colored jackets, are available throughout the aquarium and are only too happy to share their knowledge about the natural history of Monterey Bay.

The engineering feats shoring up the amazingly "natural" exhibits in the Monterey Aquarium are themselves impressive. Most remarkable are the aquatic displays, concrete tanks with unbreakable one-ton acrylic windows more than seven inches thick. The exhibits' "wave action" is simulated by a computer-controlled surge machine and hidden water jets. In the Nearshore Galleries, more than a half million gallons of fresh seawater are pumped through the various aquarium tanks daily to keep these habitats healthy. During the day, six huge "organic" water filters screen out microorganisms that would otherwise cloud the water. At night, filtration shuts down, and raw, unfiltered seawater flows through the exhibits—nourishing filter-feeders and also carrying in plant spores and animal larvae that settle and grow, just as they would in

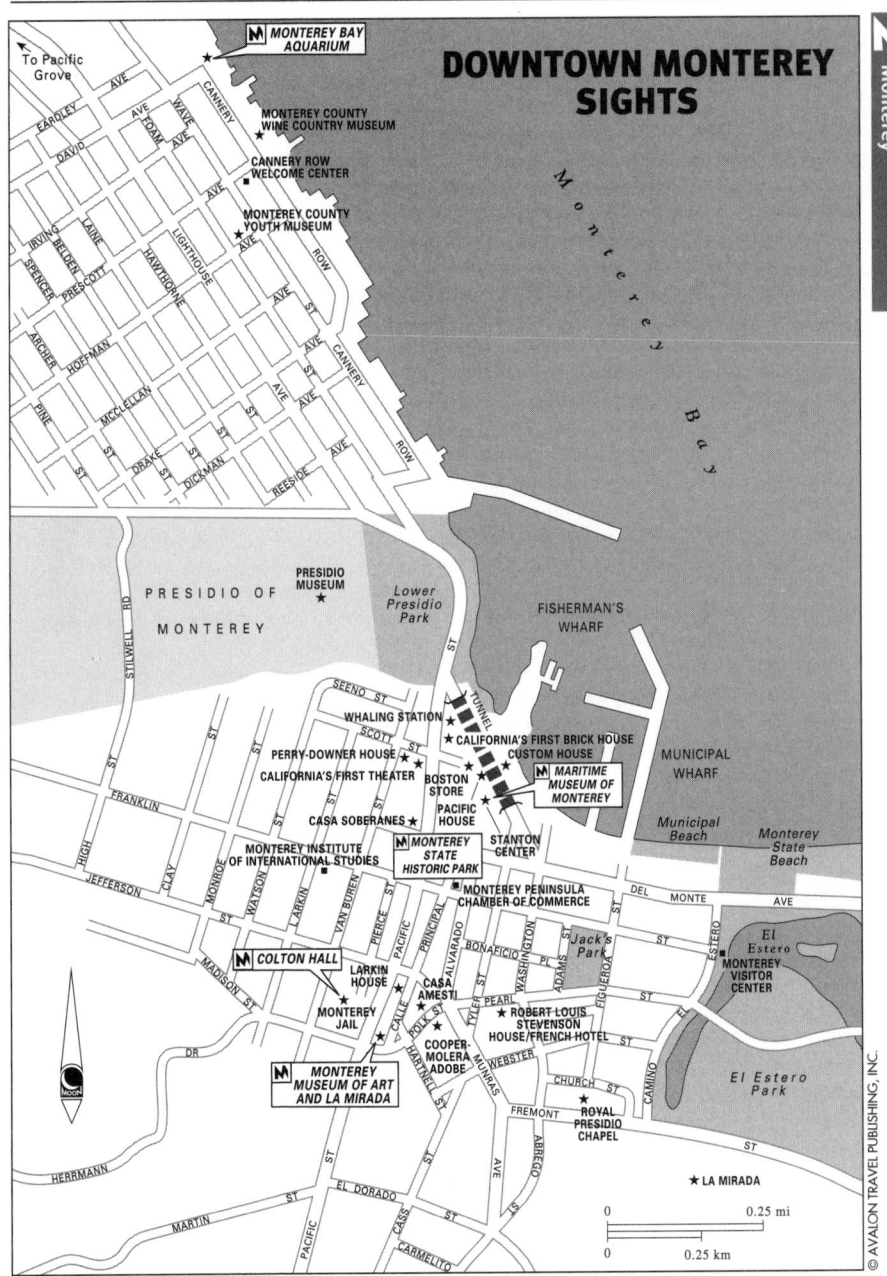

DOWNTOWN MONTEREY SIGHTS

To Pacific Grove

MONTEREY BAY AQUARIUM

MONTEREY COUNTY WINE COUNTRY MUSEUM

CANNERY ROW WELCOME CENTER

MONTEREY COUNTY YOUTH MUSEUM

EARDLEY AVE
DAVID AVE
FOAM
WAVE
CANNERY ROW
LIGHTHOUSE AVE
HAWTHORNE
SPENCER
BELDEN
IRVING
PRESCOTT
ARCHER
HOFFMAN
LINE
McCLELLAN
DRAKE
DICKMAN
REESIDE

Monterey Bay

PRESIDIO OF MONTEREY

PRESIDIO MUSEUM

STILWELL RD

Lower Presidio Park

FISHERMAN'S WHARF

FRANKLIN

SEEN D ST
SCOTT
WHALING STATION
CALIFORNIA'S FIRST BRICK HOUSE
CUSTOM HOUSE
PERRY-DOWNER HOUSE
CALIFORNIA'S FIRST THEATER
BOSTON STORE
MARITIME MUSEUM OF MONTEREY
PACIFIC HOUSE
CASA SOBERANES
MONTEREY INSTITUTE OF INTERNATIONAL STUDIES
MONTEREY STATE HISTORIC PARK
STANTON CENTER

MUNICIPAL WHARF

Municipal Beach

Monterey State Beach

JEFFERSON
HIGH
CLAY
MONROE
WATSON
LARKIN
VAN BUREN
PIERCE
PACIFIC
PRINCIPAL
ALVARADO
BONAFICIO
WASHINGTON PL
ADAMS
Jack's Park

MONTEREY PENINSULA CHAMBER OF COMMERCE

DEL MONTE AVE

El Estero
MONTEREY VISITOR CENTER

COLTON HALL
LARKIN HOUSE
CASA AMESTI
MADISON ST
MONTEREY JAIL
CALLE
POLK ST
TYLER ST
PEARL
ROBERT LOUIS STEVENSON HOUSE/FRENCH HOTEL
COOPER-MOLERA ADOBE
WEBSTER
CHURCH ST

El Estero Park

DR
MONTEREY MUSEUM OF ART AND LA MIRADA
HARTNELL
MUNRAS
FREMONT
ROYAL PRESIDIO CHAPEL
ABREGO
CAMINO

HERRMANN
EL DORADO
MARTIN
PACIFIC
CASS
CARMELITO
IS

★ LA MIRADA

0   0.25 mi

0   0.25 km

© AVALON TRAVEL PUBLISHING, INC.

nature. The Outer Bay Galleries operate as a "semiclosed" system, with water from the main intake pipes heated to 68°F and recirculated through the exhibits. Wastes are removed by biological filters and ozone treatment, and a heat-recovery system recaptures energy from the water (i.e., cools it) before it is discharged into the bay.

In the event of an oil spill or other oceanic disaster, the aquarium's 16-inch intake pipes can be shut down on a moment's notice, and the aquarium can operate as a "closed system" for up to two weeks.

Exhibits

Just in time for the aquarium's 20th anniversary in 2004 came the blockbuster **Sharks: Myth and Mystery** exhibit. In addition to a variety of other improvements, from the appealing new ticket lobby and glass-roofed atrium to the second-story gallery skywalk, more new exhibits have arrived—including the new giant Pacific octopus exhibit in the Ocean's Edge gallery—and just about all aquarium exhibits have had a celebratory spruce-up.

Just inside the aquarium's entrance, serving as an introduction to the **Nearshore Galleries,** is the 55,000-gallon, split-level **Sea Otter Tank.** These sleek aquatic clowns consume 25 percent of their body weight in seafood daily. If they're not eating or playing with toys, they're grooming themselves—and with 600,000 hairs per square inch on their pelts, it's easy to understand why otters were so prized by furriers (and hunted almost to extinction). To spot an occasional otter or two slipping into the aquarium over the seawall, or to watch for whales, head for the outdoor observation decks, which include telescopes for bay-watching. The **Outdoor Tidepool** is surrounded by the aquarium itself on three sides, on the fourth by artificial rock. It is home to sea stars, anemones, small fish—and visiting sea otters and harbor seals that occasionally shimmy up the stairs for a better look at the people. Also here are telescopes for bay-watching.

The Nearshore Galleries are being transformed into **Ocean's Edge: Coastal Habitats of Monterey Bay,** scheduled to open in mid-2005, though many of the original features remain, presented in new configurations. The three-story-tall **Giant Kelp Forest** exhibit, the aquarium's centerpiece and the first underwater forest ever successfully established as a display, offers a diver's-eye view of the undersea world. "Dazzling" is the only word for the nearby **Anchovies** exhibit, a cylindrical tank full of darting silver shapes demonstrating the "safety in numbers" philoso-

SEAFOOD WATCH

Much of the work done by the Monterey Bay Aquarium is not necessarily visible to visitors. Since the mission of the aquarium is to "inspire conservation of the oceans," public education and scientific research are high priorities.

Particularly useful for seafood fans, and accessible via the aquarium's website (www.mbayaq.org), is its *Seafood Watch—A Guide for Consumers,* a regularly updated list designed to help us all make enlightened choices about the fish and other seafood we eat. On the aquarium's "avoid" list at last report, for example, were bluefin tuna from the Atlantic and the Pacific; Chilean sea bass; Atlantic cod; lingcod; orange roughy; Pacific snapper, red snapper, and other rockfish; all sharks; all swordfish; all farmed salmon; and all imported shrimp. Con-

sumer guidance in support of sustainable fisheries worldwide is also available as a wallet-sized card, which can easily be printed from the website.

Specific research initiatives sponsored by the Monterey Bay Aquarium include the Sea Otter Research and Conservation Program (SORAC) and the Tuna Research and Conservation Center (TRCC), the latter in conjunction with Stanford University's Hopkins Marine Station. The Monterey Bay Aquarium Research Institute (MBARI) at Moss Landing initiates dozens of bay-related projects each year, and is also a full research partner in the Monterey Bay National Marine Sanctuary's Research Program. More information on all of these organizations and their programs is available via the aquarium's website.

phy. The 90-foot-long, hourglass-shaped **Monterey Bay Habitats** display is a simulated underwater slice of sea life. Sharks roam the deep among colorful anemones and sea slugs, and bat rays glide under the pier with the salmon and mackerel, accompanied by octopi and wolf eels. The craggy-shored, indoor-outdoor **Coastal Stream** exhibit has a steady rhythm all its own and provides a small spawning ground for salmon and steelhead. In the huge **Marine Mammals Gallery,** you'll see models of a 43-foot-long barnacled gray whale and her calf, plus killer whales, dolphins, sea lions, and seals.

Unusual among the predominantly bay-related exhibits, but popular, is the live chambered nautilus in the **Octopus and Kin** exhibit. Also exciting here, in a spine-tingling way, is watching an octopus suction its way across the window. But to really get "in touch" with native underwater life, visit the **Bat Ray Petting Pool,** the **Touch Tidepool** of starfish and anemones, and the **Kelp Lab.** Visitors can stroll through the **Sandy Shore** outdoor aviary to observe shorebirds.

New exhibits are continually added to the Monterey Bay Aquarium. The stunning $57 million **Outer Bay Galleries** nearly doubled the aquarium's exhibit space when they opened in early 1996. Devoted to marine life "at the edge," where Monterey Bay meets the open ocean, the centerpiece exhibit is a million-gallon "indoor sea," housing a seven-foot sunfish, sharks, barracudas, stingrays, green sea turtles, and schooling bonito—all seen through the largest aquarium window yet built, an acrylic panel some 15 feet high and 54 feet wide, weighing 78,000 pounds. Quite visually arresting in the **Drifters Gallery** is the orange and deep-blue **Sea Nettles** jellyfish exhibit, where one might stand and watch the show—something like a giant, pulsing lava lamp—for hours. Equally mesmerizing, on the way into the Outer Bay, is the swirling, endlessly circling stream of silvery mackerel directly overhead. The best way to watch—you'll notice that young children, not yet socially self-conscious, figure this out immediately—is by lying flat on your back. The **Mysteries of the Deep** exhibit studies the often bizarre creatures that inhabit the murky depths. Seldom seen in an aquarium

environment, the deep-dwelling species in this exhibit include mushroom soft coral, the predatory tunicate, the spiny king crab, and many others—a total of 40 to 60 species at any one time. In addition, daily video programs present live broadcasts from a remote submersible vehicle exploring the depths of Monterey Bay.

Other fairly recent exhibits have included **Splash Zone: Rock and Reef Homes,** designed particularly for families with small children, an interactive tour through two different shoreline habitats; **Saving Seahorses,** exploring the survival challenges of unique fish so popular in traditional Asian medicine; and **Mysteries of the Deep,** an exhibit of more than 40 species of animals collected from the depths of submarine Monterey Canyon, just offshore. **Jellies: Living Art** was a blockbuster on the scale of the new sharks exhibit. Throughout the aquarium, also expect several rotating special exhibits each year. Anytime—or at least anytime from 7 A.M. to 7 P.M.—you can get online and see what's happening via the aquarium's Live Monterey Bay Cam. And don't miss the Shark Cam.

Information

According to the Zagat Survey's 2004 *U.S. Family Travel Guide,* the Monterey Bay Aquarium is the number one aquarium in the U.S., and the nation's number three family attraction. So, do plan ahead. Advance tickets are highly recommended, especially in summer. Call 831/648-4937 or, from within California, 800/756-3737. You can also order tickets via Ticketweb. If you purchase tickets more than 10 days in advance, they can be mailed to you. Otherwise, you can order tickets online as late as 7 A.M. on the day you arrive (assuming they're available); at the aquarium, you won't need to wait in line. Simply present your email confirmation receipt at the will call/group entrance window and walk on in. You also can come on a just-show-up-and-take-your-chances basis—not advisable in summer.

The aquarium is open daily except Christmas, 10 A.M.–6 P.M. (from 9:30 A.M. in summer). At last report, admission was $19.95 for adults; $17.95 seniors; $15.95 youths age 13–17, students with college ID, and active-duty military;

$8.95 for children age 3–12 and disabled visitors; and free for tots under 3.

Free self-guided tour scripts with maps, also available in Spanish, French, German, and Japanese, are available at the aquarium's information desk, along with current "special event" details, including the exhibit feeding schedule. All aquarium facilities and exhibits are accessible to the disabled; an explanatory brochure is available at the information desk. At last report, taped audio tours had been suspended, though docent-guided aquarium tours and tours of the aquarium's research and operations facilities are available for a fee. Guided tours for school groups are free, however. For group tour information and reservations, call 831/648-4860. The steadily expanding **Aquarium Adventures** program offers behind-the-scenes fun like scuba for kids and feeding tours, as well as educational kayaking and sailing trips on Monterey Bay with museum naturalists. In summer, two-hour guided **Fishing for History Walking Tours** are offered in conjunction with the Maritime Museum of Monterey.

The aquarium's restaurant and gift/bookstores are worthwhile. The **Portola Café and Restaurant** (10 A.M.–5 P.M.) has very good food and an oyster bar—the very idea surely a shock to the aquarium's permanent residents—and is fine for a glass of wine at sunset. Along with good books, educational toys, and nature art, the aquarium gift shops have some touristy bric-a-brac and forgettable edibles like chocolate sardines.

For additional information, contact Monterey Bay Aquarium (886 Cannery Row, 831/648-4800, 831/648-4888 for 24-hour recorded information in English, 800/555-3656 for recorded information in Spanish). Or visit the "E-Quarium" (www.mbayaq.org) anytime for virtual tours and information. For more information about the bay, the **Monterey Bay National Marine Sanctuary** headquarters and information center is near the aquarium (299 Foam St. at D St., 831/647-4201, www.mbnms.nos.noaa.gov).

Avoid the worst of the human crush and come in the off-season (weekdays, if at all possible). If you do come in summer, avoid the traffic jams by riding Monterey's WAVE trolleys, which operate from late May into September.

CANNERY ROW AND FISHERMAN'S WHARF

Today, the strip is reminiscent of Steinbeck's Cannery Row only when you consider how tourists are packed in here come summertime: like sardines.

Of all the places the Nobel Prize–winning author immortalized, only "Doc's" marine lab at 800 Cannery Row still stands unchanged—a humble brown shack almost as unassuming as it was in 1948, the year marine biologist Ed Ricketts met his end quite suddenly, his car smashed by the Del Monte Express train just a few blocks away. Today, the lab is owned and preserved as a historic site by the city, and is open for guided public tours from time to time.

Wing Chong Market (835 Cannery Row), Steinbecked as "Lee Chong's Heavenly Flower Grocery," is across the street and now holds a variety of shops. The fictional "La Ida Cafe" cathouse still survives, too, in actuality as the most famous saloon on the Monterey Peninsula, **Kalisa's** (851 Cannery Row, 831/644-9316). Billed as "A Cosmopolitan Gourmet Place," Kalisa's, open since the 1950s, has really been an eclectic people's eatery. Steinbeck personally preferred the beer milkshake.

Nowadays along Cannery Row, food and wine are becoming attractions in their own right. The new, 10,000-square-foot **Culinary Center of Monterey** (625 Cannery Row, Ste. 200, 831/333-2133, www.culinarycenterofmonterey.com) bills itself as a "Fantasy Land for Foodies." Here, food lovers will find a complete food and wine center offering classes in just about everything—from classes for kids and cooking fundamentals to the latest trends, from Low Carb Recipes, Artisan Breads, Chocolate Desserts, and Cooking with Beer to Heart Healthy Cuisine and Sushi Parties. The latter might be particularly inspiring after a tour through the Monterey Bay Aquarium. (Or maybe not.) You can also dine here, at Mary's Restaurant. Gourmet takeout is also available, the choices including an in-house bakery, appetizer bar (including local wines and microbrews), and cheese market. Inside the old Monterey Canning Company cannery, wine enthusiasts can enjoy **A Taste of Monterey** (700

© SUSAN PHILIPS

Cannery Row

Cannery Row, 831/646-5446, www.tastemonterey.com), which offers tastings of regional wines, as well as local produce (there's another located in downtown Salinas); **Bargetto Winery**'s tasting room downstairs (831/373-4053, www.bargetto.com); or **Baywood Cellars** (831/645-9035, www.baywood-cellars.com), across from the Monterey Plaza Hotel.

Wine-tasting or no, adults might escort the kids to the nearby **Monterey County Youth Museum** (M.Y. Museum, 601 Wave St., 831/649-6444 or 831/649-6446, www.mymuseum.org, 10 A.M.–5 P.M. Mon.–Tues. and Thurs.–Sat., noon–5 P.M. Sun., closed Wed., $5.50, free for age 2 and under), a hands-on adventure full of interactive exhibits on science, art, and more. Older kids probably won't let you dodge the **Edgewater Packing Company Family Fun Center** (640 Wave St., 831/647-1769), full of high-tech and classic amusements—from the NASCAR simulator, virtual-reality batting cage, and Dance Dance Revolution Extreme video game to air hockey and pool. Just empty out those pockets and play along.

For more information about Cannery Row, or to seriously trace Steinbeck's steps through the local landscape, check in at the Cannery Row Foundation's **Cannery Row Welcome Center** (in the green railroad car at 65 Prescott Ave., 831/372-8512, www.canneryrow.org). Guided tours of Cannery Row can also be arranged there. The free and widely available *Official Cannery Row Visitors Guide* is well done, historically, and quite helpful. For other information, including shopping and dining options, see www.canneryrow.com.

Fisherman's Wharf

Tacky and tawdry, built up and beat up, Fisherman's Wharf is no longer a working wharf by any account. Still, a randy, ramshackle charm more honest than Cannery Row surrounds this 1846 pier, full of cheap shops, food stalls, decent restaurants, and stand-up bars indiscriminately frosted with gull guano and putrid fish scraps (the latter presumably leftovers from the 50-cent bags tourists buy to feed the sea lions). Built of stone by enslaved natives, convicts, and military deserters when Monterey was Alta California's capital, Fisherman's Wharf was originally a pier for cargo schooners. Later used by whalers and Italian-American fishing crews to

ABOUT DOC RICKETTS

Marine biologist Edward F. Ricketts (Steinbeck's character "Doc") was, according to Richard Astro, the writer's "closest friend and his collaborator on *Sea of Cortez*—his most important work of nonfiction, a volume which contains the core of Steinbeck's worldview, his philosophy of life, and the essence of a relationship between a novelists and a scientist. . . ." Much of the novelist's success, he says, is due to Ricketts's influence on Steinbeck's thinking.

According to Steinbeck himself: "[Ricketts] was a great teacher and a great lecher—an immortal who loved women. . . . He was gentle but capable of ferocity, small and slight but strong as an ox, loyal and yet untrustworthy, generous but gave little and received much. His thinking was as paradoxical as his life. He thought in mystical terms and hated and mistrusted mysticism."

To explore the world according to both Steinbeck and Ricketts, pick up a copy of *The Log from the Sea of Cortez*, published in a paperback edition by Penguin Books.

unload their catches, the wharf today is bright and bustling, full of eateries and eaters. Come early in the morning to beat the crowds, then launch yourself on a summer sightseeing tour of Monterey Bay or a winter whale-watching cruise.

Maritime Museum of Monterey

A good place to start any historic exploration is the colossal Stanton Center (5 Custom House Plaza). Inside, you'll find the Monterey History and Art Association's impressive Maritime Museum of Monterey (831/372-2608, www.montereyhistory.org, daily 10 A.M.–5 P.M., closed Thanksgiving, Christmas, and New Year's Day, $8 adults, $5 seniors and youth, free for ages 12 and under). The lobby **theater** screens a 17-minute state park–produced film about area history—a good way to quickly grasp the area's cultural context. The museum itself is an ever-expanding local maritime artifact collection—compasses, bells, ship models, the original Fresnel lens from the Point Sur lighthouse, and much more—as well as the association's maritime research library, an acclaimed ship photography collection, and a scrimshaw collection. The museum's permanent exhibits, many interactive, cover local maritime history, from the first explorers and cannery days to the present. Special exhibits in 2004 included **A Tale of Two Adobes,** curated in conjunction with the Santa Cruz Museum of Art and History. Guided group tours are available by reservation.

The Monterey History and Art Association also preserves for posterity a number of significant homes, additional outposts of local history. For more information, see the organization's website—and also see *Other Historic Homes,* below.

MONTEREY STATE HISTORIC PARK

Monterey State Historic Park (20 Custom House Plaza, 831/649-7118, www.parks.ca.gov) protects and preserves some fine historic adobes, most of which were surrounded at one time by enclosed gardens and walls draped with bougainvillea vines. Definitely worth seeing are the Cooper-Molera, Stevenson, and Larkin homes, as well as Casa Soberanes. If you have time, see them all.

Most of the park's homes and museums are open 10 A.M.–3 P.M.—though not all buildings are open on the same days—and closed Christmas, Thanksgiving, and New Year's Day. Admission to all buildings open to visitors is free. Also free are guided tours of particular homes (see below), as are general guided walking tours. Walking tours of Old Monterey begin at the Pacific House Museum and are offered on Tuesday, Wednesday, and Friday, as well as "holiday Mondays," at 10:30 A.M.; tours last about 45 minutes. Wear comfortable walking shoes. Schedules for all tours can change, for various reasons, so be sure to call to verify current tour times on the day you plan to tour the park. Historic garden tours are offered for groups only, and are scheduled well in advance; call 831/649-7109 for current fee information (usually $8–10 per person) and to schedule garden tour appointments. To poke around on your own, pick up the free self-guided walking tour map before setting out.

Available at most of the buildings and elsewhere around town, the brochure details the park's adobes, as well as dozens of other historic sights near the bay and downtown. Also stop by the Stanton Center (see above) for the short introductory Monterey history film.

Custom House and Pacific House Museums

On July 7, 1846, Commodore John Drake Sloat raised the Stars and Stripes here at Alvarado and Waterfront Streets, commemorating California's passage into American rule. The Custom House Building (10 A.M.–3 P.M. Thurs.–Mon.) is the oldest government building on the West Coast—and quite multinational, since it has flown at one time or another the flags of Spain, Mexico, and the United States. Until 1867, customs duties from foreign ships were collected here. Stop by to inspect typical 19th-century cargo.

Once a hotel, then a military supply depot, the building at Scott and Calle Principal was called Pacific House when it housed a public tavern in 1850. Later came law offices, a newspaper, a ballroom for "dashaway" temperance dances, and various small shops. Today, the recently renovated Pacific House (10 A.M.–3 P.M. Tues.–Wed. and Fri.–Sun.) includes an excellent museum of Native American artifacts (with special attention given to the Ohlone people) upstairs, and interactive historical exhibits covering the city's Spanish whaling industry, pioneer/logging periods, California statehood, and more. The Pacific House Museum is wheelchair accessible, with Braille interpretive materials and video and audio recordings available. The museum's Memory Garden connects, via wheelchair-accessible gate and pathway, to the city's Sensory Garden.

Larkin House and Others

Built of adobe and wood in 1835 by Yankee merchant Thomas Oliver Larkin, later the only U.S. consul in the territory during Mexican rule, this home became the American consulate, then later military headquarters for Kearny, Mason, and Sherman. A fine pink Monterey adobe and the model for the local colonial style, Larkin House (at Jefferson and Calle Principal, open

daily) is furnished with more than $6 million in antiques and period furnishings. For 45-minute guided tours, meet the guide here on Wednesday, Saturday, or Sunday at 2 P.M.

The tiny adobe home and headquarters of William Tecumseh Sherman is next door; it's now a museum focusing on both Larkin and Sherman. Around the corner is another Larkin building, the **House of the Four Winds** (540 Calle Principal), a small adobe built in the 1830s and named for its weathervane. The **Gutierrez Adobe** (580 and 590 Calle Principal), a typical middle-class Monterey "double adobe" home, was built in 1841 and later donated to the state by the Monterey Foundation.

Cooper-Molera Adobe

The *casa grande* ("big house" at 508 Munras Ave., open daily), a long, two-story, Monterey colonial adobe, was finished in pinkish plaster when constructed in 1829 by Captain John Bautista Rogers Cooper for his young bride, Encarnación (of California's influential Vallejo clan). The 2.5-acre complex, which includes a neighboring home, two barns, gardens, farm animals, and a visitors center, has been restored to its 19th-century authenticity. Downstairs rooms in all buildings are wheelchair accessible, as are restrooms and the Victorian garden picnic area. Stop by the **Cooper Store** here, run by the nonprofit Old Monterey Preservation Society, to sample the wares—unique books, antique reproductions, and other specialty items representing the mid-1800s. For 45-minute guided tours of Cooper-Molera Adobe, meet the guide here on Wednesday, Friday, Saturday, or Sunday at 1 P.M.

Robert Louis Stevenson House/French Hotel

Stevenson House (530 Houston St.) is scheduled to open in 2005, following renovation, but call for current details. The sickly Scottish storyteller and poet lived here at the French Hotel adobe boardinghouse for several months in 1879 while courting his American love (and later wife), Fanny Osbourne. In a sunny upstairs room is the small portable desk at which he reputedly wrote *Treasure Island*. While in Monterey,

MONTEREY'S DISTINCTIVE ARCHITECTURE

Monterey State Historic Park's **Larkin House,** a two-story redwood frame with a low shingled roof, adobe walls, and wooden balconies skirting the second floor, and the **Cooper-Molera Adobe** are both good examples of the "Monterey colonial" architectural style—a marriage of Yankee woodwork and Mexican adobe—that evolved here. Most traditional Monterey adobes have south-facing patios to absorb sun in winter, and a northern veranda to catch cool summer breezes. On the first floor are the kitchen, storerooms, dining room, living room, and sometimes even a ballroom. The bedrooms on the second floor were entered from outside stairways, a tradition subsequently abandoned. Also distinctive in Monterey are the "swept gardens"—dirt courtyards surrounded by colorful flowers under pine canopies—which were an adaptation to the originally barren home sites.

That so many fine adobes remain in Monterey today is due mostly to a long local run of genteel poverty; until recently, few developers with grandiose plans came knocking on the door. For an even better look at traditional local adobes and their gardens, come to the Monterey **Historic Adobe Tours** and **Historic Garden Tours** in late April and/or early May, when Monterey State Historic Park and many private adobes and gardens are open for special public tours.

Stevenson collected *Treasure* material on his convalescing coast walks and worked on "Amateur Immigrant," "The Old Pacific," "Capital," and "Vendetta of the West." He also worked as a reporter for the local newspaper—a job engineered by his friends, who, in order to keep the flat-broke Stevenson going, secretly paid the paper $2 a week to cover his wages. The downstairs is stuffed with period furniture. Several upstairs rooms are dedicated to Stevenson's memorabilia, paintings, and first editions. Local rumor has it that a 19th-century ghost—Stevenson's spirit, according to a previous caretaker—lives upstairs in the children's room.

Casa Soberanes

Also known as the House of the Blue Gate (336 Pacific St. at Del Monte Ave.), this is an 1830 Mediterranean-style adobe with a tile roof and cantilevered balcony, hidden by thick hedges. Home to the Soberanes family from 1860 to 1922, it was later donated to the state. Take the tour—the furnishings here are an intriguing combination of Mexican folk art and period pieces from China and New England—or just stop by to appreciate the garden and its whalebone-and-abalone-bordered flowerbeds, some encircled by century-old wine bottles buried bottoms up. Tours of Casa Soberanes, lasting about 30 minutes, are offered Tuesday at 1 P.M. and Friday at 11:30 A.M.

California's First Theater

Originally a sailors' saloon and lodging house, this small 1844 weathered wood and adobe building (at Scott and Pacific) was built by the English sailor Jack Swan. It was commandeered by soldiers in 1848 for a makeshift theater, and it later—with a lookout station added to the roof—became a whaling station. Wander through the place and take a trip into the bawdy past, complete with the requisite painting of a reclining nude over the bar, brass bar rail and cuspidor, oil lamps, ancient booze bottles, and old theatrical props and paraphernalia. A modern postscript is the garden out back. Now being restored, the building is sometimes open for tours. Call the park for current details.

Boston Store

Built by Thomas Larkin as part of his business empire, this two-story chalk and adobe building, once known as Casa del Oro (House of Gold), served a number of purposes. At one time or another, it was a barracks for American troops, a general store (Joseph Boston & Co.), a saloon, and a private residence. Rumor has it that this "house of gold" was also once a mint or, when it functioned as a saloon, that it accepted gold dust in payment for drinks—hence the name. Since the store boasted Monterey's first safe (still here), it's more likely that during the California gold rush, miners stored their wealth here. These days, it's the Boston Store (at the corner of Scott and Olivier, 831/649-3364) once more, operated by the nonprofit Historic Garden League and themed as if in the 1850s. Antiques and reproductions, including hand-crafted Russian toys and games, are on sale here. The garden league also operates the **Picket Fence** shop.

Whaling Station

The old, two-story adobe Whaling Station (391 Decatur St.), near the Custom House, now maintained and operated by the Junior League of Monterey County, was a flophouse for Por-tuguese whalers in the 1850s. Tours are some-times available (call the main state park number for information) and include access to the walled garden. The junior league also makes the house and gardens available for weddings and other special events (call 831/375-5356 for details). Whale lovers, walk softly—the sidewalk in front of the house is made of whalebone, once a com-mon sight in the U.S. and now quite rare.

California's First Brick House

This nearby building (351 Decatur St., open daily) was started by Gallant Duncan Dickenson in 1847, built with bricks fashioned and fired in Monterey. The builder left for the goldfields before the house was finished, so the home— the first brick house in California—and 60,000 bricks were auctioned off by the sheriff in 1851 for just over $1,000.

Other Historic Homes

Notable historic Monterey homes now preserved for posterity and ongoing public education in-clude a number of homes in the care of the Mon-terey History & Art Association (831/372-2608, www.montereyhistory.org). The showcase **Casa Serrano** (412 Pacific St.) was the home of Don Florencio Serrano, a Spaniard who became Mon-terey's second alcade (mayor) under American rule. Open for docent-led tours 2–4 P.M. on weekends, Casa Serrano features intact 20-inch-thick adobe walls and redwood beams, ceilings, and shingled roofs—and inside, a wealth of early California art and antiques. The 1860 **Perry-Downer Costume House** (201 Van Buren St.,

831/375-9182, 10 A.M.–3 P.M. Tues., 1–4 P.M. Sat.) is another of Monterey's great historic homes, a Victorian wood-frame house built by whaling captain Manuel Perry and his wife, Mary de Mello Silva of Boston. The house, originally one story, has been significantly remodeled over the years. The two-story house now exhibits changing fashion exhibits, such as Crazy for Pais-ley. Adjacent to the Perry House, the restored **Carriage House,** complete with stained glass ceiling, is available for private events. For Cali-forniacs, the **Mayo Hayes O'Donnell Library** (155 Van Buren St.), an impressive historical li-brary emphasizing Monterey and early California history, was originally the 1876 Saint James Epis-copal Church, built at Franklin and High Streets and later moved here for salvation from the wrecking ball of progress. The nearby 1860s **Doud House** (177 Van Buren St.) was built by Francis Doud, an Irish-born American soldier who helped arrange California's Constitutional Convention in Monterey. The association's small, two-story adobe **Fremont House** was long been thought to be headquarters for John C. Fremont when he and his "heavily armed topographers" came to Monterey in July 1846. Now it's be-lieved that Fremont and his wife Jessie stayed here in 1849, when he served as a delegate to the new state's Constitutional Convention.

◼ COLTON HALL

The Reverend Walter Colton, Monterey's first American alcalde, or local magistrate, built this impressive, pillared "Carmel Stone" structure (351 Pacific, between Madison and Jefferson, 831/646-5640, www.monterey.org/museum, daily 10 A.M.–noon and 1–5 P.M., closed Thanksgiv-ing, Christmas, and New Year's Day) as a school-house and public hall. Colton and Robert Semple published the first American newspaper in Cali-fornia here, cranking up the presses on August 15, 1846. California's Constitutional Conven-tion took place here during September and Oc-tober 1849, and the state constitution was drafted upstairs in Colton Hall, now a city museum.

Next door is the 1854 **Monterey jail** (en-trance on Dutra Street), a dreary, slot-windowed

Monterey

Colton Hall

prison once home to gentleman bandit Tiburcio Vasquez and killer Anastacio Garcia, who "went to God on a rope" pulled by his buddies.

MONTEREY MUSEUM OF ART AND LA MIRADA

The fine Monterey Museum of Art at the Civic Center (559 Pacific, 831/372-5477, www.montereyart.org, 11 A.M.–5 P.M. Wed.–Sat., 1–4 P.M. Sun., closed holidays, $5), across the street from Colton Hall, offers an excellent collection of California and regional art—and Western art, including bronze cowboy-and-horse statues by Charles M. Russell. The Fine Arts collection includes folk art, high-concept graphics, photography, paintings, sculpture, and other contemporary art in changing exhibits. The admission price for the Monterey Museum of Art also gets you into La Mirada.

An impressive Monterey-style adobe, the amazing **La Mirada** (720 Via Mirada, 831/372-5477, 11 A.M.–5 P.M. Wed.–Sat., 1–4 P.M. Sun., $5), the onetime Castro Adobe and Frank Work Estate, is now home to the museum's Asian art and artifacts collection. The home itself is exquisite, located in one of Monterey's oldest neighborhoods. The original adobe portion was the residence of Jose Castro, one of the most prominent citizens in California during the Mexican period. Purchased in 1919 by Gouverneur Morris—author/playwright and descendant of the same-named Revolutionary War figure—the adobe was restored and expanded, with the addition of a two-story wing and huge drawing room, to host artists and Hollywood stars. The Dart Wing, added in 1993, was designed by architect Charles Moore.

These days, the 2.5-acre estate overlooking El Estero still reflects the sensibilities of bygone eras. The house itself is furnished in antiques and early California art, and the gardens are perhaps even more elegant, at least in season, with a walled rose garden (old and new varieties), traditional herb garden (medicinal, culinary, fragrant, and "beautifying"), and a rhododendron garden with more than 300 camellias, azaleas, rhododendrons, and other flowering perennials and trees. Changing exhibits are displayed in four contemporary galleries that complement the original estate.

The price of admission also gets you into the Monterey Museum of Art, described above. Come 1:30–3:30 P.M. on the first Sunday of each month for **First Sunday at La Mirada,** offering light refreshments (wine available) and free admission to the gardens and art galleries.

MONTEREY INSTITUTE OF INTERNATIONAL STUDIES

This prestigious, private, and nonprofit graduate-level college (425 Van Buren, 831/647-4100, www.miis.edu, visitors welcome 8:30 A.M.–5 P.M. Mon.–Fri.) specializes in foreign-language instruction. Students prepare for careers in international business and government, and in language translation and interpretation. Fascinating and unusual is the school's 200-seat auditorium, set up for simultaneous translations of up to four languages. Most of the institute's programs—including guest lectures—are open to the public.

PRESIDIO OF MONTEREY

One of the nation's oldest military posts, the Presidio of Monterey is the physical focal point of most early local history. The original complex, now gone, was founded by Portolá in 1770 to protect the Spanish mission (later moved to Carmel) and was located in the area defined these days by Webster, Fremont, Abrego, and El Estero Streets. History buffs, head for 26-acre **Lower Presidio Historic Park** and note the commemorative monuments to Portolá, Junípero Serra, Vizcaíno, and Commodore Sloat, plus late-in-the-game acknowledgment of native peoples. (When Lighthouse Avenue was widened through here, most of what remained of a 2,000-year-old Rumsen village was destroyed, leaving only a ceremonial rain rock, a rock mortar for grinding acorns, and an ancient burial ground marked by a tall wooden cross.) The 31-foot-tall granite Sloat Monument sits at the base of the Civil War–era Fort Mervine, a diamond-shaped fortress. The fort's forward ravelin is all that remains. Also here: incredible panoramic views of Monterey Bay.

The new **Presidio Museum** (Building 113, Cpl. Ewing Rd., just off Artillery Street, 831/646-3456, www.monterey.org/museum /pom, 10 A.M.–1 P.M. Mon., 10 A.M.–4 P.M. Thurs.–Sat., 1–4 P.M. Sun.), at the base of the bluff beneath the Sloat Monument, was once a tack house. So, it seems appropriate that it's now filled with cavalry artifacts, uniforms, pistols, cannons, photos, posters, and dioramas about the U.S. Cavalry and local history, beginning with Native Americans and the arrival of the Spanish and continuing into Monterey's Mexican, then American, periods. Call for driving directions. To reach the museum, it's not necessary to pass through a security checkpoint.

The Presidio's main gate at Pacific and Artillery Streets leads to the **Defense Language Institute Foreign Language Center** (831/242-5000, http://pom-www.army.mil), top drawer for foreign language education.

PITCHING THE MONTEREY PINE

Eons ago, Monterey pines blanketed much of California's coastline. Today, only a few native stands remain in California—and within a decade, at least 80 percent of these trees will be gone, done in by a fungus. That fungus, known as pine pitch canker, was first discovered in Alameda and Santa Cruz Counties in the mid-1980s. Since then, it has spread throughout California via contaminated lumber and firewood, Christmas trees, infected seedlings, pruning tools, insects, birds, and wind. There is no known cure. Afflicted trees first turn brown at the tips of their branches, then erupt in pitchy spots; within the tree, water and nutrients are choked off. The open infections attract bark beetles, which bore into tree trunks and lay eggs, an invasion that hastens tree death. Usually within four years, an infected tree is completely brown and lifeless. The United Nations has declared the Monterey pine an endangered species.

Enjoy the majestic groves of Monterey pine near Monterey while they still stand, endangered as they are both by disease and further development plans. Also take care to avoid being an unwitting "carrier" for the disease; don't cart home any forest products as souvenirs. Pine pitch canker has been found in at least eight other species, including the Ponderosa pine, sugar pine, and Douglas fir, though it appears the Monterey pine is most susceptible. The California Department of Forestry is justifiably concerned that the disease will soon spread—or is already spreading—into the Sierra Nevada and California's far northern mountains.

ROYAL PRESIDIO CHAPEL

Originally established as a mission by Father Junípero Serra in June 1770, this building (550 Church Street, near Figueroa) became the Royal Presidio Chapel of San Carlos Borromeo when the mission was relocated to Carmel. A national historic landmark, the chapel was originally wood but rebuilt with stone and adobe, this version 1791–1795.

After secularization in 1835, it became the San Carlos Cathedral, a parish church. The cathedral's interior walls are decorated with Native American and Mexican folk art. Above, the upper gable facade is the first European art made in California, a chalk-carved Virgin of Guadalupe tucked into a shell niche. To get here, turn onto Church Street just after Camino El Estero ends at Fremont—a district once known as Washerwoman's Gulch.

Recreation

The 18-mile **Monterey Peninsula Recreation Trail** is a spectacular local feature—a walking and cycling path that stretches from Asilomar State Beach in Pacific Grove to Castroville. Scenic bay views are offered all along the way, as the trail saunters past landmarks, including Point Pinos Lighthouse, Lovers Point, the Monterey Bay Aquarium, Cannery Row, Fisherman's Wharf, Custom House Plaza, and Del Monte Beach. The 14-acre **Monterey Beach** is not very impressive (day use only), but you can stroll the rocky headlands on the peninsula's north side without interruption, traveling the Monterey Peninsula Recreation Trail past the **Pacific Grove Marine Gardens Fish Refuge** and **Asilomar State Beach,** with tidepools, rugged shorelines, and thick carpets of brightly flowered (but nonnative) ice plants.

For ocean swimming, head south to **Carmel River State Beach,** which includes a lagoon and bird sanctuary, or to **China Cove** at Point Lobos. **El Estero Park** in town—bounded by Del Monte Avenue, Fremont Boulevard, and Camino El Estero—has a small, horseshoe-shaped lagoon with ducks, pedal boat rentals, picnic tables, a par course, hiking and biking trails, and the **Dennis the Menace Playground,** designed by cartoonist Hank Ketcham. (Particularly fun here is the hedge maze.) Also at El Estero is the area's first **French Consulate,** built in 1830, moved here in 1931, and now the local visitor information center. The **Don Dahvee Park** on Munras Avenue (one leg of local motel row) is a secret oasis of picnic tables with a hiking/biking trail.

For information on local parks and beaches—including the new **Palo Corona Ranch Regional Park,** gateway to Big Sur, set to open to the public in spring 2005—contact the **Monterey Peninsula Regional Park District** (831/372-3196, www.mprpd.org).

JACKS PEAK COUNTY PARK

The highest point on the peninsula (but not *that* high, at only 1,068 feet) and the focal point of a 525-acre regional park, Jacks Peak (25020 Jacks Peak Park Rd., 888/588-2267, at least 10 A.M.–5 P.M. daily) offers great views, good hiking and horseback trails, and picnicking, plus fascinating flora and wildlife. Named after the land's former owner—Scottish immigrant and entrepreneur David Jacks, best known for his local dairies and their "Monterey Jack" cheese—the park features marked trails, including the self-guided **Skyline Nature Trail.** Almost 8.5 miles of riding and hiking trails wind through Monterey pine forests to breathtaking ridge-top views. From Jacks Peak, amid the Monterey pines, you'll have spectacular views of both Monterey Bay and Carmel Valley—and possibly the pleasure of spotting American kestrels or red-shouldered hawks soaring on the currents. The park's first 55 acres were purchased by the Nature Conservancy, and the rest were bought up with county, federal, and private funds. To get here, take Olmstead County Road (from Highway 68 near the Monterey Airport) for two miles.

GOLF AND BIKING

Monterey and vicinity are most famous, of course, as an elite golfing oasis. For information on public access to area courses, which are primarily private—including Clint Eastwood's course (see the *Monterey Peninsula Golfing* sidebar in the *Pacific Grove* chapter).

Otherwise, get some fresh air and see the sights by bicycle. Either bring your own or rent one at any of several local outfits. Bike rentals and pedal-powered surreys are the specialties of **Wheel Fun**

Rentals @ Bay Bikes (on the bike path at 585 Cannery Row and also at 99 Pacific St., just above Fisherman's Wharf, 831/655-2453, www.baybikes.com). Or tool around on a moped, available for rent through Monterey Moped Adventures (1250 Del Monte Ave., 831/373-2696), which also rents bikes.

WATER SPORTS

The coolest place to get ready to hang five or ten is On the Beach Surf Shop (693 Lighthouse Ave., New Monterey, 831/646-9283). Another way to see Monterey Bay is by getting right in it is by kayak. Monterey Bay Kayaks (693 Del Monte Ave., 831/649-5357 or 800/649-5357, www.montereybaykayaks.com) offers tours—bay tours, sunset tours, full-moon tours, and even trips into Elkhorn Slough and along the Salinas River—as well as classes and rentals of both open and closed kayaks. Wetsuits, paddling jackets, life jackets, water shoes, and a half hour of on-land instruction are included in the basic all-day rental price. AB Seas Kayaks (32 Cannery Row #5, 831/647-0147 or 866/824-2337, www.montereykayak.com) offers similar services at similar prices, including guided wildlife and birding tours. Adventures by the Sea (299 Cannery Row, 831/372-1807 or 831/648-7236, www.adventuresbythesea.com) also offers kayak rentals and tours, in addition to bike rentals and bike trips, inline skate rentals, and custom beach parties. Carrera Sailing (66 Fisherman's Wharf at Randy's Fishing Trips, 831/375-0648, www.sailmontereybay.com) offers the comfortable 32-foot sloop Carrera for nature tours, sunset cruises, and chartered sails. Scenic Bay Sailing School and Yacht Charters (831/372-6603, www.montereysailingcharters.com) offers sailing lessons and is also willing to sail off into the sunset. Another possibility for photo and nature outings, dinner cruises, even extreme sailing, is Monterey Bay Sailing & Diving (Cannery Row, 831/372-7245, www.montereysailing.com).

Other boating companies also offer bay tours (including cocktail cruises), year-round whale-watching, and fishing trips. Discount coupons are often available at local visitors information

centers. Recommended for whale-watching by the Monterey Bay Aquarium, Sanctuary Cruises (now located at Moss Landing Harbor, 831/917-1042, www.sanctuarycruises.com) offers weekend and some weekday whale-watching aboard the Princess of Whales, a double-decked power catamaran that holds up to 149 people. And by the way: The Princess fuels up on biodiesel—and even features an ADA-compliant restroom, along with full onboard galley serving organic, free-trade coffee and other goodies, plus full bar. Some weekday trips are offered onboard the Sanctuary.

Other good choices include Monterey Whale Watching Cruises (96 Fisherman's Wharf No. 1, 831/372-2203 or 800/200-2203, www.montereywhalewatching.com); Randy's Fishing Trips (66 Fisherman's Wharf #1, 831/372-7440 or 800/251-7440, www.randysfishingtrips.com), which also offers Point Sur fishing charters; and Chris' Fishing Trips (48 Fisherman's Wharf #1, 831/375-

BEACHCOMBING BY THE BAY

Beachcombing is finest in February and March after winter storms—especially if you're searching for driftwood, agates, jasper, and jade—and best near the mouths of creeks and rivers. While exploring tidepools, refrain from taking or turning over rocks, which provide protective habitats for sea critters (like the monarch butterfly, other animals don't like being molested, either). Since low tide is the time to "do" the coast, coastwalkers, beachcombers, and clammers need a current tide table (useful for a range of about 100 coastal miles), available at local sporting goods stores and dive shops. Also buy a California fishing license, since a permit is necessary for taking mussels, clams, and other sea life. Finally, know the rules: Many regulations are enforced to protect threatened species, and others are for human well-being. There's an annual quarantine on mussels, for example, usually from May through October, to protect omnivores from nerve paralysis caused by the seasonal "red tide."

5951, www.chrissfishing.com), which offers a fleet of four big boats, including the 70-foot *New Holiday*.

Another way to see the bay is to get a fish's-eye view. The **Aquarius Dive Shop** (2040 Del Monte Ave., 831/375-1933, www.aquarius-divers.com), at home here since 1970, is your best bet for rentals, instruction, equipment, and repairs. Aquarius also offers guided underwater tours (specializing in photography and video) and can provide tips on worthwhile dives worldwide. Another possibility is the **Monterey Bay Dive Center** (225 Cannery Row, 831/656-0454 or 800/607-2822, www.montereyscubadiving.com), which offers rentals and lessons, chartered dive trips, guided dives and snorkeling, and night dives.

Adrenaline junkies can get a bird's-eye view of the bay by throwing themselves out of an airplane with **Skydive Monterey Bay** (3261 Imjin Rd., Marina, 831/384-3483 or 888/229-5867, www.skydivemontereybay.com, daily, year-round, $199 per jump). No experience is necessary; after a bit of instruction, you'll make a tandem jump harnessed to a veteran skydiver.

SAND DUNE CITIES

The sand-dune city of **Marina** was once the service center supporting Fort Ord. The U.S. Army base is now closed, replaced by the fledgling campus of California State University at Monterey Bay. So, Marina, the peninsula's most recently incorporated city (1975), is also being transformed. Marina now boasts a new municipal airport, sports arena, and state beach popular for hang-gliding and surfing. On the ground, explore the nearby dunes; they're serene in a simple, stark way, with fragile shrubs and wildflowers. Some are quite rare, so don't pick. The new **Fort Ord Dunes State Park** (831/649-2836), once part of Fort Ord, features a four-mile stretch of beachfront, though not yet open to the public at last report.

The University of California at Santa Cruz (UCSC) is beginning to have a notable local presence, too, starting with its **Monterey Bay Education, Science & Technology Center** (MBEST, near the airport, just off Reservation Road east of the city at 3180 Imjin Rd., 831/582-1020, www.ucmbest.org), a 500-acre research and development technology park. Off to a slow

SUCH A DEAL: SEASIDE AND MARINA

The secret may no longer be much of a secret, but just in case: People who live on the Monterey Peninsula know that prices for both food and lodging can be considerably lower in the "sand dune cities" of Seaside and Marina.

Ethnic eateries abound, most of them quite good. In Seaside, the wonderful **Fishwife Seafood Cafe** (789 Trinity at Fremont, 831/394-2027) is everyone's favorite for seafood. The Fishwife offers quick and interesting seafood, pastas, and other California cuisine standards with a Caribbean accent, fresh Salinas Valley produce, and homemade desserts. (There's another Fishwife in Pacific Grove, near Asilomar.) For more exceptional seafood in Seaside, consider the Salvadoran **El Migueleño,** (1066 Broadway, 831/899-2199). The house specialty, Playa Azul, combines six different kinds of seafood with ranchera sauce, white wine, and mushrooms, served with white rice and beans.

Yum. Seaside's **La Tortuga Torteria** (1257 Fremont, 831/394-8320) is known for intriguing tortas, like the nopalitos con huevo, an egg sandwiched between cactus paddles. But do try at least one of the licuados: milk, sugar, and cinnamon blended with fruit—banana, papaya, mango, peach, strawberry, or cantaloupe. Yum again.

But there are more nationalities to sample in Seaside. For Chinese food, there's excellent **Chef Lee's Mandarin House** (2031 N. Fremont St., 831/375-9551). Or head for University Plaza (1760 N. Fremont), not all that aesthetic, but something of a haven for fans of ethnic eateries. Other fine bets include **Fuji Japanese Restaurant and Sushi Bar** (831/899-9988), with good lunch specials; **Orient Restaurant** (831/394-2223) for Chinese and Vietnamese specialties, notably an abundance of soup and noodle dishes; and **Barn Thai** (831/394-2996), where a great lunch goes for about $5.

start, given the doldrums even in Silicon Valley these days, the center offers extension classes, showcases various community collaborations, and supports "technology transfer"—such as the onsite **Swords to Plowshares** program, developed in conjunction with UCSC's Center for Agroecology and Sustainable Food Systems, in which Dynasty Farms is cultivating a large-scale organic farm on former military lands. Artistic highlights include the **Monterey Sculpture Center** (711 Neeson Rd., 831/384-2100), a bronze sculpture foundry that offers the wheelchair-accessible Sculpture Habitat at Marina, a collection of original sculptures by both local and world-renowned artists scattered throughout the grasslands, live oaks, and chaparral shrubs.

Likewise, locals laud the new **California State University Monterey** (www.csumb.edu) campus—the school's mascot is the sea otter—which has to date taken over some 2,000 acres at Fort Ord (of the 13,065 set aside for it) and is expected to grow to a student population of 13,000 to 15,000 by 2015. The emphasis at California's 21st state university campus is fairly unconventional. The focus here is on mastering subjects, rather than simply amassing course credits. Students are expected to become fluent in a second language, as well as fully computer-literate, and to engage in community service work, along with mastering more than a dozen other essential skills. For information and reservations (required) for 45-minute guided tours of campus, usually offered Monday–Friday at 10 A.M. and 2 P.M. and Saturday at 10 A.M., call 831/582-3518 at least two weeks in advance. Also worth exploring are some 50 miles of trails open to the public, now known as **Fort Ord Public Lands.** The 16,000 acres, administered by the U.S. Bureau of Land Management, are just about the last truly wild areas remaining on the Monterey Peninsula. Two fishable lakes and picnic areas are also available. As fun as it is to be out and about in these wide-open spaces, hikers, bikers, and horseback riders should take care to stick only to authorized trails; military explosives and other hazards are found in restricted areas, and habitat restoration is underway. Some 35 rare and endangered species inhabit Fort Ord Public Lands. For current trail information, contact the BLM field office in Hollister (831/630-5000, www.ca.blm.gov/hollister).

Marina offers great possibilities, too —starting with the new **Marina Everyone's Harvest Certified Farmers' Market,** just west of Highway 1 at the Marina Transit Station (280 Reservation Rd., 831/384-6961, 10 A.M.–P.M. Sun.). Great for quickie authentic Mexican and all the essential ingredients is **El Rancho Market** (346 Reservation Rd., 831/384-5151). Then there's **Café Pronto! Italian Grill** (330-H Reservation Rd., 831/883-1207), where pastas, pizzas, and seafood specialties star. For Korean, head for **Nak Won** (831/883-2302), also in the 330 Reservation complex.

For accommodations, less expensive choices in Seaside include the **Thunderbird Motel** (1933 Fremont Blvd., 831/394-6797, some rates under $50). Good rooms are available for $50–100 at the **Best Western Magic Carpet Lodge** (1875 Fremont Blvd., 831/899-4221); the **Pacific Best Inn** (1141 Fremont Blvd., 831/899-1881); the **Seaside Inn** (1986 Del Monte Blvd., 831/394-4041); and the **Sand Castle Motel** (1101 La Salle Ave., 831/394-6556).

The newest resort on the Monterey Peninsula is in Marina: the plush, 30-room **Marina Dunes Resort,** in the dunes just west of Highway 1 (3295 Dunes Dr., 831/883-9478 or 877/944-3863, www.marinadunes.com, $100 and up). Rooms and suites in these beachfront bungalows feature California King beds, oversized furnishings, gas fireplaces, fully tiled baths with pedestal sinks, and either a private patio or balcony. Extras include a heated pool, lap pool, hydrotherapy, and complete spa services—plus the opportunity to stroll on the beach for miles in either direction. The lodge building offers meeting facilities and the **A.J. Spurs** restaurant and tapas bar.

Seaside and **Sand City,** to Marina's north, share ownership of former Fort Ord and the new CSU Monterey campus—and all three cities, the peninsula's traditionally low-rent neighborhoods, are still feuding with more affluent Monterey, Pacific Grove, and Carmel over future development plans. Opponents contend that proposed new hotels, golf courses, conference and shopping centers, and housing developments in these northern towns will adversely affect limited area water supplies, roads and other public infrastructure, and the environment.

Head inland on Canyon del Rey Road to **Work Memorial Park** and the nearby **Frog Pond Natural Area** (entrance in the willows near the Del Rey Oaks City Hall), a seasonal freshwater marsh home to birds and the elusive inch-long Pacific tree frog. Or take Del Monte Avenue off Highway 1 to **Del Monte Beach,** one of the least bothered beaches of Monterey Bay (no facilities).

Del Monte Avenue also takes you past the **U.S. Naval Post-Graduate School** (831/656-2441, www.nps.edu or www.nps.navy.mil), a navy preflight training school during World War II and now a military university offering doctorates. It's housed on the grounds of the stately, 1880 Spanish-style **Del Monte Hotel.** The state's oldest large resort and once queen of American watering holes for California's nouveau riche, the Del Monte was built by Charles Crocker and the rest of the railroading Big Four. You can tour the university grounds 8 A.M.–4:30 P.M. daily. Downstairs in the old hotel is the school's **museum** (11 A.M.–2 P.M. Mon.–Fri., closed on major holidays), with memorabilia from the Del Monte's heyday.

Worth stopping for in Seaside is the tranquil **Monterey Peninsula Buddhist Temple** (1155 Noche Buena, 831/394-0119), surrounded by beautiful Asian-style gardens and carp-filled ponds. Come in May for the bonsai show.

For the present, at least, accommodations are considerably less expensive here than elsewhere on the Monterey Peninsula. For example, RVers can hole up at the spiffed-up **Marina Dunes RV Park** (3330 Dunes Dr. in Marina, 831/384-6914, www.marinadunesrv.com), which has sites with full hookups (including cable TV), as well as tent sites. It's just nine miles from Monterey, making this a good potential base of operations. And the new **Marina Dunes Resort** (831/883-9478, www.marinadunes.com) is the first new resort hotel built in the greater Monterey area in 20 years.

For more information about the sand dune cities, contact the **Marina Chamber of Commerce** (211 Hillcrest, 831/384-9155, www.marinachamber.com) and the **Seaside/Sand City Chamber of Commerce** (505 Broadway in Seaside, 831/394-6501, www.seaside-sandcity.com).

Accommodations

CAMPING

Right in downtown Monterey, RV campers can plug in at **Cypress Tree Inn** (2227 N. Fremont St., 831/372-7586 or 800/446-8303 in California, www.cypresstreeinn.com, under $50). Otherwise a pleasant motel, the Cypress Tree features concrete for RVers too, plus amenities, including water and electric hookups, showers, restrooms, a washer and dryer, and use of the motel's hot tub and sauna. Also in Monterey, if you're feeling lucky—or desperate—try pitching a tent in year-round **Veterans Memorial Park** (831/646-3865, $20 per night, three-day maximum stay) on Via del Rey, adjacent to the presidio. First-come, first-camped; 30 of the 40 sites can accommodate trailers. Hiker/biker sites are available, too. Facilities include restrooms and hot showers. No hookups. (Best bet: Arrive before 3 P.M. and get a permit from the attendant.)

Outside town on the way to Salinas is the **Laguna Seca Recreation Area,** at the **Mazda Raceway at Laguna Seca** just off Highway 68, with some 93 tent sites and 102 spots for

Monterey

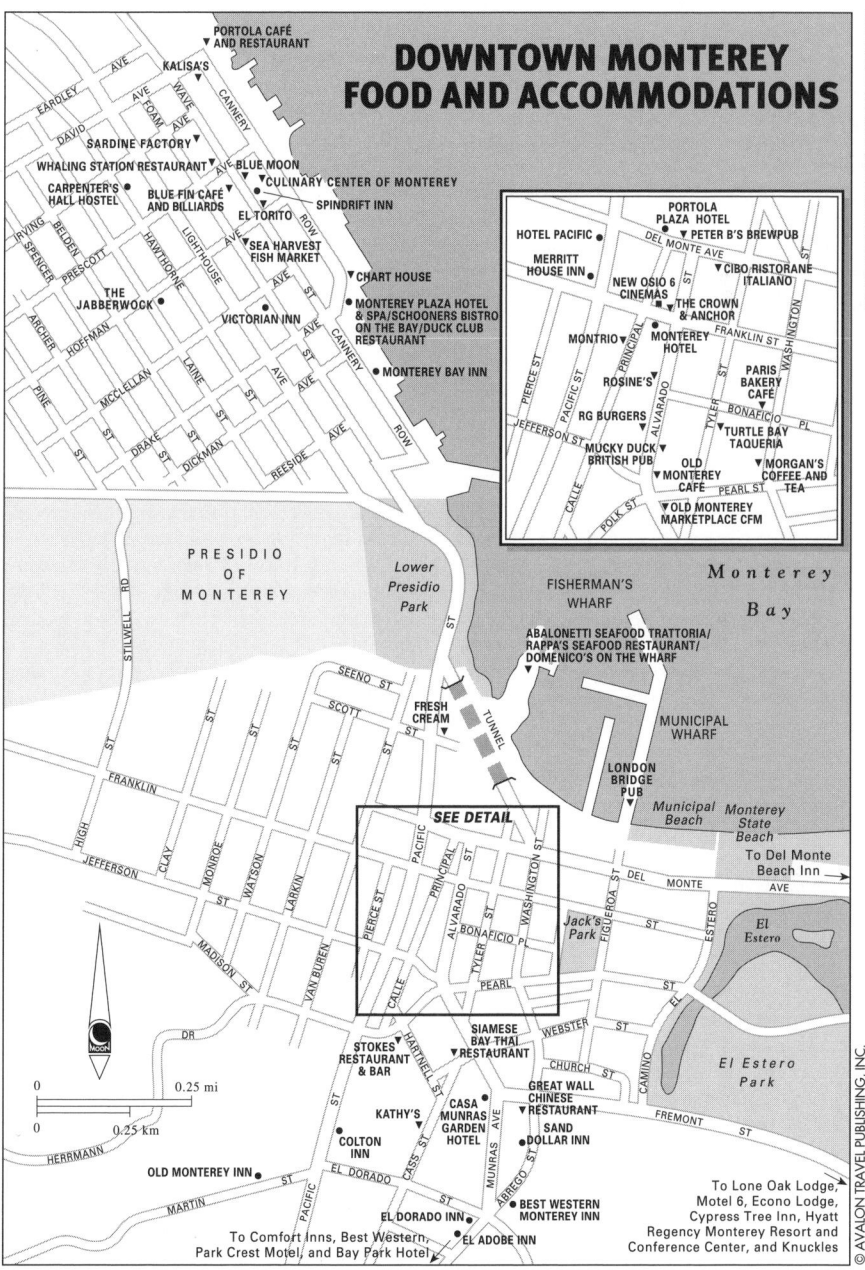

DOWNTOWN MONTEREY
FOOD AND ACCOMMODATIONS

PORTOLA CAFÉ
AND RESTAURANT
KALISA'S
SARDINE FACTORY
WHALING STATION RESTAURANT
BLUE MOON
CARPENTER'S
HALL HOSTEL
BLUE FIN CAFÉ
AND BILLIARDS
CULINARY CENTER OF MONTEREY
EL TORITO
SPINDRIFT INN
SEA HARVEST
FISH MARKET
THE
JABBERWOCK
CHART HOUSE
VICTORIAN INN
MONTEREY PLAZA HOTEL
& SPA/SCHOONERS BISTRO
ON THE BAY/DUCK CLUB
RESTAURANT
MONTEREY BAY INN

EARDLEY AVE
DAVID AVE
IRVING
SPENCER
BELDEN
PRESCOTT
ARCHER
HOFFMAN
PINE
MCCLELLAN
DRAKE
DICKMAN
LAINE
HAWTHORNE
LIGHTHOUSE AVE
WAVE
FOAM AVE
CANNERY
ROW
RESIDE AVE
CANNERY
ROW

HOTEL PACIFIC
PORTOLA
PLAZA HOTEL
DEL MONTE AVE
PETER B'S BREWPUB
MERRITT
HOUSE INN
CIBO RISTORANTE
ITALIANO
NEW OSIO 6
CINEMAS
THE CROWN
& ANCHOR
MONTRIO
MONTEREY
HOTEL
PARIS
BAKERY
CAFÉ
ROSINE'S
RG BURGERS
TURTLE BAY
TAQUERIA
MUCKY DUCK
BRITISH PUB
OLD
MONTEREY
CAFÉ
MORGAN'S
COFFEE AND
TEA
OLD MONTEREY
MARKETPLACE CFM

PIERCE ST
PACIFIC ST
PRINCIPAL
ALVARADO
FRANKLIN ST
WASHINGTON ST
JEFFERSON ST
TYLER
BONAFICIO PL
CALLE
PEARL ST
FOLK ST

PRESIDIO
OF
MONTEREY

STILWELL RD

Lower
Presidio
Park

Monterey
Bay

FISHERMAN'S
WHARF

ABALONETTI SEAFOOD TRATTORIA/
RAPPA'S SEAFOOD RESTAURANT/
DOMENICO'S ON THE WHARF

SEENO ST
SCOTT ST
FRESH
CREAM
TUNNEL

MUNICIPAL
WHARF

LONDON
BRIDGE
PUB

Municipal
Beach

Monterey
State
Beach

To Del Monte
Beach Inn

FRANKLIN ST
HIGH ST
CLAY ST
JEFFERSON ST
MONROE ST
WATSON ST
LARKIN ST
MADISON ST
VAN BUREN ST

SEE DETAIL

PACIFIC
PIERCE ST
PRINCIPAL ST
ALVARADO
BONAFICIO
TYLER
PEARL
WASHINGTON ST

Jack's
Park

DEL MONTE AVE
FIGUEROA ST
ESTERO ST
ESTERO ST

El
Estero

MOON

DR

HERRMANN

0   0.25 mi
0   0.25 km

OLD MONTEREY INN

MARTIN

STOKES
RESTAURANT
& BAR
KATHY'S
COLTON
INN
HARTNELL ST
PACIFIC ST
EL DORADO
CASS ST
MUNRAS AVE

SIAMESE
BAY THAI
RESTAURANT
CASA
MUNRAS
GARDEN
HOTEL
GREAT WALL
CHINESE
RESTAURANT
SAND
DOLLAR INN
WEBSTER ST
CHURCH ST
ABREGO ST

CAMINO EL

EL ESTERO ST

El Estero
Park

FREMONT ST

EL DORADO INN
BEST WESTERN
MONTEREY INN

EL ADOBE INN

To Comfort Inns, Best Western,
Park Crest Motel, and Bay Park Hotel

To Lone Oak Lodge,
Motel 6, Econo Lodge,
Cypress Tree Inn, Hyatt
Regency Monterey Resort and
Conference Center, and Knuckles

RVs. The various campgrounds, some offering private, oak-shaded sites, look down on the track. The park is not recommended for light sleepers when the races are on. For information and reservations during non-race times, contact Laguna Seca County Recreation Area in Salinas (831/422-6138 for information, 831/755-4899 for reservations, or 888/588-2267, www.co.monterey.ca.us/parks or www/laguna-seca.com). When races aren't scheduled, the day-use fee is $6 per day. RV camping is $30 per night, and tent sites are $22 per night (each plus $5 reservation fee). To reserve camping during race periods, call the ticket office (800/327-7322). Premier and Reserved sites are reservable in advance; others are first-come, first-camped.

For other camping options, head south to Carmel.

HOSTELS

It's happened at last: Monterey's onetime Carpenter's Union Hall, now the town's long-awaited 45-bed hostel, is finally open. Thanks to the Monterey Hostel Society, travelers can now bunk in separate women's and men's dorms (shared bathrooms) just four blocks from Cannery Row. Among its other features, the HI-USA **Carpenter's Hall Hostel** (778 Hawthorne St., 831/649-0375, www.montereyhostel.org, info@montereyhostel.org, office open 8–10 A.M. and 5–10 P.M., under $50) offers the latest in water conservation technology—token-operated showers, metered faucets, ultra-low-flow, half-gallon Microphor toilets, and water-saving appliances. The price includes a pillow, sheets, and a blanket; bring your own sleep sack for a $1 discount (no sleeping bags allowed). Family rooms and private "group rooms" (for up to 35 people) are available. For groups, discounts on overnight fees are available for youth and children. Given the area's popularity, advance reservations are usually essential. (Call, email, or see the website for reservation details.) Reserve with personal check or Visa/MasterCard. Free onsite parking. To avoid adding to local traffic woes, leave your vehicle here and take public transportation.

Now that there is genuinely affordable accommodation available in Monterey, there are debts to be paid. Please express your gratitude by sending an extra contribution to the Monterey Hostel Fund, in care of the hostel.

If you'll be continuing north, excellent HI-USA hostels are available in Santa Cruz, just north, and also farther along the San Mateo County coastline. If you're heading south, there's also a great hostel in San Luis Obispo. For current details on these and other hostels in California, see http://hostelweb.com/california.htm.

MOTELS AND HOTELS

Current complete listings of accommodations (including prices) and restaurants in Monterey proper are available free from the convention and visitors bureau. Discounts of 50 percent or more are available at many inns, hotels, and motels during off-season promotions.

Monterey has a reasonable supply of decent motels, with most rooms in the $100–150 range, but many are much more. Most offer all modern amenities, and many establishments provide complimentary breakfast and other extra services. If you're here for the Jazz Festival, plan to stay at a motel in Marina or Seaside and vicinity, or on Fremont Street (motel and fast-food row), just a block from the fairgrounds. Motels on Munras are generally pricier. Be on the lookout, especially during high season, for "floating" motel rates, wherein the price may double or triple long *after* you've made your reservation. When in doubt, request written reservation and price confirmation.

For assistance in booking midrange to high-end accommodations in and around Monterey, contact **Resort II Me Room Finders** (800/757-5646, www.resort2me.com), a firm with a good track record in matching peninsula visitors with appropriate local lodgings.

$50–100

Motels with at least some lower-priced rooms include the **Lone Oak Lodge** (2221 N. Fremont St., 831/372-4924 or 800/283-5663, www.loneoaklodge.com) and pleasant **El Adobe Inn** (936 Munras Ave., 831/372-5409, www.el-adobe-inn.com); amenities include in-room coffeemakers and refrigerators. Another possibility is the **Motel 6** (2124 N. Fremont St., 831/646-8585), which is clean, has a pool, and isn't far from the downtown action—reachable on any eastbound bus (take number 1). It's popular, so make reservations six months or more in advance, or stop by at 11 A.M. or so to check for cancellations. There's another Motel 6 in the same price range (a bit less expensive) just outside Monterey proper (100 Reservation Rd., Marina, 831/384-1000). For reservations at any Motel 6, call 800/466-8356 or try www.motel6.com.

Quite nice, quite reasonably priced, and surprisingly homey are the locally owned Comfort Inns on Munras Avenue. **Comfort Inn-Carmel Hill** (1252 Munras Ave., 831/372-2908) features 30 cheery rooms with the usual amenities and electronic door locks. Adjacent is the **Comfort Inn-Munras** (1262 Munras Ave., 831/372-8088 or 888/970-7666 for reservations at either, www.stayatmonterey.com). Both are close enough—but not too close—to local attractions, especially if you look forward to some vigorous walking. The best thing about the location, which is quite close to Highway 1 and the Del Monte Shopping Center, is its walkability. Directly across the way, flanking Munras all the way back downtown to its junction with Abrego, is long, narrow **Dan Dahvee Park,** with its pleasant trees, flowers, birds, and walking paths.

Other motel options include the 15-room **El Dorado Inn** (900 Munras Ave., 831/373-2921) and the very nice **Best Western Park Crest Motel** (1100 Munras Ave., 831/372-4576 or 888/829-0092, www.bestwesterncalifornia.com), where rooms include in-room coffeemakers and refrigerators, and extras include TVs with free HBO, a pool, a hot tub, and free continental breakfast. There are also a number of good motels off Fremont.

$100–150

Most of the area's less expensive motels, including those listed above, also offer pricier rooms. Centrally located near Highway 1 and within easy reach of all area towns is the **Bay Park Hotel** (1425 Munras Ave., 831/649-1020 or 800/338-3564, www.bayparkhotel.com), featuring in-room

coffeemakers, refrigerators, and hair dryers, plus onsite extras, including fitness facilities and a restaurant, pool, and hot tub. Rates for family-friendly rooms with two double beds can drop to $79. The nonsmoking, downtown **Best Western Monterey Inn** (825 Abrego St., 831/373-5345 or 877/373-5345, www.montereyinnca.com) is quite pleasant, with 80 spacious rooms—some with fireplaces, all with in-room coffeemakers and refrigerators. The motel also has a heated pool and hot tub. Another solid bet is the nearby **Sand Dollar Inn** (755 Abrego St., 831/372-7551 or 800/982-1986, www.sanddollarinn.com), with pool, hot tub, and some fireplace rooms.

$150–250

Set to debut in September 2005, following an $8 million renovation and expansion, downtown's historic **Monterey Hotel** (831/375-3184 or 800/966-6490 for reservations, www.montereyhotel.com) now boasts a main entrance on Calle Principal, in addition to its previous address at 406 Alvarado Street, and is all set for a spiff centennial. The new Monterey Hotel shows off much of its original 1904 Victorian bone structure, yet now includes a total of 69 rooms (an increase of 24), a 1,200-square-foot fitness facility, additional meeting space, and extra parking. There's also a new pedestrian walkway linking Alvarado and Calle Principal. Rooms feature custom-made armoires (with TV sets), hand-carved furnishings, plantation shutters, ceiling fans, telephones, private marble baths with tub showers, and tasteful yet subtle decorating touches, all individualized. Every floor features an outdoor landing and deck area, and the third-floor interior landing boasts an intimate atrium parlor lit by a skylight. See the website for renovation news.

Offering good value in comfortable accommodations on acres of lovely landscape is the **Casa Munras Garden Hotel** (700 Munras Ave., 831/375-2411, 800/222-2446 in California, or 800/222-2558 nationwide, www.casamunras-hotel.com), conveniently located close to historic downtown. A restaurant is onsite.

Another good deal, right downtown, is the attractive and accommodating **Colton Inn** (707

Pacific St., 831/649-6500 or 800/848-7007, www.coltoninn.com), where the basics include VCRs with free videos and phones with data ports, and extras include a sauna and sundeck. Some rooms have real fireplaces and whirlpool tubs. The comfortable **M Portola Plaza Hotel** (formerly the Doubletree Hotel, 2 Portola Plaza, adjacent to the Convention Center downtown at Pacific St. and Del Monte, 831/649-4511 or 888/222-5851 for reservations, www.portolaplazahotel.com) boasts an onsite brewpub, restaurant, bar, full-service fitness center, 370 rooms, and 10 suites—all brightly redecorated in fall 2002. Plus it's convenient to just about everything, especially if you prefer walking to the sights. Some great specials and packages are available, too.

$250 and Up

For definite bayside luxury, head for the 290-room, Craftsman-style **M Monterey Plaza Hotel & Spa** (400 Cannery Row, 831/646-1700 or 800/368-2468, www.woodsidehotels.com). The Monterey Plaza's fine accommodations include Italian Empire and 18th-century Chinese furnishings, every convenience (even a complete fitness center with six Nautilus stations), and exceptional food service, including the Duck Club, one of the area's finer restaurants. The 15 Grand Suites feature grand pianos. Great onsite restaurants and rental bikes and kayaks are available. Recently, the Monterey Plaza added a $6 million, 10,000-square-foot, Eurostyle, rooftop full-service spa and three spa-level suites. Coming soon to the neighborhood is a new IMAX theater.

Also deluxe and downtown is the contemporary, faux-adobe-style **Hotel Pacific** (300 Pacific St., 831/373-5700 or 800/554-5542, www.hotelpacific.com). All rooms are suites and feature hardwood floors, separate sitting areas, balconies or decks, fireplaces, wet bars, honor bars, in-room coffeemakers, irons, ironing boards, two TVs, two phones, and terrycloth bathrobes. The tiled bathrooms have a separate shower and tub. Some rooms have a view. Continental breakfast, afternoon tea, and free underground parking are included.

Surprisingly appealing is the **Spindrift Inn** a onetime bordello (652 Cannery Row at Hawthorne, 831/646-8900 or 800/841-1879,www.spindriftinn.com). Rooms feature hardwood floors, wood-burning fireplaces, TVs with VCRs, second telephones in the tiled bathrooms, marble tubs, featherbeds (many canopied), goose-down comforters, all-cotton linens, and terry bathrobes. In the morning, continental breakfast and the newspaper of your choice are delivered to your room. With a rooftop garden and sky-high atrium, the Spindrift also offers a luxurious lobby with Oriental rugs and antiques.

The huge (575-room) **Hyatt Regency Monterey Resort and Conference Center** (1 Old Golf Course Rd., 831/372-1234, 800/824-2196 in California, or 800/233-1234 for central reservations, www.monterey.hyatt.com) is definitely a resort, and a newly renovated one. The spacious grounds here include the 18-hole Del Monte Golf Course, six tennis courts (extra fee for both), two pools, whirlpools, and a fitness center—the works. In summer, there's even a jazz festival. The sports bar here, **Knuckles,** offers 200 satellite channels, 11 TV monitors, and entire lifetimes of sports memorabilia. There's also the quieter **Café Monterey** lobby bar, and the **Peninsula Restaurant** for steaks and seafood.

Other upscale stays in town include the **Monterey Bay Inn** (242 Cannery Row, 831/373-6242 or 800/424-6242, www.montereybayinn.com), offering contemporary accommodations right on the bay (many view rooms with balconies). Near the Row is the 68-room **Best Western Victorian Inn** (487 Foam St., 831/373-8000 or 800/232-4141, www.victorianinn.com), where spa fireplaces, complimentary continental breakfast, and afternoon wine and cheese are among the amenities. Concierge-level rooms include featherbeds and robes; some feature whirlpool tubs. Two family suites are available.

BED-AND-BREAKFASTS

Monterey's showcase country inn is the gorgeous, ivy-covered 1929 English Tudor **M Old Monterey Inn** (500 Martin St., 831/375-8284 or 800/350-2344, www.oldmontereyinn.com,

$250 and up), featuring 10 elegant rooms and suites, most with fireplaces. All have sitting areas, featherbeds, CD players, a whirlpool tub for two, special touches, such as skylights and stained glass, and an abundance of amenities—making this a destination of choice for special-event getaways. As if the inn itself weren't appealing enough, it is shaded by a specimen oak amid stunning gardens. You'll also enjoy marvelous full breakfasts and a sunset wine hour.

The Jabberwock (598 Laine St., 831/372-4777 or 888/428-7253, www.jabberwockinn.com, $100–250) is a seven-room "post-Victorian" with a Victorian name and an Alice-through-the-looking-glass sensibility. Some rooms share baths. Rates include full breakfast (imaginative and good), plus cookies and milk at night.

A classic in inimitable Monterey style is downtown's historic **Merritt House Inn** (386 Pacific St., 831/646-9686 or 800/541-5599, www.merritthouseinn.com). The original adobe, built in 1830, features three suites ($250 and up) with 19th-century sensibility and modern bathrooms. The 22 surrounding motel-style rooms are more contemporary ($150–250).

At the European-style **Del Monte Beach Inn** (1110 Del Monte Ave., 831/649-4410, $50–100), close to Monterey Bay, rooms share baths—there are one or two clean, individual bathrooms per floor—which means this place is quite appealing and affordable for people who don't normally do B&Bs. Rates include continental breakfast.

Food

In Monterey, eating well *and* fairly inexpensively is easier than finding low-cost lodgings. Picnicking at the beaches or local parks is hard to beat. Happy hour—at the wharf, on the Row, and elsewhere—is a big deal in the area. In addition to cheap drinks, many bars serve good (free) food from 4 to 7 P.M. Due to an abundance of reasonably priced (and generous) breakfast places, an inexpensive alternative to three meals a day is skipping lunch (or packing simple picnic fare), then shopping around for early-bird dinners, a mainstay at many local restaurants. Do-it-yourselfers can pick up whatever suits their culinary fancy at the open-air **Old Monterey Marketplace Certified Farmers Market** (Alvarado Street at Pearl, 831/665-8070, 4–8 P.M. Tues. year-round, until 7 P.M. in winter). Great food, great fun. On Thursday, head for the **Monterey Bay Peninsula College CFM** (980 Fremont St. at Fisher, 831/728-5060, 2:30–6 P.M. year-round). For fresh seafood, the place is **Sea Harvest Fish Market** (598 Foam St., 831/646-0547; also located on the highway in Moss Landing, 831/633-8300). Your best bet for gourmet ingredients and organic produce—though there is a Trader Joe's in adjacent Pacific Grove—is probably the **Whole Foods Market** in the Del Monte Shopping Center (831/333-1600).

No doubt helped along by the abundance of fresh regional produce, seafood, cheese and other dairy products, poultry, and meats, the Monterey Peninsula has also become a sophisticated dining destination. Some of the area's great restaurants are listed below. But to get a true "taste" of the Monterey Peninsula, consider dining in nearby Pacific Grove and Carmel as well.

STANDARDS

By "standard," we mean places people can happily—and affordably—frequent. The **M Old Monterey Cafe** (489 Alvarado St., 831/646-1021, 7 A.M.–2:30 P.M. daily) serves all kinds of omelettes at breakfast—try the chile verde—plus unusual choices like calamari and eggs, lingüiça and eggs, and pigs in a blanket. Just about everything is good at lunch, too, from homemade soups, hearty shrimp Louie, and the Athenian Greek salad (with feta cheese, Greek olives, shrimp, and veggies) to the three-quarter-pound burgers and steak or calamari sandwiches. Fresh-squeezed juices and espresso and cappuccino are featured beverages. Breakfast is served until closing.

Nearby **Rosine's** (434 Alvarado St. near Bonifacio, 831/375-1400) is locally loved at breakfast, lunch, and dinner. In addition to good pancakes, waffles, and other standards, at breakfast here you can get veggie Benedict (with avocado, sautéed mushrooms, and tomatoes instead of Canadian bacon). Lunch features homemade soups, salads, sandwiches, and burgers. Pasta, chicken, seafood, and steak appear on the menu at dinner, with prime rib available on Friday and Saturday nights. Wonderful desserts.

Great for burgers and fries is kid-friendly **RG Burgers** (470 Alvarado St., 831/647-3100; also at 201 Crossroads Blvd., Carmel, 831/626-8054), where you can get all kinds, from the biggest and beefiest to the turkey guacamole burger and lemon pepper falafel. Still reasonable (and delicious) for all-American fare is **Kathy's** (700 Cass St., 831/647-9540), located south of Webster and west of Munras, amid the warren of oddball downtown streets. Pick any three items for a fluffy omelette. Your meal includes home fries, cheese sauce, bran muffins, and homemade strawberry jam for around $5. Sandwiches, similarly priced, are best when eaten on the patio.

ℳ Turtle Bay Taqueria (431 Tyler St. at Bonifacio, 831/333-1500) is a sibling of the region's hot Fishwife restaurants, and serves fast, good, very reasonably priced coastal Mexican fare, from grilled meat and seafood to flautas and tacos. Great selection of salsas, too. (There's another Turtle Bay in Seaside at 1301 Fremont, 831/899-1010.) Thai food fanatics should try **Siamese Bay Thai Restaurant** (131 Webster St., 831/373-1550). You can make a meal of the appetizers—such things as veggie tempura with plum sauce and crushed peanuts. The **Great Wall Chinese Restaurant** (724 Abrego St., 831/372-3637) has wonderful soups and an extensive vegetarian menu.

Stop in at **ℳ Morgan's Coffee and Tea** (498 Washington, 831/373-5601), a pretty darned hip coffeehouse serving superb coffees as well as organic green, black, and herb teas—not to mention sweets like mixed nut cake and pear tarts. Unusual sandwiches and a great $4.95 pizza are available at lunch. You can get your WiFi fix here, too. Morgan's offers pleasant outdoor street seating, complete with tables, chairs, and umbrellas. One block away is another reasonable breakfast or lunch stop, **Paris Bakery Café** (271 Bonifacio Place, 831/646-1620). The lunch menu includes sandwiches, salads, and soups, and the breads and pastries are wonderful.

PUBS

A notable beer lovers' destination is the fairly new **English Ales Brewery & Pub** (223 Reindollar Ave., Marina, 831/883-3000), which serves some impressive British-style homebrews, such as Ramsay's Fat Lip Ale—grand stuff, already served on tap in the Bay Area and at other sophisticated locales.

With a logo depicting a one-eyed jack doing the proverbial 12-ounce curl, **Peter B's Brewpub** (2 Portola Plaza, in the alley behind the Doubletree Hotel, 831/649-4511) is a real find in Monterey proper, offering great microbrews on tap and good pub grub. The Brit-style pub in Monterey is **The Crown & Anchor** (across from the Marriott at 150 W. Franklin St., 831/649-6496), dark and inviting, with a brassy seagoing air. The full bar features 20 beers on tap, and the food is pretty darn good and reasonably priced—from the fish and chips or bangers and mash to spicy meatloaf, curries, cottage pie, and steak-and-mushroom pie. You'll also find salads and sandwiches and a special menu for the "powder monkeys" (Brit sailor slang for kids). Open for lunch and dinner daily, with the full menu available until midnight. Or consider the **London Bridge Pub** (Municipal Wharf, north of Fisherman's Wharf, at Del Monte and Figueroa, 831/655-2879), which specializes in authentic British cuisine and pours more than 60 different beers (the "Hall of Foam") to wash it down.

AT THE WHARF

Named for tender squid, breaded and then sautéed in butter, TV chef John Pisto's **Abalonetti Seafood Trattoria** (57 Fisherman's Wharf, 831/373-1851) offers relaxed lunch and dinner—primarily seafood (especially calamari) and standard Italian fare. The restaurant is fairly inexpensive, with a nice view. Out on the end of the secondary pier at the wharf is the very good **Rappa's Seafood Restaurant** (Fisherman's Wharf #1, 831/372-7562), an oceanside oasis with outdoor dining, reasonable prices, good food, and early-bird dinners. Equally good **Domenico's on the Wharf** (50 Fisherman's Wharf #1, 831/372-3655), another Pisto outpost, has a Southern Italian accent. The menu features fresh seafood, homemade pasta, chicken, steak, and veal dishes, with an award-winning, very California wine list and a full bar. The oyster bar is open from 10 A.M. daily.

CANNERY ROW

If you're spending most of the day at the Monterey Aquarium, try the **Portola Café and Restaurant** there, or head out onto the Row. Many of the places along Cannery Row offer early-bird dinners, so if price matters, go shopping for deals before you get hungry.

Get your margarita fix and decent Mexican fare at **El Torito** (600 Cannery Row, 831/373-0611). Jose Cuervo flaming fajitas, anyone? For something simple, an interesting choice for "views, brews, and cues" is the **Blue Fin Café and Billiards** (685 Cannery Row, 831/375-7000). In addition to salads, sandwiches, and full dinners, the Blue Fin boasts a full bar, emphasizing bourbons and scotches and also serving some 40 beers, including 22 ales and lagers on tap. There's plenty to do besides eat and drink, too, thanks to 18 pool tables, snooker, foosball, darts, and shuffleboard. Live music and DJs also. No cover.

Naturally enough, seafood is the predominant dinner theme along the Row. The **Chart House** (444 Cannery Row, 831/372-3362) brings its trademark casually elegant, nautical-themed decor to the Row, serving primarily seafood, steaks, and prime rib—predictably tasty. A bit inland, but still looking to the sea for inspiration, is TV chef John Pisto's casual **Whaling Station Restaurant** (763 Wave St., 831/373-3778, daily), another locally popular dinner house offering everything from seafood and homemade pastas to mesquite-grilled Black Angus steaks Pisto's Paradiso Trattoria has been

replaced by the elegant, Far East-themed **Blue Moon** (654 Cannery Row, 831/375-4155), which still includes seafood and Italian specialties like cioppino and crab risotto.

The exceptional and expensive **Ñ Sardine Factory** (701 Wave St., 831/373-3775, dinner nightly) serves New American regional fare, from seafood and steaks to pasta and other specialties, in an elegant setting. Seafood served here, by the way, is included on the Monterey Bay Aquarium's approved "sustainable fisheries" list. Full bar.

Another upscale Row restaurant going for the nautical theme is much more casual: **Schooners Bistro on the Bay** (400 Cannery Row at the Monterey Plaza Hotel, 831/372-2628), specializing in California cuisine at lunch and dinner. Another possibility is the hotel's renowned but still casual **Ñ Duck Club Restaurant** (831/646-1706, daily), which serves outstanding bay views and superb American regional cuisine for breakfast and dinner.

FINE DINING

Ñ Fresh Cream (upstairs at 100-C Heritage Harbor, 99 Pacific St., 831/375-9798), across from Fisherman's Wharf, features wonderful French country cuisine lightened a bit by a fresh California sensibility. Fresh Cream has won so many awards, people can't keep track of them all—not even all those consecutive years of the *Wine Spectator*'s Award of Excellence. Everything is worthy of a recommendation, from the mushroom bisque, duckling in blackcurrant sauce, and Holland Dover sole meunière to the Grand Marnier soufflé. Great views of Monterey Bay are served, too. One of the Monterey Peninsula's best restaurants, Fresh Cream is also dressier than most. Meals are expensive, but even travelers light in the pocketbook can afford dessert and coffee. Open for dinner only; menu changes daily. Call for information and reservations.

Still popular is the relaxed, kid-friendly all-American bistro **Ñ Montrio** (414 Calle Principal at Franklin, 831/648-8880, lunch Mon.–Sat., dinner daily), another of Monterey's favorite restaurants, this one at home in a onetime firehouse. You might start with fire-roasted artichokes, terrine of eggplant, or Dungeness crab cakes, then continue with grilled gulf prawns, lamb tenderloins, or Black Angus New York steak. Vegetarians can dig into the oven-roasted portobello mushroom over polenta and veggie ragout. At last report, Monday was still cioppino night. You'll also enjoy marvelous sandwiches at lunch, exquisite desserts, a full bar (good bar menu), and a great wine list.

Equally stylish is the historic 1833 **M Stokes Restaurant & Bar** (500 Hartnell St. at Madison, 831/373-1110, lunch Mon.–Sat., dinner daily), its exteriors—including the gardens—preserving that Monterey colonial style, its impressive interiors suggesting the Old World. But the excellent food is the thing. On the menu here is rustic, refined, and reasonably affordable California-style, country Northern Mediterranean cuisine made from the freshest available local ingredients, from savory soups, salads, and tapas to seafood, chicken, lamb, and beef. Small plates might feature choices such as homemade mozzarella and ciabatta bread served with herbed olive oil, and oven-roasted spinach gratin with mussels and herbed breadcrumbs. Large plates might include pasta tubes with homemade fennel sausage, manila clams, and spinach aioli; seared hanger steak with spinach cheese tart; or perhaps grilled lavender pork chops with leek-lemon bread pudding. Full bar, good wines.

Other Mediterranean possibilities include relaxed, kid-friendly **Cibo Ristorante Italiano** (301 Alvarado St., 831/649-8151), serving rustic but stylish Sicilian fare—plenty of pizzas and pastas—including the specialty bay shrimp in pesto, vodka, and cream sauce—and good homemade desserts. A three-course fixed-price menu is served nightly 5 to 7 P.M.

Serving up stylish "American country" fare, **Tarpy's Roadhouse** (831/647-1444, lunch and dinner daily, plus brunch on Sun.), inside the historic stone Ryan Ranch homestead three miles off Highway 1 on Highway 68 (at Canyon del Rey), is not to be confused with some cheap-eats-and-beer joint. The point here is reinterpreting American classics—and that's no cheap-eats tale. Dinner includes such things as Indiana duck, Dijon-crusted lamb loin, baby back ribs, and grilled vegetables with succotash. Great desserts; salads and sandwiches at lunch; full bar.

Entertainment and Events

Still a fairly new pleasure in Monterey are the cool **New Osio 6 Cinemas** (350 Alvarado St., 831/644-8171, www.osiocinemas.com), next to the Crown & Anchor, screening five or more indie and foreign films every week.

Viva Monterey (414 Alvarado St., 831/646-1415) is the favorite for rockin' out, though Viva is branching out into blues, funk, and reggae, too. **Sly McFly's** (700 Cannery Row, 831/649-8050) is the best blues club, though you might also catch hot salsa bands some nights. For jazz, head for **Cibo Ristorante Italiano** (301 Alvarado St., 831/649-8151). Locals say the best local dance club is **Club Octane** (321 Alvarado St., 831/646-9244).

The Monterey Peninsula also offers an impressive year-round calendar of theater, arts, lectures, museum and gallery exhibits, and other cultural events. See local newspapers for current listings.

EVENTS

Visitors have a whale of a time at January's free **Whalefest** weekend, held at Fisherman's Wharf. Come in February for **A Day of Romance in Old Monterey**—"living history" storytelling, with 19th-century Monterey characters holding forth from the Cooper-Molera and Diaz Adobes, Larkin House, and Sherman Quarters—and the Valentine's Day **Love at the Aquarium.** In late February, come for the **Steinbeck Cannery Row Birthday Celebration** (there's another bash in Salinas). In early March, **Dixieland Monterey** brings three days of Dixie and swing to various venues around town. Later in March, come for the waterfront's **Clam Chowder Festival.** April brings the **Sea Otter Classic,** one of the world's best cycling parties, designed for both mountain bike and road racers, and the **Monterey Wine Festival,** when more than 200 California wineries strut their stuff. Traditionally, though, April is adobe month in Monterey, with the popular **Adobe Tour** through public and private historic buildings toward the end of the month. In late April or early May, begin Monterey's **Historic Garden Tours,** beginning at the Cooper-Molera Adobe and including the Stevenson and (usually) Larkin Houses, which continue into September. At least tangentially related is the Earth Day–focused **Elkhorn Slough Mud Stomp,** just north of town in Moss Landing, organized to create nesting holes for endangered snowy plovers in the slough's salt flats. The **Old Monterey Plein Air Painting and Art Promenade** is also in April.

Come in May for the **Marina International Festival of the Winds,** which includes the annual **Tour de Ford Ord** bike ride, and for the free Memorial Day weekend **Red, White & a Little Blues** music festival, staged at Custom House Plaza and along Alvarado Street in Monterey. Also in May: the **Ed "Doc" Ricketts Birthday Party** and the once-a-year **Ed "Doc" Ricketts Lab Tours** on Cannery Row, plus the **Block Party on Cannery Row.** In late May, the Kiwanis-sponsored **Great Monterey Squid Festival** is a chic culinary indulgence for those with calamari cravings, plus arts, crafts, and entertainment.

June brings the acclaimed **Monterey Bay Blues Festival,** and also the **Monterey Bay TheatreFest** at Custom House Plaza, which includes an arts and crafts festival, a family-oriented theater festival, historical reenactments, and "the Human Chess Game" on the waterfront. The **Fourth of July** celebration here is fun, with fireworks off the Coast Guard Pier, music in historic Colton Hall, and living history in Old Monterey. Neighboring Seaside starts a day early, with its community-wide **Festival of Patriots** block party on July 3. Come mid-month for the **Rock & Art Festival** at the Monterey Fair-

ground, a celebration of rock 'n' roll. There's almost always something going on at nearby Mazda Racetrack Laguna Seca, too, including July's **Honda International Superbike Classic** and August's **Rolex Monterey Historic Automobile Races.** Also in August, the **Monterey County Fair** comes to the fairgrounds, bringing amusement rides, livestock shows, and young faces sticky with cotton candy. Also come in August for **Otter Days,** at the Monterey Bay Aquarium, and the annual **Winemaker's Celebration** in Custom House Plaza.

Come in September for the fastest weekend of them all, the **Grand Prix of Monterey,** at Mazda Raceway Laguna Seca. In mid-September, it's time for the city's most famous event of all: the **Monterey Jazz Festival,** the oldest continuous jazz fest in the nation. Not as daring as others, it nonetheless hosts legendary greats and up-and-coming talent. This is the biggest party of the year here, so get tickets and reserve rooms well in advance (four to six months). Another big deal in September is artist Equity's annual three-day **Artists Studio Tour,** a self-guided exploration of more than 70 Monterey County studios.

October possibilities include the annual **Old Monterey Seafood & Music Festival** and the **California Constitution Day** reenactment of California's 1849 Constitutional Convention. In mid-November are the **Great Wine Escape Weekend,** when area wineries all hold open houses, and the **Cannery Row Christmas Tree Lighting.** The **Christmas in the Adobes** yuletide tour in mid-December is another big event, with luminaria-lit tours of 15 adobes, each dressed up in period holiday decorations. Festivities are accompanied by music and carolers. Also come in December for the **Brighten The Harbor** boating parade of lights and the annual **Cowboy Poetry & Music Festival.** Celebrate New Year's Eve through the arts at **First Night Monterey,** immensely popular here.

Shopping

For more shopping ideas and other visitor information, contact the **Monterey County Convention & Visitors Bureau** (831/648-5373, 831/626-1426, or 888/221-1010, www.montereyinfo.org) and the **Old Monterey Business Association** (321 Alvarado St. Ste. G, 831/655-8070, www.oldmonterey.org).

CANNERY ROW

Cannery Row is the obvious starting point for most visiting shoppers. Wander the Row's shops on the way to and from the aquarium. Don't overlook the gift and book shop at the nonprofit **Monterey Bay Aquarium** itself (886 Cannery Row, 831/648-4800), which offers good books and a wonderful selection of educational and "eco" items. Proceeds support the aquarium and its educational and research mission. The **Monterey Soap & Candle Works** (685 Cannery Row Ste. 109, 831/644-9425) offers natural, handmade coconut, glycerin, and specialty soaps, as well as beeswax candles. Great for antiques is the **Cannery Row Antique Mall** (471 Wave St., 831/655-0264).

ANTIQUES AND VINTAGE

The Monterey area boasts its fair share of antique and "heritage" shops, but consider actively supporting the preservation of local history. A few shops within downtown's Monterey State Historic Park actually operate out of park buildings—to help generate funds for historic preservation, garden development, and other improvements. Worth a look along Monterey's Path of History is the **Cooper Shop** in the Cooper-Molera Adobe (Polk and Munras Sts., 831/649-7111), operated by the nonprofit Old Monterey Preservation Society, which offers quality 1800s-vintage reproductions, from toys to furniture. The **Boston Store** (or Casa del Oro, at the corner of Scott and Olivier, 831/649-3364) is run by the nonprofit Historic Garden League

and offers antiques, collectibles, and reproductions. The garden league also operates the **Picket Fence,** an upscale garden shop.

There are many great shops downtown, and just wandering around is an enjoyable way to find them. Great for secondhand and vintage clothing, accessories, and other treasures is eclectic **Blue Moon Trading Company** (75 Bonifacio Plaza, east of Alvarado, 831/641-0616). Another possibility for previously loved clothing is **Nice Twice** (397 Calle Principal, 831/373-5665). The unique **California Views Historical Photo Collection** (469 Pacific St., 831/373-3811) offers more than 80,000 historical photographs of California and Monterey.

BOOKS

A first stop for books and magazines is **Bay Books** (316 Alvarado St., 831/375-1855), with a nice selection of Steinbeck and titles of local or regional emphasis. Used-book possibilities include **Book End** (245 Pearl St., 831/373-4046); **The Book Haven** (559 Tyler St., 831/333-0383); and the **Cannery Row Old Book Company** (471 Wave St., 831/656-9264). **Carpe Diem Fine Books** (502 Pierce St., 831/643-2754) specializes in rare and out-of-print books and is open only by appointment. A destination in its own right for used-book aficionados is **Lighthouse Avenue** in New Monterey. The unusual used bookstores here include **Books & Things** (224 Lighthouse Ave., 831/655-8784); the **Book Worm** (600 Lighthouse, 831/375-4208); **Old Capitol Books** (639 Lighthouse, Ste. A, 831/375-2665); **Basset Books** (800 Lighthouse Ave., Ste. C, 831/655-3433); and **Lighthouse Books** (801 Lighthouse, 831/372-0653).

MARKETS AND CENTERS

In addition to gathering up fresh produce and bakery items, head for downtown's Tuesday **Old Monterey Market Place** (Alvarado St. and Bonafacio Place, 4–7 or 8 P.M.) for quality crafts.

The best all-purpose shopping center just happens to be conveniently installed astride motel row, Munras Avenue—the **Del Monte Shopping Center** (1410 Del Monte Center, 831/373-2705), where you'll find coffee, food, boutiques, books, and furniture, plus Macy's and Mervyn's. The center's **Avalon Beads** (831/643-1847, www.avalonbeads.com) features beads from around the globe, as well as imported jewelry.

Information

The **Monterey Visitor Center** (Camino El Estero at Franklin, 831/648-5373, 9 A.M.–6 P.M. Mon.–Sat., 9 A.M.–5 P.M. Sun., Apr.–Oct.; 9 A.M.–5 P.M. Mon.–Sat., 10 A.M.–4 P.M. Sun. Nov.–Mar.) is staffed by the Monterey County Convention & Visitors Bureau and offers personal expertise, as well as reams of flyers on just about everything in and around the region. You can also stop by the "mini-center," downtown at the Visitor & Convention Bureau's main office (150 Oliver St., 831/626-1426, 10 A.M.–5:30 P.M. Mon.–Fri.) There are also CVB satellite centers in Salinas and King City. For additional area information, including a current visitor guide, call 888/221-1010 or visit www.montereyinfo.org. Via the website, you can also book a room at more than 100 area motels and hotels; request a meeting planner; send an e-postcard; and get up to speed on attractions, arts, and events. Other resources include the **Monterey Peninsula Chamber of Commerce** (380 Alvarado St., 831/648-5360, www.mpcc.com) and the **Old Monterey Business Association** (321 Alvarado St. Ste. G, 831/655-8070, www.oldmonterey.org).

The *Monterey County Herald* (www.montereyherald.com) is the mainline community news source. For an alternative view of things, pick up the free *Monterey County Weekly* (www.coastweekly.com), also offering entertainment (including clubs) and events information.

GETTING AROUND

Getting around by car can be a problem; even finding streets is confusing, due to missing signs, complex intersections and traffic signals, and one-way routes. Local traffic jams can be horrendous. So, save yourself some headaches and avail yourself of local public transportation (see below). Drivers, park at the 12-hour meters near Fisherman's Wharf—the cheapest lots are downtown—and walk (or bike) elsewhere. Or take the shuttle or bus. For more specific parking advice, pick up the free *Smart Parking in Monterey: How to Find Affordable Legal Public Parking* brochure at area visitors centers.

By Bicycle

Bicycling is another way to go. The local roads are narrow and bike paths are few, but you can get just about everywhere by bike if you're careful. Rent bikes at **Wheel Fun Rentals @ Bay Bikes** (640 Wave St. on Cannery Row, 831/646-9090, www.baybikes.com), where you can opt for mountain bikes, touring bikes, or four-wheel covered surreys known as pedalinas. You can also rent bikes at **Adventures by the Sea** (299 Cannery Row, 831/372-1807, www.adventuresbythesea.com), which offers guided bike tours, as well as rental mountain bikes, bikes built for two, and pedalinas; and **A B Seas Kayaks** (32 Cannery Row, Ste. 5, 888/371-6035, www.montereykayak.com).

By Shuttle and Bus

Once parked, from Memorial Day through Labor Day, you can ride Monterey-Salinas Transit's **MST Trolley** (10 A.M.–7 P.M. daily)—a free, rubber-tired trolley system connecting the Tin Cannery shopping center (at the edge of Pacific Grove), the Monterey Bay Aquarium, Cannery Row, Fisherman's Wharf, and the town's historic downtown adobes with the downtown conference center, nearby motels and hotels, and parking garages. See a Monterey-Salinas Transit guide or MST's website (www.mst.org) for a route map (MST trolley) and schedule. A separate MST

MONTEREY FOG

It is the Pacific that exercises the most direct and obvious power upon the climate. At sunset, for months together, vast, wet, melancholy fogs arise and come shoreward from the ocean. From the hilltop above Monterey the scene is often noble, although it is always sad. The upper air is still bright with sunlight; a glow still rests upon the Gabelano Peak; but the fogs are in possession of the lower levels; they crawl in scarves among the sand-hills; they float, a little higher, in clouds of a gigantic size and often of a wild configuration; to the south, where they have struck the seaward shoulder of the mountains of Santa Lucia, they double back and spire up skyward like smoke. Where their shadow touches, color dies out of the world. The air grows chill and deadly as they advance. The trade-wind freshens, the trees begin to sigh, and all the windmills in Monterey are whirling and creaking and filling their cistern with the brackish water of the sands. It takes but a little while till the invasion is complete. The sea, in its lighter order, is submerged the earth. Monterey is curtained in for the night in thick, wet, salt, and frigid clouds; so to remain till day returns; and before the sun's rays they slowly disperse and retreat in broken squadrons to the bosom of the sea. And yet often when the fog is thickest and most chill, a few steps out of town and up the slope the night will be dry and warm and full of inland perfume.

Excerpted from Robert Louis Stevenson's "The Old Pacific Capital," Fraser's Magazine, 1880

trolley route serves adjacent Pacific Grove (10 A.M.–7 P.M. Tues.–Sat.).

To get around on public buses otherwise, contact **Monterey-Salinas Transit** (1 Ryan Ranch Rd., 831/899-2555 or 831/424-7695 from Salinas, www.mst.org), though most buses roll out from the downtown transit center. "The Bus" serves the entire area, including Pacific Grove, Carmel, and Carmel Valley, from Watsonville south to Salinas. Local buses can get you just about anywhere, but some run spo-

radically. Pick up the free Rider's Guide schedule at the downtown **Transit Plaza** (where most buses stop and where Alvarado, Polk, Munras, Pearl, and Tyler Streets converge) or at motels, the chamber of commerce, and the library. The standard single-trip fare (one zone) is $1.75; exact change required; free transfers. Some longer routes traverse multiple zones and cost more. Seniors, the disabled, and children can ride for $.85 with the transit system's courtesy card. Children under age 5 ride free. A regular adult day pass costs $3.50, and a super day pass (valid on all routes and all zones) is $7; seniors and students pay half price. In April, for the Big Sur Marathon—and for other special events—and otherwise from late May through early September, bus 22 runs south to famous Nepenthe in Big Sur (two buses per day in each direction; $3.50 one way).

Keep in mind that Monterey-Salinas Transit buses can get you to and from the **Amtrak** station in Salinas (11 Station Place, 831/422-7458 for depot or 800/872-7245, www.amtrak.com). Call or check the website for reservations and schedule information, including information on Amtrak's Thruway bus connections from Monterey and vicinity, a service included in some fares.

You'll also find a **Greyhound** station (1042 Del Monte Ave., 831/373-4735 or 800/231-2222 for systemwide information and reservations, www.greyhound.com, 8 A.M.–10 P.M. daily).

Tours

An unusual thrill: cruising town in a facsimile Model A or Phaeton from **Rent-A-Roadster** (229 Cannery Row, 831/647-1929, www.rent-a-roadster.com). The basic rate is about $30–40 an hour (with weekday deals), but you can arrange half-day and full-day tours, too—and head south to Big Sur and San Simeon in style.

Ag Venture Tours in Monterey (831/643-9463 or 888/643-9463, www.whps.com/agtours) specializes in winery tours in the Monterey Wine Country, Carmel Valley, Salinas Valley, and Santa Cruz Mountains. A typical daylong tour includes tasting at three different wineries, a vineyard walk, and a picnic lunch.

Pacific Grove

Pacific Grove began in 1875 as a prim, proper tent city founded by Methodists who, Robert Louis Stevenson observed, "come to enjoy a life of teetotalism, religion, and flirtation." No boozing, waltzing, zither-playing, or reading Sunday newspapers were allowed. Dedicated inebriate John Steinbeck lived here for many years in the next century, but had to leave town to get drunk. Pacific Grove was the last dry town in California: Alcohol has been legal here only since 1969. The first Chautauqua in the western states was held here—bringing "moral attractions" to heathen Californians—and the hall where the summer meeting tents were stored still stands at 16th and Central Avenues.

Nicknamed Butterfly City, U.S.A., in honor of migrating monarchs—there's a big fine and/or six months in jail for "molesting" one—Pacific Grove dazzles with its rocky shoreline and wonderful tidepools, and sparkles with Victorians and modest seacoast cottages, community pride, and an absolutely noncommercial Butterfly Parade in October. Also here is Asilomar, a well-known retreat—now a state-owned conference center—with its own beautiful beach. In addition to impressive accommodations and restaurants, the town also offers some great bargains, especially for secondhand shoppers. Trendy **Time After Time** (301 Grand Ave., 831/643-2747) and **Encore Boutique** (125 Central Ave., 831/375-1700) are good places to start. And don't miss all those used bookstores along Lighthouse Avenue.

Pacific Grove is well served by Monterey-Salinas Transit buses (see *Monterey* chapter). For events, accommodations, restaurants, and other current information, stop by the **Pacific Grove Information Center** at Forest and Central, or contact the **Pacific Grove Chamber of Commerce** (831/373-3304 or 800/656-6650, www.pacificgrove.org). Another interesting web portal is www.93950.com. The **Pacific Grove Public Library** (550 Central at Fountain, 831/648-3160, 10 A.M.–8 P.M. Mon.–Thurs., 10 A.M.–5 P.M. Fri.–Sat.) is also a useful resource.

Must-Sees

M **"Three-Mile Drive"—or Walk:** This jaunt along Ocean View Boulevard offers notable community parks, crashing surf, craggy shorelines, picnicking, and wildlife watching. And, unlike the more famous 17-Mile Drive, this one's free (page 51).

M **Pacific Grove Museum of Natural History:** Another great Pacific Grove freebie, the natural history museum showcases local wonders, from sea otters and seabirds to rare insects and native plants. Kids especially love *Sandy,* the gray whale sculpture right out front (page 51).

M **Asilomar:** Originally established as a YWCA retreat in 1913, now a state-owned retreat center, Asilomar just happens to sit astride a stunning public beach. The landmark buildings here were designed by architect Julia Morgan, best known for Hearst's San Simeon estate (page 53).

M **17-Mile Drive:** The famed rubbernecker's tour of golf courses and gargantuan homes also showcases some grand vistas, as well as the landmark Lone Cypress—the official (trademarked) emblem of the Monterey Peninsula (page 53).

the Lone Cypress

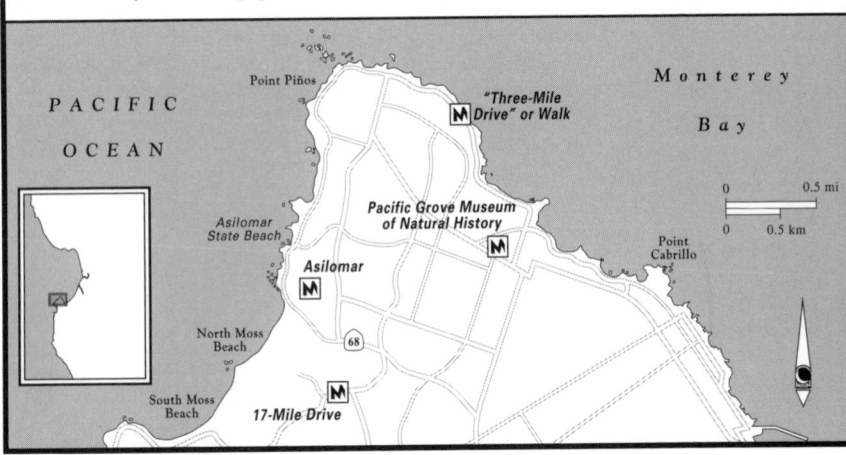

Sights

From Pacific Grove, embark on the too-famous 17-Mile Drive in adjacent Pebble Beach. But better (and free), tour the surf-pounded peninsula as a populist. The city of Pacific Grove is one of few in California to own its beaches and shores, all dedicated to public use. Less crowded and hoity-toity than 17-Mile Drive, but just as spectacular and absolutely free, are a walk, bike ride, or drive along Ocean View Boulevard. Or take the Monterey Peninsula Recreation Trail as far as you want; this path for walkers, joggers, bicyclists, skaters, and baby-stroller-pushers runs all the way from Marina to Pebble Beach. It's paved in places (right through downtown Monterey, for example) and dirt in others. Or cycle from here to Carmel on the Del Monte Forest ridge via Highway 68 (the Holman Highway) for a spectacular view of the bay, surrounding mountains, and the 17-Mile coastline to the south.

◼ "THREE-MILE DRIVE"—OR WALK

Along the Ocean View route are Berwick Park, Lovers Point, and Perkins Park; altogether, Pacific Grove boasts 13 community parks. These areas (and points in between) offer spectacular sunsets, crashing surf, craggy shorelines, swimming, sunbathing, and picnicking, plus whale-watching in season, sea otters, sea lions, seals, shorebirds, and autumn flurries of monarch butterflies. Stanford University's **Hopkins Marine Station** on Point Cabrillo (China Point) is also along the way, the crystal offshore waters and abundant marine life attracting scientists and students from around the world. This is the first marine laboratory on the Pacific coast. (An aside for Steinbeck fans: This was the location of Chin Kee's Squid Yard in *Sweet Thursday*.) As for **Lovers Point,** the granite headland near Ocean View Boulevard and 17th Street, there is considerable disagreement over whether Pacific Grove could have been *sexual* in Methodist days, when it was named. The popular local opinion, still, is that the name was originally Lovers

of Jesus Point. But conscientious researchers have established that the reference is to romance—and was, at least as far back as 1890. (For help in divining other arcane area details, pick up a copy of *Monterey County Place Names: A Geographical Dictionary,* by Donald Thomas Clark; and its companion. *Santa Cruz County Place Names*—if you can find them.) Trysting spot or no, Lovers Point is not a safe place to be during heavy weather; entirely too many people have been swept away to their deaths. Picnic at **Perkins Point** instead, or wade or swim there (safe beach). **Marine Gardens Park,** an aquatic park stretching along Ocean View, with wonderful tidepools, is usually a good spot for watching sea otters frolic in the seaweed just offshore.

◼ PACIFIC GROVE MUSEUM OF NATURAL HISTORY

Pacific Grove's Museum of Natural History (165 Forest Ave. at Central, 831/648-5716, www.pg-museum.org. 10 A.M.–5 P.M. Tues.–Sun., free admission but donations greatly appreciated) showcases local wonders of nature, including sea otters, seabirds (a huge collection with more than 400 specimens), rare insects, and native plants. A fine array of Native American artifacts is on rotating display. Particularly impressive is the relief map of Monterey Bay, though youngsters will probably vote for *Sandy,* the gray whale sculpture right out front. Besides the facsimile butterfly tree, the blazing, feathery dried seaweed exhibit is a must-see. Many traveling exhibits visit this museum throughout the year, such as 2004's *Portraits of the Great Apes,* by Robert Cooper. The museum's annual **Wildflower Show** on the third weekend in April is excellent. Contact the museum for information.

POINT PIÑOS LIGHTHOUSE

Built of local granite and rebuilt in 1906, this is the oldest continuously operating lighthouse on the Pacific coast, listed on the National Register

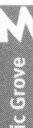

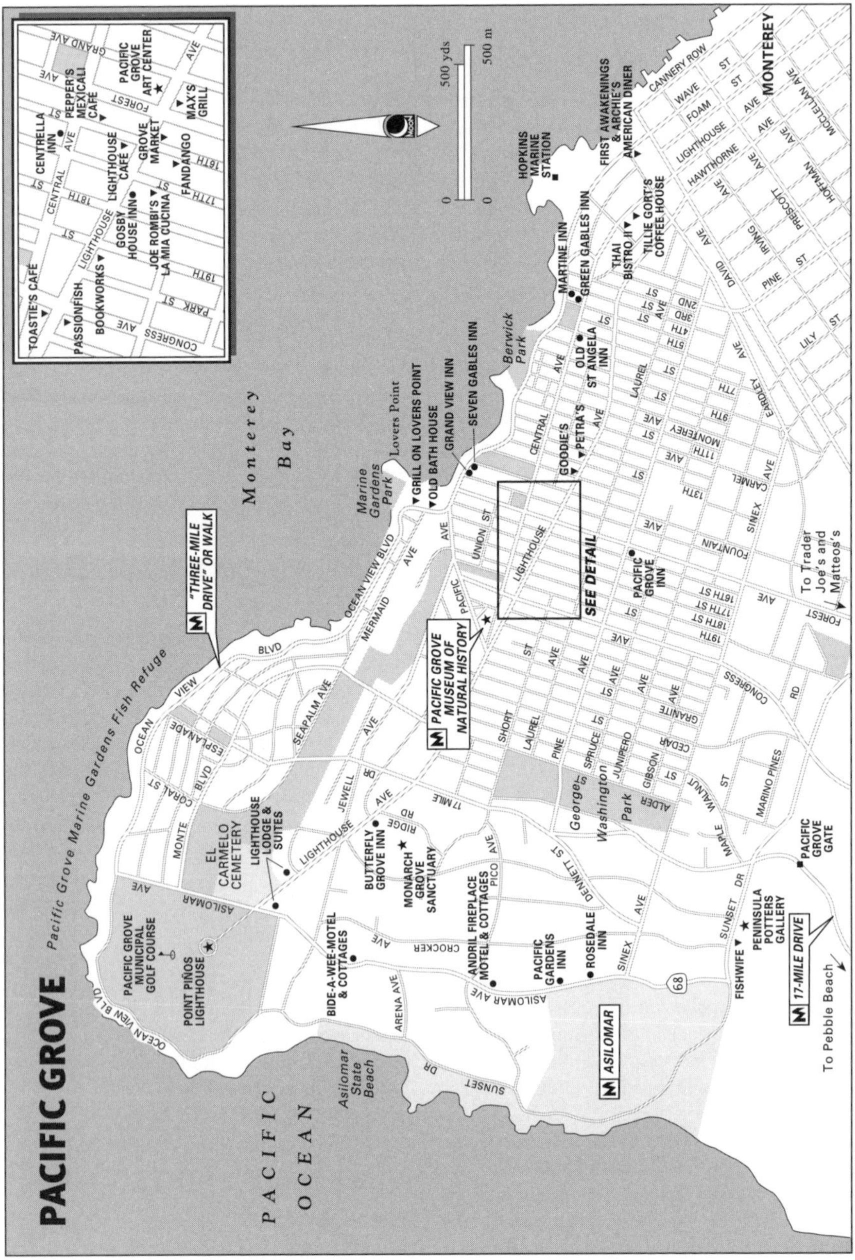
PACIFIC GROVE
PACIFIC OCEAN
Monterey Bay
Pacific Grove Marine Gardens Fish Refuge
"THREE-MILE DRIVE" OR WALK
PACIFIC GROVE MUSEUM OF NATURAL HISTORY
SEE DETAIL
ASILOMAR
17-MILE DRIVE
PACIFIC GROVE MUNICIPAL GOLF COURSE
POINT PIÑOS LIGHTHOUSE
EL CARMELO CEMETERY
LIGHTHOUSE LODGE & SUITES
BUTTERFLY GROVE INN
MONARCH GROVE SANCTUARY
BIDE-A-WEE-MOTEL & COTTAGES
ANDRIL FIREPLACE MOTEL & COTTAGES
PACIFIC GARDENS INN
ROSEDALE INN
FISHWIFE
PENINSULA POTTERS GALLERY
PACIFIC GROVE GATE
Asilomar State Beach
George Washington Park
Marine Gardens Park
Lovers Point
Berwick Park
GRILL ON LOVERS POINT
OLD BATH HOUSE
GRAND VIEW INN
SEVEN GABLES INN
GOODIE'S
PETRA'S
OLD ST ANGELA INN
PACIFIC GROVE INN
MARTINE INN
GREEN GABLES INN
THAI BISTRO II
TILLIE GORT'S COFFEE HOUSE
HOPKINS MARINE STATION
FIRST AWAKENINGS & ARCHIE'S AMERICAN DINER
MONTEREY
CANNERY ROW
To Trader Joe's and Matteos's
To Pebble Beach
0 500 yds
0 500 m
TOASTIE'S CAFE
PASSIONFISH
BOOKWORKS
GOSBY HOUSE INN
LIGHTHOUSE CAFE
CENTRELLA INN
PEPPER'S MEXICALI CAFE
GROVE MARKET
JOE ROMBI'S LA MIA CUCINA
FANDANGO
MAX'S GRILL
PACIFIC GROVE ART CENTER
OCEAN VIEW BLVD
LIGHTHOUSE AVE
SUNSET DR
ASILOMAR AVE
FOREST AVE
CENTRAL AVE
17 MILE DR
© AVALON TRAVEL PUBLISHING, INC.

Point Piños Lighthouse

ASILOMAR

The Young Women's Christian Association's national board of directors coined this Spanish-sounding nonword from the Greek *asilo* ("refuge") and the Spanish *mar* ("sea") when they established this facility as a YWCA retreat in 1913. **Asilomar State Beach** has tidepools and wonderful white-sand beaches, shifting sand dunes, wind-sculpted forests, spectacular sunsets, and sea otters and gray whales offshore. Not to mention all those surfers. Inland, many of Asilomar's original buildings—designed by architect Julia Morgan, best known for Hearst's San Simeon estate—are now historical landmarks. Primarily a conference center offering meeting rooms and accommodations for groups, Asilomar is now a nonprofit unit of the California state park system; subject to room availability, the general public can also stay here. Guest or not, anyone can fly kites or build sandcastles at the beach, stop to appreciate the forest of Monterey pine and cypress, and watch for deer, raccoons, gray ground squirrels, hawks, and owls.

For current information, contact Asilomar Conference Center (800 Asilomar Blvd., Pacific Grove, 831/372-8016 or 831/642-4242 to make reservations for leisure travelers, www.visitasilomar.com). You can book online. To stay here, make reservations up to 90 days in advance, or call—not more than a week in advance—to inquire about cancellations. Rates are $100–150, with full country-style breakfast included. Children ages 3–12 can stay (in the same room with an adult) for $5 more.

17-MILE DRIVE

The best place to start off on the famed 17-Mile Drive—technically in Pebble Beach—is in Pacific Grove, or, alternatively, the Carmel Hill gate off Highway 1. Not even 17 miles long anymore, since it no longer loops up to the old Del Monte Hotel, the drive still skirts plenty of ritzy digs in the 5,300-acre, privately owned Del Monte Forest in the four-gated "town" of Pebble Beach. Note the Byzantine castle of the banking/railroading Crocker family. Believe it or not,

of Historic Places. The beacon and mournful foghorn here have been warning seagoing vessels away from the point since February 1, 1855. The original French Fresnel lenses and prisms are still in use, though the lighthouse is now powered by electricity and a 1,000-watt lamp instead of whale oil. The lighthouse and the **U.S. Coast Guard Museum** inside (both open 11:30 A.M.–5 P.M. daily in summer, 1–4 P.M. Thurs.–Sun. the rest of the year, free or small donation) are located two blocks north of Lighthouse Avenue on Asilomar Boulevard. **Doc's Great Tidepool,** yet another Steinbeck-era footnote, is near the foot of the lighthouse. For information, contact the Pacific Grove Museum (see above).

Across from the lighthouse parking lot is fascinating **El Carmelo Cemetery,** a de facto nature preserve for deer and birds. For more bird-watching, amble down to freshwater **Crespi Pond,** near the golf course at Ocean View and Asilomar Boulevards.

MONARCH BUTTERFLIES

Pacific Grove is the best known of the 20 or so places where monarch butterflies winter. Once partial to Monterey pine or cypress trees for perching, monarchs these days prefer eucalyptus introduced from Australia. Adults arrive in late October and early November, their distinctive orange-and-black, Halloweenish wings sometimes tattered and torn after migrating thousands of miles. But they still have that urge to merge, first alighting on low shrubs, then meeting at certain local trees to socialize and sun themselves during the temperate Monterey Peninsula winter, before heading north to Canada to mate in the spring and then die. Their offspring metamorphose into adult butterflies the following summer or fall and—mysteriously—make their way back to the California coast without ever having been here. Milkweed eaters, the monarchs somehow figured out this diet made them toxic to bug-loving birds, who subsequently learned to leave them alone.

Even when massed in hundreds, the butterflies may be hard to spot: With wings folded, their undersides provide neutral camouflage. But if damp from the fog, monarchs will spread their wings to dry in the sun and "flash"—a priceless sight for any nature mystic.

Pacific Grove loves its monarch butterflies.

the estate's private beach is heated with underground pipes.

From **Shepherd's Knoll,** there's a great panoramic view of both Monterey Bay and the Santa Cruz Mountains. **Huckleberry Hill** does have huckleberries, but botanically more fascinating is the unusual coexistence of Monterey pines, Bishop pines, and Gowen and Monterey cypress. Sadly, these days pitch canker disease is taking its toll in the forest, killing off even venerable specimen trees. **Spanish Bay,** a nice place to picnic, is named for Portolá's confused land expedition from Baja in 1769; Portolá was looking for Monterey Bay, but he didn't find it until his second trip. **Point Joe** is a treacherous, turbulent convergence of conflicting ocean currents, wet and wild even on calm days. ("Joe" has been commonly mistaken by mariners as the entrance to Monterey Bay, so countless ships have gone down on these rocks.) Both **Seal Rock** and **Bird Rock** are aptly named. **Fanshell Beach** is a secluded spot, good for picnics and fishing, but dangerous for swimming.

Most famous of all is the landmark **Lone Cypress**—the official (trademarked) emblem of the Monterey Peninsula—at the route's midpoint. No longer lonely, this craggy old-timer is visited by millions each year; it's now "posed" with supporting guy wires, fed and watered in summer, and recovering well from a recent termite attack. At **Pescadero Point,** note the cypress bleached ashen and ghostlike by sun, salt spray, and wind.

From Pacific Grove by car, the tour costs $8, map included. The drive is open for touring from sunrise to 30 minutes before sunset year-round. For more information, call 831/647-5235 and ask for the concierge.

PEBBLE BEACH

Very private Pebble Beach has seven world-class golf courses made famous by Bing Crosby's namesake tournament. The Crosby, now called the **AT&T Pebble Beach National Pro Am Golf Tournament,** is held each year in late January or early February. For golfing information or reservations, contact the course (800/654-9300, www.pebblebeach.com). Only guests at the ultra-upscale resort accommodations can reserve a tee more than 24 hours in advance. (And some guests book their stays one to two years in advance.) Other facilities are

open to the public, including jogging paths and beautiful horse trails. Just about everything else—country clubs, yacht clubs, tennis courts, swimming pools—is private (and well guarded), though the public is welcome to stay here and play here, for a price. If you're here in August, join in the **Scottish Highland Games** or take in the **Concours d'élégance** classic car fest at The Lodge.

MONTEREY PENINSULA GOLFING

Golfers from around the globe make a point of arriving on the Monterey Peninsula, clubs in tow, at some point in their lives. The undisputed golf capital of the world, the Pebble Beach area between Carmel and Pacific Grove is also the most famous, largely due to "The Crosby," which is now the **AT&T Pebble Beach National Pro-Am Golf Tournament** (www.attpbgolf.com). Making headlines in 1999 was news that the Pebble Beach Company and its four world-class courses had been bought by a high-powered American investor group—Clint Eastwood, Richard Ferris, Arnold Palmer, and Peter Ueberroth—for $820 million. Just before, Clint Eastwood debuted his superb **Tehama** golf club (25000 Via Malpaso in Carmel Valley, 831/622-2200), a private course with an invitation-only membership of 300. Heady days at the head of the food chain.

It may cost a pretty penny—the green fee at Pebble Beach Golf Links, for example, is more than $350—but the public is welcome at private **Pebble Beach Golf Links,** ranked the number one public course in America by *Golf Digest* in 2003–2004. Other options include the **Links at Spanish Bay, Spyglass Hill Golf Course,** the **Peter Hay Par 3,** and the 1897 **Del Monte Golf Course** in Monterey, the oldest course in continuous operation west of the Mississippi. All are associated with Pebble Beach Resorts, headquartered at The Lodge at Pebble Beach on 17-Mile Drive. For more information on any of these courses and to make reservations, see www.pebblebeach.com or call 800/654-9300.

There is affordable golf around as well, however, the best thing going being the unpretentious

Pacific Grove Municipal Golf Links (77 Asilomar Ave., 831/648-5777), serving up Pebble Beach views at a fraction of the cost. The first nine holes were designed by Chandler Egan in classic rural-England style, and the back nine by Jack Neville, the original designer of the Pebble Beach Golf Links. Fees for 18 holes are $32 on weekdays, $38 in weekends. Great for beginners. Reservations can be made no more than seven days in advance.

Also open to the public are the **Poppy Hills Golf Course** (3200 Lopez Rd., just off 17-Mile Dr., 831/624-2035), designed by Robert Trent Jones, Jr.; the **Bayonet** and **Black Horse Golf Courses** (on North-South at former Fort Ord, 831/899-7271); and the Robert Trent Jones (Sr. and Jr.) **Laguna Seca Golf Club** (on York Road between Monterey and Salinas, 831/373-3701 or 888/524-8629).

Though Pebble Beach is world-renowned for its golf courses and golf events, Carmel Valley and vicinity have nearly as many courses—most of them private in the country-club model, and most recognizing reciprocal access agreements with other clubs. The **Rancho Cañada Golf Club** (about a mile east of Hwy. 1 via Carmel Valley Rd., 831/624-0111 or 800/536-9459) is open to the public, however. As part of accommodations packages, nonmembers can golf at **Quail Lodge Resort & Golf Club** (8000 Valley Greens Dr., 831/624-2888) and at **Carmel Valley Ranch** (1 Old Ranch Rd. in Carmel, 831/625-9500), which features an 18-hole Pete Dye course. And you can always try to find someone who knows someone who knows someone who's a member of Tehama, Clint's club described above, to see if they can get you in.

Accommodations

To maintain its "hometown America" aura, Pacific Grove has limited its motel development. The local chamber of commerce provides accommodations listings. Bed-and-breakfast inns are popular in Pacific Grove—see separate listings, below—and these comfortable, often luxurious home lodgings compared in price to much less pleasant alternatives elsewhere on the peninsula.

HOTELS AND INNS: $100–150

The state-owned **Asilomar Conference Center** (800 Asilomar Ave., Pacific Grove, 831/372-8016 or 831/642-4242 for reservations for leisure travelers, fax 831/372-7227, www.asilomar-center.com, $100–150, children age 3–12 stay in same room with adult for $5 more) enjoys an incredible 60-acre setting on the Pacific Ocean, complete with swimming pool, volleyball nets, horseshoe pits, and miles of beaches to stroll. When it's not completely booked with business-people, conferences, and other groups, it can be a reasonably priced choice for leisure travelers. Adding to the earthy appeal: Architect Julia Morgan designed many of the resort's pine lodges. Generally less expensive are the older, rustic cottages, though all have private bathrooms. Some units have kitchens and fireplaces. Call ahead for reservations, up to 90 days in advance, or hope for last-minute cancellations. Rates include a full country breakfast. Asilomar now offers T-1 high-speed Internet access, so guests can check their email in the lobby, and a new patio with bonfire ring—s'mores, anyone?—and regulation sand volleyball court.

Otherwise, closest to the beach are the 1930s-style cottages at **Bide-a-Wee-Motel & Cottages** (near Asilomar at 221 Asilomar Blvd., 831/372-2330, www.bideaweemotel.com, some rooms under $100 in off-season). Some of the cottages have kitchenettes. Also family-owned and across from Asilomar is comfortable, woodsy **Andril Fireplace Motel & Cottages** (569 Asilomar Blvd., 831/375-0994, www.andrilcottages.com), which feature all the comforts and an outdoor whirlpool tub, too. Cottages have full kitchens, fireplaces (wood provided), free DVDs, even private decks. Some of the larger cottage configurations—such as two bedroom with a separate living room—are more than $150, but still a good deal for families or couples traveling together.

Near Asilomar is the **Pacific Gardens Inn** (701 Asilomar Blvd., 831/646-9414 or 800/262-1566 in California, www.pacificgardensinn.com), where the contemporary rooms feature wood-burning fireplaces, refrigerators, TVs, and phones—even popcorn poppers and coffeemakers. Suites feature full kitchens and living rooms. Complimentary continental breakfast and evening wine and cheese are offered. Very nice. Right across from Asilomar is the recently renovated, all-suites **Rosedale Inn** (775 Asilomar Blvd., 831/655-1000 or 800/822-5606, www.rosedaleinn.com), where all rooms have a ceiling fan, fireplace, large whirlpool tub, wet bar, refrigerator, microwave oven, in-room coffeemaker, remote-control color TV and VCR, and even a hair dryer. Some suites have two or three TVs and/or a private patio. Especially if the monarchs are in town, consider a stay at the **Butterfly Grove Inn** (1073 Lighthouse Ave., 831/373-4921 or 800/337-9244, www.butterflygroveinn.com, some rooms under $100). Butterflies are partial to some of the trees here. The inn is quiet, with a pool, a spa, some kitchens, and fireplaces. Choose rooms in a comfy old house or motel units.

HOTELS AND INNS: $150 AND UP

The **Lighthouse Lodge and Suites** (1150 and 1259 Lighthouse Ave., 831/655-2111 or 800/858-1249, www.lhls.com) are two adjoining properties. The 31 Cape Cod–style suites feature abundant amenities—king beds, large whirlpool tubs, plush robes, mini-kitchens with stocked honor bars—and are the most expensive. The 64 lodge rooms feature many comforts, too, and are family-friendly, with extras including large-screen TV with cable, refrigerator, microwave, in-room coffee, even breakfast and a complimentary poolside barbecue in the afternoon (weather permitting). Lower rates are offered in the off-season, and there's a two-night minimum on summer weekends.

Those super-swank choices in adjacent Pebble Beach are definitely beyond the reach of most people's pocketbooks. But if you win the lottery, check 'em out. At **The Inn at Spanish Bay** (2700 17-Mile Dr. at the Scottish Links Golf Course, 831/647-7500), rooms are ultra-deluxe, with gas-burning fireplaces, patios, and balconies with views. Amenities include the usual luxuries, plus beach access, a pool, saunas, whirlpools, a health club, tennis courts, and a putting green. (By the way, the Inn at Spanish Bay's hotel lobby is a swell place to lounge around and at least pretend you're a swell, what with the spectacular views, gorgeous interiors, inviting couches in front of the fireplace, and open-air patio. That bagpiper playing at sunset is an unexpected bonus.)

Also an unlikely choice for most travelers is **The Lodge at Pebble Beach** (17-Mile Drive, 831/624-3811), another outpost of luxury. (If you don't stay, peek into the exclusive shops here.) A recent addition are the elegant, estate-style cottages at the 24-room  **Casa Palmero,** near both The Lodge and the first fairway of the Pebble Beach Golf Links. For still more pampering, the **Spa at Pebble Beach** is a full-service spa facility. For reservations at any of these Pebble Beach Resort facilities, contact 800/654-9300 or visit www.pebblebeach.com.

BED-AND-BREAKFASTS

Victoriana is particularly popular in Pacific Grove. The most famous Victorian inn in town is the elegant **Seven Gables Inn** (555 Ocean View Blvd., 831/372-4341, www.pginns.com, $150 and up), which offers ocean views from all 14 rooms and an abundance of European antiques and Victorian finery. Rates include a fabulous full breakfast and afternoon tea. Sharing the garden and offering equally exceptional, if more relaxed, Victorian style next door is the sibling **Grand View Inn** (557 Ocean View Blvd.,

831/372-4341, $150 and up). The view from all 11 rooms, with their antique furnishings and luxurious marble bathrooms, is indeed grand. Full breakfast, afternoon tea.

The lovely **Green Gables Inn** (104 Fifth St., 831/375-2095 or 800/722-1774, www.foursisters.com, $150–300) is a romantic, gabled Queen Anne. The seaside "summer house" offers marvelous views, five rooms upstairs, a suite downstairs, and five rooms in the carriage house. Of these, seven feature private bathrooms. Rates include continental breakfast. The **Gosby House Inn** (643 Lighthouse Ave., 831/375-1287 or 800/527-8828, $100 and up) is another of the Four Sisters—this one a charming (and huge) Queen Anne serving up fine antiques, a restful garden, homemade food, and fresh flowers. All 22 rooms boast great bayside views, and most feature private bathrooms. Some have fireplaces, whirlpool tubs, and TVs.

The 1889 **Centrella Inn** (612 Central Ave., 831/372-3372 or 800/233-3372, www.centrellainn.com, $150–300), a national historic

Pacific Grove Inn

landmark, offers 20 rooms plus a whirlpool-tub-equipped garden suite and five cottages with wood-burning fireplaces and wet bars. The cottage-style gardens are quite appealing, especially in summer. Rates include complimentary morning newspaper, full buffet breakfast, and a social hour in the afternoon (wine and hors d'oeuvres).

The Cape Cod–style **Old St. Angela Inn** (321 Central Ave., 831/372-3246 or 800/748-6306, www.sueandlewinns.com, $100–250) is a converted 1910 country cottage featuring eight guestrooms decorated with antiques, quilts, and other homey touches. Amenities include a garden hot tub, solarium, living room with fireplace, complimentary breakfast, and afternoon wine or tea and hors d'oeuvres. The historic three-story (no elevator) **Pacific Grove Inn** (581 Pine at Forest, 831/375-2825 or 800/732-2825, www.pacificgrove-inn.com, $150–250) is a 1904 Queen Anne. Some rooms have ocean views, most have fireplaces, and all have private baths and modern amenities like color TVs, radios, and telephones. Breakfast buffet every morning.

Food

A good Pacific Grove grocery stop is **Grove Market** (242 Forest Ave., 831/375-9581). For edible eclectica—the usual impressive selection—plus affordable wine, Pacific Grove has a **Trader Joe's** (1170 Forest Ave., 831/656-0180), though if you want to go local, consider **Tillie Gort's** on Central (see below), a very popular natural foods restaurant that opened an associated market in 2004. The best place around for a deli sandwich is **Goodie's** (518 Lighthouse Ave., 831/655-3663), at home in what served as Red Williams' gas station in John Steinbeck's novel *Cannery Row*, sharing space with a produce market. Ham and baked brie, anyone?

BREAKFAST AND COFFEE

A local favorite for breakfast, just a stroll from the Monterey Bay Aquarium, is **First Awakenings** (125 Oceanview Blvd., 831/372-1125, breakfast and lunch daily), in the American Tin Cannery, where you can fill up on "bluegerm pancakes" (blueberry with wheat germ), omelettes, and crêpes. Sandwiches such as the "chicado"—grilled chicken, avocado, and cheese—star at lunch. Eat inside or out.

You can get marvelous crêpes for breakfast or lunch, as well as good waffles and homemade soups, at **Toastie's Cafe** (702 Lighthouse Ave., 831/373-7543, 7 A.M.–2 P.M. daily). Also good for breakfast is the **Lighthouse Café** (602 Lighthouse, 831/372-7006), inside the onetime Winston Hotel. Or try the vegetarian and vegan dishes at **Tillie Gort's Coffee House** and art gallery (111 Central, 831/373-0335), just a stroll from Cannery Row. The Mediterranean frittata, cinnamon raisin French toast, and tofu and various other scrambles shine at breakfast, though sides of chicken apple sausage, bacon, and Canadian bacon are available. If the Summer of Love is just a vague memory, one you'd like to revisit, you'll love this place. Tillie Gort's is locally famous for those decadent black-bottom cupcakes, too, though try to hold off on those until lunch or dinner. Live music sometimes, too. Plus, there's now a natural foods market.

For lattes, cappuccinos, espressos, or just a good cuppa joe, head to the dual-purpose **Bookworks** (667 Lighthouse Ave., 831/372-2242), where you can sample the wares in the bookstore as well as the coffeehouse. **Patisserie Bechler** (1225 Forest Ave., 831/375-0846) is the place for French bakery goods.

LUNCH AND DINNER

Already revered is **Matteo's** trattoria (1180 Forest, 831/333-1035), an authentic and welcoming Sicilian café, the creation of Matteo Enea and his wife Cheryl, tucked into a little shopping center. Enjoying Southern Italian comfort food is the whole point here. Everything is homemade, from the panini and flavorful sauces to the eggplant parmigiana.

Thai Bistro II (159 Central Ave., 831/372-8700, lunch and dinner daily) is the place to go for outstanding Thai food. Those with a fireproof palate will love the restaurant's spicy dishes, and vegetarians will appreciate the large number of meatless entrées. (There's another Thai Bistro in Carmel Valley at 55 W. Carmel Valley Rd., 831/659-5900.) The locals' favorite for white-tablecloth Italian is **Joe Rombi's La Mia Cucina** (208 17th St., 831/373-2416); for Mediterranean, try **Petra's** (477 Lighthouse Ave., 831/649-2530).

A popular burger option in the same neighborhood is the Tin Cannery's **Archie's American Diner** (831/375-6939), just the place to load up on Monterey burgers and garlic fries. Another good bet for burgers, not to mention that view, is the fast-food **Grill on Lovers Point** (618 Oceanview Blvd., 831/649-6859).

Locals say the homemade *chiles rellenos* at immensely popular **Peppers MexiCali Cafe** (170 Forest Ave., 831/373-6892, daily except Tues. for dinner, daily except Tues. and Sun. for lunch) are the best on the peninsula, but you won't go wrong with any of the Mexican and seafood specialties here, including tamales, seafood tacos, or spicy prawns. Beer and wine are served. Excellent for seafood with a Caribbean flair is the relaxed, reasonably priced, and family-friendly **ℕ Fishwife** (1996-1/2 Sunset Dr. at Asilomar, 831/375-7107, lunch and dinner daily) in the Beachcomber Inn, where such things as Boston clam chowder and grilled Cajun snapper fill out the menu. Full bar.

Dinner-only **ℕ Passionfish** (701 Lighthouse Ave., 831/655-3311) is another seafood hot spot, this one serving only seafood from fisheries currently considered sustainable. Meals are quite reasonable priced, at $20 or less for most entrées, from wild Monterey Bay salmon to tilapia in sweet roasted red pepper vinaigrette over veggie risotto. Save room for some homemade dessert. Wine is an adventure here, too, especially since the selections are priced at retail. You can also order by the glass—even dessert wines—from an ever-changing international selection.

FINE DINING

Among the Monterey Peninsula's hottest new restaurants, at last report, was casually dressy **ℕ Max's Grill** (209 Forest Ave., 831/375-7997, 5–9:30 P.M. Tues.–Sun., closed Mon.), where most of the produce and other main ingredients are regional and fresh, and just about everything else, down to the breads and pastas, is homemade. Chef Hisayuki "Max" Muramatsu was most recently executive chef at Carmel's Anton & Michel; before that, he was an award-winning chef in Tokyo, cooking at Maxim's of Paris. The menu changes regularly, yet house specialties such as grilled farm-fresh baby abalone with citrus capers in white wine sauce and Max's own "surf and turf," coconut-encrusted prawns plus broiled filet mignon in red wine sauce with potatoes Maxim's, are always on the menu. Quite reasonable prices, too, and a nice wine list. A truly great deal, especially for smaller appetites, is Max's fixed-price Sunset Menu, served 5–6 P.M. For $13.95, you get soup or salad and your choice of a handful of entrées, including blackened salmon, grilled calamari, and chicken piccata. Reservations are essential at Max's on Friday and Saturday nights.

For boisterous Basque food, try **Fandango** (in the stone house at 223 17th St. off Lighthouse Ave., 831/372-3456, lunch and dinner daily, Sun. brunch). One of the best restaurants around, Fandango serves wonderful Mediterranean country fare—from mesquite-grilled seafood, steak, and rack of lamb to tapas, pastas, and paella—in several separate dining rooms warmed by fireplaces. Try the chocolate nougatine pie or *vacherin* for dessert. Sunday brunch here is superb. Dressy attire prevails at dinner in the smaller dining rooms, but everything is casual in the Terrace Room.

A longtime local favorite for that special night out is romantic, welcoming, and fairly expensive **ℕ The Old Bath House** (at Lovers Point, 620 Ocean View Blvd., 813/375-5195, nightly for dinner), beloved for its lively Northern Italian and French fare, exceptional desserts, and appetizing views. Full bar, venerable Scotch list, extensive wine list. Early Dinner and Children's Menus, too.

Entertainment and Shopping

Pacific Grove boasts more than 75 local art galleries, enough to keep anyone busy. The **Peninsula Potters Gallery** (2078 Sunset Dr., 831/372-8867, 10 A.M.–4 P.M. Mon.–Sat.) is the place to appreciate the potter's art. Also worth a stop is the excellent **Pacific Grove Art Center** (568 Lighthouse, 831/375-2208).

EVENTS

There are hometown-style events happening year-round. The renowned Pacific Grove **Wildflower Show,** an exhibit of more than 600 native species (150 outdoors) in bloom at the Pacific Grove Museum of Natural History, is held the third week in April. Also in April is the **Pacific Grove Poetry Festival.** In March or April, the **Good Old Days** celebration brings a parade, Victorian home tours, and arts and crafts galore. In late July, come for the annual **Feast of Lanterns,** a traditional boat parade and fireworks ceremony that started when Chinese fishermen lived at China Point (their village was torched in 1906).

Pacific Grove's biggest party comes in October, with **Welcome Back Monarch Day.** This native, naturalistic, and noncommercial community bash heralds the return of the migrating monarchs and includes the **Butterfly Parade,** carnival, and bazaar, all to benefit the PTA. Not coinci-

dentally, from October to February, the most popular destination in town is the **Monarch Grove Sanctuary** on Ridge Road (just off Lighthouse), where docent-led tours are offered daily; for reservations, call 831/375-0982 or 888/746-6627. Otherwise, come in October for the **Pacific Grove Victorian Home Tour,** or in November for the **State Championship High School Marching Band Festival.** In December, check out **Christmas at the Inns,** when several local B&Bs, decorated for the holidays, hold an open house and serve refreshments. Here, as in Monterey, **First Night** is everyone's favorite kickoff for the new year.

SHOPPING

Shopping is good in adjacent Pacific Grove, too—starting right next to Cannery Row at the **American Tin Cannery Premium Outlet** mall (125 Ocean Ave., 831/372-1442), where shops include Carole Little, Carter's Children's Wear, Nine West, and Woolrich, not to mention specialty shops like Windborne Kites. **The First Noel** (562 Lighthouse Ave., 831/648-1250) specializes in all things Christmas, with other holidays thrown in for good measure. The best boutique around for women's clothing is **The Clothing Store** (510 Lighthouse Ave., 831/649-8866).

Carmel

Vizcaíno named the river here after Palestine's Mount Carmel, probably with the encouragement of several Carmelite friars accompanying his expedition. The name Carmel-by-the-Sea distinguishes this postcard-pretty coastal village of almost 5,000 souls from affluent Carmel Valley, 10 miles inland, and Carmel Highlands, just south of Point Lobos on the way to Big Sur. Everything about all the Carmels, though, says one thing quite clearly: money. Despite its bohemian beginnings, modern-day Carmel tends to crankily guard its quaintness while cranking up the commercialism. (Shopping is the town's major draw.) Still free at last report are the beautiful city beaches and visits to the elegant old Carmel Mission. Almost free: tours of Robinson Jeffers's **Tor House** and fabulous **Point Lobos,** just south of town.

Carmel hasn't always been so crowded or so crotchety. Open-minded artists, poets, writers, and other oddballs were the community's original movers and shakers—most of them shaken up and out of San Francisco after the 1906 earthquake. Upton Sinclair, Sinclair Lewis, Robinson Jeffers, and Jack London were some of the literary lights who once twinkled in this town. Master photographers Ansel Adams and Edward Weston were more recent residents. But, as often happens in California, land values shot up, and the original bohemians were priced right out of the neighborhood. Still, the arts are still proud local residents.

Must-Sees

ᴍ **Carmel Walks:** This two-hour guided walk showcases the onetime homes of bohemians, classic fairytale cottages, architecture by Bernard Maybeck and Charles S. Greene, and even Doris Day's pet-friendly hotel (page 63).

ᴍ **Carmel Mission:** California's second mission features an evocative 1797 baroque stone church, one of the state's most graceful buildings, complete with a four-bell Moorish tower, arched roof, and star-shaped central window (page 65).

ᴍ **Robinson Jeffers's Tor House:** Now a national historic landmark, this medieval-looking granite retreat presides over Carmel Bay. Tor House was built by the famed California poet Robinson Jeffers, who helped haul the huge stones up from the beach below with horse teams (page 65).

ᴍ **Point Lobos:** A jewel in the crown of California's state parks, Point Lobos, just south of Carmel, offers miles of pounding surf and a dramatic, cypress-fringed, rocky coastline (page 68).

© ROBERT HOLMES/CALTOUR

Carmel Mission

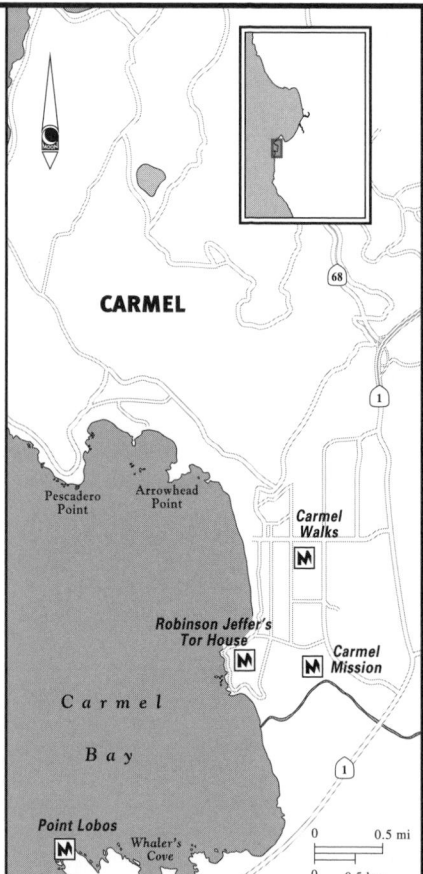

In summer and on most warm-weather weekends, traffic on Highway 1 can back up for a mile or more in either direction, due to the Carmel "crunch." At such times, parking is usually nonexistent. (Even if you do find a parking spot in downtown Carmel, don't dawdle; parking is limited to one hour, and you risk a steep fine if you're late getting back.) Sane people take the bus, ride bikes, or walk. Better yet, come for the weekend and pretend you live here. That's really the only way to appreciate the town's unique characteristics—including the absence of streetlights, traffic signals, street signs, sidewalks, house numbers, mailboxes, neon signs, and jukeboxes.

Another thing about Carmel: It's gone to the dogs. For one thing, dogs can run free on Carmel Beach. For another, dogs are not only welcome, but pampered at many hostelries and eateries around town, and many shopkeepers pass out doggie treats with no prompting. There's even a dogs-only drinking fountain in town, the **Fountain of Woof** at Carmel Plaza. And don't miss the doggie boutiques.

Sights

To get oriented, take a walk. Carmel has a few tiny parks hidden here and there, including one especially for walkers: **Mission Trails Park,** featuring about five miles of trails winding through redwoods, willows, and wildflowers (in season). Finding it is challenging, since Carmel doesn't believe in signs. To do the walk the easy way, start at the park's cleverly concealed Flanders Drive entrance off Hatton Road (appreciate the **Lester Rowntree Memorial Arboretum** just inside) before strolling downhill to the Rio Road trailhead near the mission. Then visit the mission or head downtown. Carmel's shops and galleries alone are an easy daylong distraction for true shoppers, but local architecture is also intriguing. The area between Fifth and Eighth Streets and Junipero and the city beach is packed with seacoast cottages, Carmel gingerbread "dollhouses," and adobe-and-post homes typical of the area.

CARMEL WALKS

For a great two-hour guided walk, Carmel Walks (831/642-2700, www.carmelwalks.com, $20 per person) tours walkers past the town's original fairytale cottages, architecture by Bernard Maybeck and Charles S. Greene, onetime homes of bohemians, the local doings of photographers Edward Weston and Ansel Adams, and oddities such as a house made entirely of doors and another built from pieces of old ships. The tour also visits Doris Day's pet-friendly hotel, includes tales of locally famous dogs, and notes local restaurants where dogs are permitted to dine with the family out on the patio. At last report, walks were offered at 10 A.M. Tuesday–Friday and at 10 A.M. and 2 P.M. Saturday. Reservations required.

BEACHES

The downtown crescent of **Carmel Beach City Park** is beautiful—steeply sloping, blinding-white sands and aquamarine waters—but too cold and dangerous for swimming. It's also a tourist zoo in summer. (A winter sunset stroll is wonderful, though.) A better alternative is to take Scenic Road (or Carmelo Street) south from Santa Lucia off Rio Road to **Carmel River State Beach** (831/649-2836), fringed with eucalyptus and cypress and often uncrowded, but quite dangerous in high surf. This is where locals go to get away. The nearby marsh is a bird sanctuary providing habitat for hawks, kingfishers, cormorants, herons, pelicans, sandpipers, snowy egrets, and sometimes flocks of migrating ducks and geese. Still part of the park, just beyond, yet almost a secret, are **Middle Beach,** a curving, sandy crescent on the south side of the Carmel River, and **Monastery Beach** at San Jose Creek, just south. Middle is accessible year-round by taking Ribera Road from Highway 1; in summer or fall, you can also get there by walking across the dry riverbed and following the trail. Safety note: Mid-

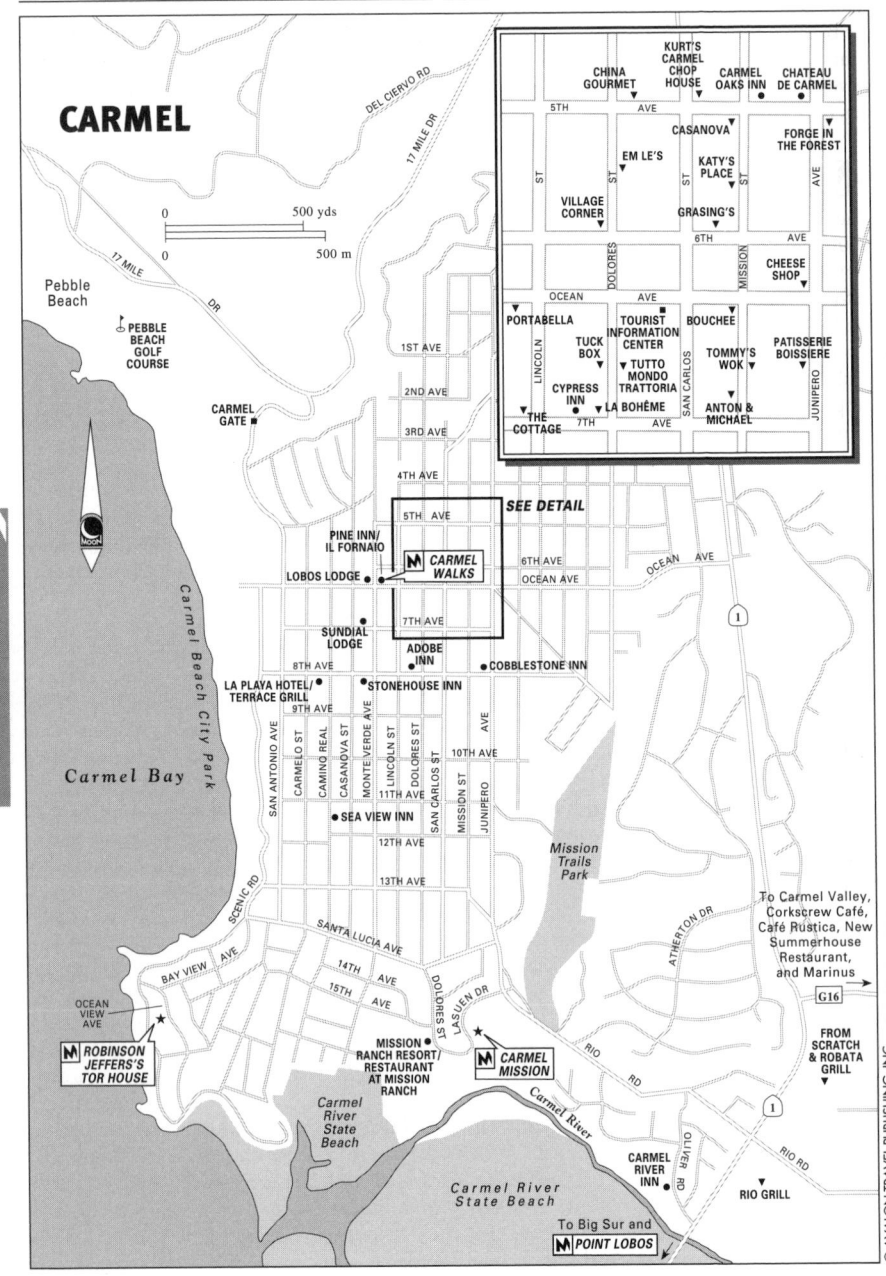

CARMEL

Carmel

Pebble Beach

PEBBLE BEACH GOLF COURSE

CARMEL GATE

DEL CIERVO RD

17 MILE DR

17 MILE DR

0   500 yds
0   500 m

1ST AVE
2ND AVE
3RD AVE
4TH AVE
5TH   AVE

SEE DETAIL

PINE INN/ IL FORNAIO
LOBOS LODGE

CARMEL WALKS

6TH AVE
OCEAN AVE
7TH AVE

OCEAN   AVE

SUNDIAL LODGE
ADOBE INN
8TH AVE
9TH AVE

COBBLESTONE INN

LA PLAYA HOTEL/ TERRACE GRILL
STONEHOUSE INN

Carmel Beach City Park

SAN ANTONIO AVE
CARMELO ST
CAMINO REAL
CASANOVA ST
MONTE VERDE AVE
LINCOLN ST
DOLORES ST
SAN CARLOS ST
MISSION ST
JUNIPERO
SCENIC RD

10TH AVE
11TH AVE

Carmel Bay

SEA VIEW INN

12TH AVE
13TH AVE

Mission Trails Park

SANTA LUCIA AVE

BAY VIEW   AVE

14TH   AVE
15TH   AVE

DOLORES ST
LAS UEN DR

OCEAN 1

ATHERTON DR

To Carmel Valley, Corkscrew Café, Café Rustica, New Summerhouse Restaurant, and Marinus

G16

OCEAN VIEW AVE

ROBINSON JEFFERS'S TOR HOUSE

MISSION RANCH RESORT/ RESTAURANT AT MISSION RANCH

CARMEL MISSION

FROM SCRATCH & ROBATA GRILL

Carmel River State Beach

Carmel River

RIO RD

Carmel River State Beach

CARMEL RIVER INN

OLIVER RD

RIO RD

RIO GRILL

1

To Big Sur and
POINT LOBOS

Detail inset:

CHINA GOURMET
KURT'S CARMEL CHOP HOUSE
CARMEL OAKS INN
CHATEAU DE CARMEL

5TH   AVE

CASANOVA
FORGE IN THE FOREST

EM LE'S
KATY'S PLACE

ST
ST
ST
ST
AVE

VILLAGE CORNER
GRASING'S

DOLORES

6TH   AVE

MISSION

CHEESE SHOP

OCEAN   AVE

PORTABELLA

TOURIST INFORMATION CENTER
BOUCHEE
PATISSERIE BOISSIERE

LINCOLN

TUCK BOX
TUTTO MONDO TRATTORIA
TOMMY'S WOK

SAN CARLOS

JUNIPERO

CYPRESS INN
LA BOHÈME
ANTON & MICHAEL

THE COTTAGE
7TH   AVE

© AVALON TRAVEL PUBLISHING, INC.

dle Beach is hazardous for swimming and sometimes even for walking, due to freak 10-foot waves. Monastery Beach is popular for scuba diving, but its surf conditions are equally treacherous.

CARMEL MISSION

The Carmel Mission (3080 Rio Rd., 831/624-3600 for gift shop or 831/624-1271 for rectory, www.carmelmission.org, open for self-guided tours 9:30 A.M.–4:30 P.M. Mon.–Fri., 10:30 A.M.–4:15 P.M. Sat.–Sun., $4 adults and seniors, $1 children 5–17, free for children under 5, additional donations appreciated), properly called Mission Basilica San Carlos Borroméo del Rio Carmelo, is wonderful and well worth a visit. California's second mission, it was originally established at the Monterey Presidio in 1770, then moved here the following year. Located just a few blocks west of Highway 1, it is the onetime headquarters and favorite foreign home of Father Junípero Serra, whose remains are buried at the foot of the altar in the sanctuary. The mission's magnificent, vine-draped cathedral is the first thing to catch the eye. The romantic Baroque stone church, one of the state's most graceful buildings, complete with a four-bell Moorish tower, arched roof, and star-shaped central window, was completed in 1797.

Most of the buildings here are reconstructions, however, since the Carmel Mission fell to ruins in the 1800s. But these "new" old buildings, painstakingly rebuilt and restored in the 1930s under the direction of Sir Harry Downie, fail to suggest the size and complexity of the original bustling mission complex: an odd-shaped quadrangle with a central fountain, gardens, kitchen, carpenter and blacksmith shops, soldiers' housing, and priests' quarters. The native peoples attached to the mission—a labor force of 4,000 Christian converts—lived separately in a nearby village. More than 3,000 "mission Indians" are buried in the silent, simple cemetery. Most graves in these gardens are unmarked, but some are decorated with abalone shells. The gardens themselves, started by Downie, are fabulous, with old-fashioned plant

Carmel Mission

varieties, from bougainvillea to bird of paradise, fuchsias, and "towers of jewels."

The Carmel Mission has three museums. The "book museum" holds California's first unofficial library—the 600 volumes Padre Serra brought to California in 1769. The silver altar furnishings are also originals, as are the ornate vestments, Spanish and native artifacts, and other mission memorabilia. By contrast, Serra's simple priest's cell is a lesson in modern materialism.

ROBINSON JEFFERS'S TOR HOUSE

A medieval-looking granite retreat on a rocky knoll above Carmel Bay, Tor House (26304 Ocean View Ave., 831/624-1813, www.torhouse.org) was built by family man and poet Robinson Jeffers, who hauled the huge stones up from the beach below with horse teams. The manual labor, he said, cleared his mind, and "my fingers had the art to make stone love stone." California's dark prince of poetry, Jeffers was generally aloof from the peninsula's other "seacoast bohemians." On the day he died here, January 20, 1962, it

© ROBERT HOLMES/CALTOUR

CROWN OF CARMEL HIKING: PALO CORONA

Now that the Monterey Peninsula Regional Park District has acquired a portion of the vast Palo Corona Ranch, a spectacular community park offers public access to property known locally as "the Old Fish Ranch." The new **Palo Corona Ranch Regional Park,** accessible from the foothills near Carmel and opened in spring 2005, starts with the ranch's stunning northern slopes, covering some 680 acres. Ultimately, Palo Corona Park will total 4,300 acres and provide access for hiking, biking, dog walking, and horseback riding.

Ranging from near sea level to more than 3,000 feet in elevation, the property offers outstanding views of Santa Cruz, both Carmel and Monterey Bays, Pebble Beach, Point Lobos, and the Big Sur coastline, as well as Fremont Peak and the Pinnacles Range.

The entire Palo Corona Ranch, at nearly 10,000 acres, was purchased in 2002 by The Nature Conservancy and The Big Sur Land Trust. Still serving as the gateway to Big Sur, the ranch connects 13 previously conserved lands, protects 20 rivers, and preserves a 70-mile wildlife corridor between Carmel and Hearst Ranch near San Simeon.

Since Palo Corona Ranch Regional Park is new and public access in its infancy, be sure to get current details before setting out. For information, contact the **Monterey Peninsula Regional Park District** (831/372-3196, www.mprpd.org).

snowed—a rare event along any stretch of California's coast. James Karman's literary biography, **_Robinson Jeffers: Poet of California,_** offers wonderful insight into Jeffers's life and work.

You can only begin to appreciate Tor House from the outside (it's just a short walk up from Carmel River Beach, on Ocean View Avenue between Scenic Road and Stewart Way). Jeffers built the three-story Hawk Tower, complete with secret passageway, for his wife, Una. The mellow redwood paneling, warm oriental rugs, and lovely gardens soften the impact of the home's bleak tawny exterior—the overall effect somehow symbolizing Jeffers's hearth-centered life, seemingly far removed

from the world's insanity. Almost whimsical is the collection of 100-plus unicorns the poet gathered. Now a national historic landmark—don't go snooping around on your own—Tor House is open for small-group guided tours on Friday and Saturday, advance reservations required. Adults pay $7, full-time college students $4, high school students $2. The first tour begins at 10 A.M. and the final tour at 3 P.M. Tours are limited to six people; no children under 12 are allowed. Make reservations by phone or email (see the website for details).

The Tor House Foundation also offers a full schedule of events, from its annual poetry prize, readings, and sunset garden parties to the Robinson Jeffers Seminars, Jeffers Country Bus Tour (of Big Sur), and Jeffers Poetry Walk.

CARMEL VALLEY

The sunny (and warmer), sprawling "village" of Carmel Valley stretches some 14 miles inland via Carmel Valley Road, a well-designed but hellacious highway, at least between Carmel and these affluent suburbs and golf and tennis farms (including John Gardiner's Tennis Ranch). Locals curse tourists and others who drive the speed limit.

The village area has definite diversion value for the wealthy and wannabes—note the shopping centers—but the valley has always been the one Carmel's just plain folks were most likely to inhabit. In 1939, Rosie's Cracker Barrel on Equiline Road became the valley's general store, and soon the unofficial community center. Though Rosie's was always the place to pick up picnic supplies and whatnot, there was also a bar out back where locals held forth—definitely not a tourist joint. Rosie's is closed now; plans to reopen it as a museum are in the works. Still, some notable before-the-wealthy Carmel Valley traditions remain, like wide-open spaces. Outdoorsy types will appreciate **Garland Ranch Regional Park** (north of town at 700 W. Carmel Valley Rd., 831/659-4488). The park offers hiking trails on 4,500 hilly acres; you'll get an astounding view from the top of Snively's Ridge.

For more information about Carmel Valley and vicinity, contact the **Carmel Valley Chamber of Commerce** (91 W. Carmel Valley Rd., 831/659-4000, www.carmelvalleychamber.com).

ROBINSON JEFFERS MEETS UNA

If William Hamilton Jeffers [his father] was the archetypal wise old man in Robinson's life, then Una Call Kuster was, in Jungian terms, his anima ideal. Robinson met Una the first year he attended USC [the University of Southern California], in 1906. They were in Advanced German together, reading *Faust*. Una was strikingly beautiful and very intelligent. She was also three years older than Robinson and married. Nevertheless, a friendship developed that was nurtured by a mutual love for literature and ideas. She gave him Arthur Symons' *Wordsworth and Shelley* to read, and the two spent many hours discussing this and other essays, books, and poems.

When Jeffers left USC for the University of Zurich, he sent her an occasional note. When he returned to begin medical studies, the friendship resumed and deepened.

At this time in her life, Una was struggling to define her own identity. Several years before, at eighteen, she had left Mason, Michigan, in order to enter the University of California at Berkeley. She met a young attorney there, Edward ("Teddie") Kuster, whom she promptly married. When they moved to the Los Angeles area, she lived the life of a successful lawyer's wife—with golf at the San Gabriel Country Club, social events, even road races in big, expensive cars taking up most of her time. But something was missing. . . .

Inevitably, her marriage fell apart. Her husband, trying to explain to an interested public what had happened, blamed the breakdown on Una's unconventional ideas. As he says in an interview that appeared in the February 28, 1913, edition of the *Los Angeles Times*, "my wife seemed to find no solace in the ordinary affairs of life; she was without social ambition, and social functions seemed a bore to her. Her accomplishments are many, and she sought constantly for a wider scope for her intelligence. She turned to philosophy and the school of modern decadents, and she talked of things beyond the ken of those of us who dwelt upon the lower levels."

Though Teddie could not understand his wife, he knew there was someone who could—a "vile poetaster" named Robinson Jeffers.

From the first time they met, Robinson had listened to Una and shared her enthusiasms. His own extensive background in languages, philosophy, religion, and literature made him a perfect conversation partner. Moreover, he was a handsome man, rugged, poetic, melancholy, and intense.

And Una listened to Robinson. She was perhaps the only person he had ever known who could understand and appreciate the complex thoughts he brooded on. Moreover, she was unconventional and passionate. While the fashionable women wore their hair in high pompadours topped by large hats, Una often wore hers in a braid that fell loose down her back.

In time, their casual friendship grew more rich. "Without the wish of either of us," says Una, "our life was one of those fatal attractions that happen unplanned and undesired."

—Excerpted with permission from the literary biography Robinson Jeffers: Poet of California, *by James Karman (Ashland, OR: Story Line Press, 1995)*

TASSAJARA ZEN MOUNTAIN CENTER

Tassajara Hot Springs, established in 1869 beyond Carmel Valley Road, was long a respected area resort. (The Tassajara Road turnoff is off Cachagua Road, near the southward intersection with Tularcitos.) According to Native American legend, these curative springs first flowed from the eyes of a young chief seeking help for his dying sister. Offering himself as a sacrifice to the sun, he turned to stone, and his tears became the hot springs.

Now the monastic Tassajara Zen Mountain Center (www.sfzc.com), affiliated with the **San Francisco Zen Center,** this is the first Soto Zen monastery outside of Asia, open to the general public from April or May until early September. Guest stays require "a commitment to explore Zen practice," and summer work stays can also be arranged. Otherwise, people can apply to come here as day guests for the hot springs (bathing suits required), fabulous wilderness access, and marvelous vegetarian meals. With confirmed reservations, the center will send a map and directions. For current details, see the Zen Center's website. There is no phone at Tassajara, and no cell phones, radios, tape players, TVs, or cars are allowed.

Not far from Tassajara, on Cachagua Road, is the onetime site of the 10-story, 34-ton AT&T **Jamesburg Earth Station,** an impressive parabolic COMSAT dish antenna which once transmitted (via satellite) more than half the phone calls between the U.S. and Asia. Long a popular stop for space technology fans, the station was unplugged in October 2003 by AT&T, since the transmission task had been taken over by fiber optic cables laid down on the ocean's floor.

For an excursion, take Tularcitos Road until it joins Arroyo Seco Road, then jog southwest toward the backside of Big Sur and the Arroyo Seco River canyon. There you can enjoy camping, picnicking, and hiking. Backpackers can head west on a long but rewarding trek to remote, undeveloped **Sykes Hot Springs,** near Horse Bridge Camp.

MIRA OBSERVATORY

If for some reason you decide to drive the last six miles of unpaved Tassajara Road, this is where you'll end up. Not officially open to the public, the MIRA Observatory, built atop Chews Ridge by the Monterey Institute for Research in Astronomy (MIRA, 831/883-1000, www.mira.org), is a barrel-shaped, rolltop professional observatory 12 miles inland from Big Sur. MIRA's earth-tone, two-story, corrugated Oliver Observing Station—named after a retired Hewlett-Packard vice president who kicked in some cash, some advanced electronics, and a 36-inch telescope—includes office and living space. It has earned design awards from the American Institute of Architects. Monthly summer and early fall tours of the observing station and occasional guest lectures are offered. The institute is now developing the **Richard W. Hamming Astronomy Center** on the old site of Fort Ord, near the new CSU Monterey Bay campus.

Recreation

⋈ POINT LOBOS

One of the crown jewels of California's state parks, Point Lobos State Reserve (831/624-4909, http://pt-lobos.parks.state.ca.us, ptlobos @mbay.net, day use only, sunrise–sunset in summer, until 5 P.M. in winter) is a 1,250-acre coastal wonderland about four miles south of Carmel. Pack a picnic; this is the best the Monterey area has to offer. The relentless surf and wild winds have pounded these reddish shores for millennia, sculpting six miles of shallow aquamarine coves, wonderful tidepools, aptly named Bird Island, and jutting points: Granite, Coal, Chute, China, Cannery, Pinnacle, Pelican, and Lobos itself. From here, look to the sea, as Santa Cruz poet William Everson has, "standing in cypress and surrounded by cypress, watching through its witchery as the surf explodes in unbelievable beauty on the granite below." Local lore has it that Point Lobos inspired Fort Ord, near the Robert

dramatically beautiful Point Lobos

Louis Stevenson's Spyglass Hill in *Treasure Island*. The muse for Robinson Jeffers's somber "Tamar" definitely lived (and lives) here.

Sights

From the dramatic headlands, watch for whales in winter. Many other marine mammals are year-round residents. Brown pelicans and cormorants preen themselves on offshore rocks. Here, the sea otters aren't shy: They boldly crack open abalone and dine in front of visitors. (The entire central coast area, from San Francisco south to beyond Big Sur, is protected as part of the **Monterey Bay National Marine Sanctuary.** And by order of former President Bill Clinton, the state's entire coastline is now protected as the California Coastal National Monument.) If you're heading south into Big Sur country, watch offshore otter antics—best with binoculars—from highway turnouts. Harbor seals hide in the coves. The languorous, loudly barking sea lions gave rise to the original Spanish name Punta de los Lobos Marinos ("Point of the Sea Wolves"). Follow the crisscrossing reserve trails for a morning walk

through groves of bonsai Monterey cypress and pine, accented by colorful seasonal wildflowers (300 species, best in April). Watch for poison oak, which thrives here, too. Whalers Cove, near the picnic and parking area, was once a granite quarry, then a whaler's cove—the cabin and cast-iron rendering pot are still there—and an abalone cannery. It's something of a miracle that the Point Lobos headland exists almost unscarred, as cattle grazed here for decades. Fortunately for us all, turn-of-the-20th-century subdivision plans for Point Lobos were scuttled.

Head for Whalers Cove to bone up on local history. **Whalers Cabin Museum,** "the shack" overlooking Whalers Cove, built by Chinese fishermen, tells the story of Point Lobos and vicinity. The adjacent **Whaling Station Museum,** once a garage, features displays about shore whaling along California's central coast—everything from harpoons and whale-oil barrels to historic Monterey Peninsula whaling photos. Both museums are open as staffing allows, usually 11 A.M.–3 P.M. Guided hikes are also offered at Point Lobos; see the monthly schedule posted at the park's entrance. Curious students of history and natural history can also get an impressive area introduction via the park's website.

Safety

Point Lobos is considered one of the state's "underwater parks," in recognition of its aquatic beauty. Scuba and free diving are popular, but allowed by permit only; call for reservations (831/624-8413), or see the park's website. Diver safety is a major concern of park staff. Get permits and current information about what to expect down below before easing into the water. People aren't kidding when they mention "treacherous cliff and surf conditions" here, so think first before scrambling off in search of bigger and better tidepools. Particularly dangerous, even in serene surf, is the Monastery Beach area, near San Jose Creek just beyond the reserve's northern border; there's a steep offshore drop-off into submarine Carmel Canyon, and unstable sand underfoot. Children should be carefully supervised, and even experienced

Carmel

SEA OTTERS DECLINING AGAIN

Sea otters range north along the coast to Jenner in Sonoma County, and south to Cambria (and beyond). Watching otters eat is quite entertaining; to really see the show, binoculars are usually necessary. Carrying softball-sized rocks in their paws, sea otters dive deep to dislodge abalone, mussels, and other shellfish, then return to the surface and leisurely smash the shells and dine while floating on their backs, "rafting" at anchor in forests of seaweed. They feed heartily, each otter consuming about two and a half tons of seafood per year—much to the dismay of commercial shellfish interests.

Such scenes are still fairly common, yet the California sea otter, listed as a threatened species under the federal Endangered Species Act, is declining again. In 1995, the U.S. Fish and Wildlife Service counted 2,377 sea otters. By 1998, the population had dropped to 1,937—and some 200 dead otters washed ashore on area beaches, for reasons unknown. The average spring-count population declined at a rate of about four percent per year between 1985 and 1994, but since the mid-1990s, the annual decline has averaged eight percent. Scientists are still figuring out why.

Obvious ongoing hazards include coastal pollution, infectious disease, natural toxins (such as red tide algae), entrapment in fishing nets or wire fishing pots, and even occasional shark attacks. Yet recent research suggests parasitic disease is the primary culprit, causing fatal illness in the brains and nervous systems of sea otters and other animals. Two primary parasites have been discovered: *Toxoplasma gondii,* its spores introduced by cat feces flushed into sewage systems, and *Sarcocystis neurona,* spread through opossum feces.

In past centuries, an estimated population of almost 16,000 sea otters along the California coast was decimated by eager fur hunters. A single otter pelt was worth upward of $1,700 by 1910, when it was generally believed that sea otters were extinct here. But a small pod survived off the coast near Carmel, a secret well guarded by biologists until the Big Sur Highway opened in 1938.

Until the 1990s, the sea otters seemed to be making a comeback; their range had expanded widely up and down the coast. Much to the chagrin of the south coast commercial shellfish industry, sea otters had even started moving south past Point Conception into shellfish waters.

divers and swimmers might think twice before going into the water.

Practicalities

Point Lobos is beautiful—and popular. It can be crowded in summer and sometimes on spring and fall weekends. Since only 450 people are allowed into the park at one time, plan your trip accordingly, and come early in the day (or wait in long lines along Highway 1—not fun). Admission (parking) is $8 per car, a fee waived for walk-ins and bike-ins. Small fee for trail brochures. Bikes must stay on pavement in the park, which means no trail riding.

You can also get to Point Lobos on Monterey-Salinas Transit's bus 22 (to Big Sur). From Carmel, it's a fairly easy bike ride. The weather can be cold, damp, and windy, even in summer, so bring a sweater or jacket in addition to good walking shoes (and, if you have them, binoculars). The park's informative brochure is printed in five languages. Guided tours are offered daily. To better appreciate local flora and the 200-plus species of birds spotted at Point Lobos, pick up the plant and bird lists at the ranger station. In May, the Department of Fish and Game's **Marine Resources and Marine Pollution Studies Laboratory** at Granite Canyon sponsors an open house.

Accommodations

CAMPING

Mary Austin's observation that "beauty is cheap here" may apply to the views, but little else in the greater Carmel area—with the exception of camping and the fine local elder hostel.

Carmel by the River RV Park (27680 Schulte Rd. off Carmel Valley Road, 831/624-9329, www.carmelrv.com) is well away from it all. Some 35 attractively landscaped sites sit right on the Carmel River, with full hookups, cable TV, laundry facilities, a rec room, and other amenities. Also at the end of Schulte Road, nearby **Saddle Mountain Recreation Park** (831/624-1617) offers both tent and RV sites (reservations accepted for weekends only), restrooms, showers, picnic tables, a swimming pool, a playground, and other recreational possibilities, including nearby hiking trails. Another option is **Veterans Memorial Park** (see *Camping* in the *Monterey* chapter).

In the primitive-and-distant category, you can camp southeast of Carmel Valley at the U.S. Forest Service **White Oaks Campground** at Chews Ridge, which has seven sites, or nearby **China Camp,** with six sites; both are free and first-come, first-camped, best suited for wilderness trekkers. Farther on, you'll find **Tassajara Zen Mountain Center** (415/865-1899 after April 1, www.sfzc .com) often offering camping and other accommodations in summer by advance reservation. The nearby Forest Service **Arroyo Seco Campground** has 46 sites. Camping is also plentiful to the south in Big Sur (see below). The Forest Service sites require purchase of a daily (or annual) Adventure Pass, available at Forest Service ranger stations and many sporting goods stores and other vendors. For more information on local Forest Service campgrounds, contact the Monterey District of Los Padres National Forest (831/385-5434, www.fs.fed.us/r5/lospadres).

Those who qualify as elders can sign on for a very affordable, very educational Carmel stay, thanks to the **Elderhostel at Hidden Valley** (831/659-3115, www.hiddenvalleymusic.org/ehostel.htm or www.elderhostel.org), a program of Carmel Valley's Hidden Valley Music Center. The five-night stays include room, board, and programs such as *The Eden Steinbeck Was East Of, Birding at Monterey Bay,* and *Wine, Wonderful Wine,* all for less than $100 per day. Such a deal.

HOTELS AND INNS: $100–150

"Classic" is the only word for the historic **Pine Inn** (downtown on Ocean between Monte Verde and Lincoln, 831/624-3851 or 800/228-3851, www.pine-inn.com). This small hotel offers comfortable "Carmel Victorian" accommodations and fine dining at the onsite **Il Fornaio** restaurant and bakery; there's even a gazebo with a rollback roof for eating alfresco, fog permitting. Even if you don't stay here, sit on the terrace, act affluent, and sip Ramos fizzes.

The **Carmel River Inn** (26600 Oliver Rd., south of town on Hwy. 1 at the Carmel River Bridge, 831/624-1575 or 800/882-8142, www.carmelriverinn.com, $85 and up, two-night minimum on weekends) is a pleasant, 10-acre, riverside spread with a heated pool, 24 cozy, family-friendly cottages and duplexes (some with wood-burning fireplaces and kitchens), and 19 motel rooms. Pets welcome for a $25-per-pet fee.

Other above-average Carmel accommodations—and there are plenty to choose from—include the **Carmel Oaks Inn** (Fifth and Mission, 831/624-5547 or 800/266-5547, www.carmeloaksinn.com), attractive and convenient and a bargain by local standards, and the **Lobos Lodge** (Monte Verde and Ocean, 831/624-3874, www.loboslodge.com). Another option is the recently upgraded, 20-room, Victorian-style **Chateau de Carmel** (Fifth and Junipero, 831/624-1900 or 800/325-8515, www.chateaudecarmel.com), a restyled, two-story motel offering some lower-priced rooms.

HOTELS AND INNS: $150–250

The **Sundial Lodge** (Monte Verde and Seventh, 831/624-8578, www.sundiallodge.com) is a cross between a small hotel and a bed-and-breakfast. Each of the 19 antique-furnished rooms has a private bath, TV, and telephone. Other amenities include lovely English gardens and a courtyard, continental breakfast, and afternoon tea.

The landmark 1929 **M Cypress Inn,** (downtown at Lincoln and Seventh, 831/624-3871 or 800/443-7443, www.cypress-inn.com, $125–425) is a charming, gracious, and intimate place; another small hotel with a bed-and-breakfast sensibility, recently updated. Pets are allowed—invited, actually—since actress-owner Doris Day is an animal-rights activist. (Dog beds provided.) And when hotel staff place a mint on your pillow at turn-down, they'll also leave a treat for your dog or cat. How's *that* for service? Rates include a continental breakfast.

Très Carmel, and a historic treasure, is the Mediterranean-style 1904 **M La Playa Hotel** (Camino Real and Eighth, 831/624-6476 or 800/582-8900, www.laplayahotel.com, $175 and up), where lush gardens surround guestrooms and cottages on the terraced hillside. Recently remodeled, rooms at La Playa feature evocative Spanish-style furnishings. The five cottages (starting at $335) feature fireplaces, oceanview decks, and separate living areas. Especially enjoyable when the gardens are in their glory is the onsite **Terrace Grill.**

BED-AND-BREAKFASTS

Local inns offer an almost overwhelming amount of choice, though that "inn" in Carmel may be a revamped motel. Local bed-and-breakfast inns are comparable in price to most Carmel area motels, and they're usually much homier. Two-night stays are usually required on weekends.

A notable value is the relaxed yet stylish **M Carmel Country Inn** (Dolores at Third, 831/625-3263 or 800/215-6343, www.carmel-countryinn.com, $150 and up), where the well-tended gardens are also an attraction. All rooms feature private bathrooms (some with whirlpool tubs) and come with quilted bed coverings, down comforters, country-pine furniture, gas fireplaces, color TV with cable, in-room coffee makers, and

refrigerators. Continental breakfast included. Pets and well-behaved children welcome.

The **M Cobblestone Inn** (Junipero near Eighth, 831/625-5222 or 800/833-8836, www.foursisters.com, $125 and up) is a traditional Carmel home now transformed into a Four Sisters inn—complete with a cobblestone courtyard, gas fireplaces in the guestrooms, and English country-house antiques. Rates include a full breakfast buffet, complimentary tea, and hors d'oeuvres. A Carmel classic is the ivy-draped **Stonehouse Inn** (Eighth and Monte Verde, 831/624-4569 or 877/748-6618, www.carmelstonehouse.com, $100–250), constructed by local Indians. All six rooms here are named after historical local luminaries, including writers, and all but two share bathrooms. Rates include full Southern-style breakfast, wine and sherry, and hors d'oeuvres.

The **Adobe Inn** (downtown at Dolores and Eighth, 831/624-3933 or 800/388-3933, www.adobeinn.com) features just about every inn-style comfort. Large rooms include elegant furnishings and gas fireplaces, wet bars with refrigerators, patios or decks, color TVs, phones, and data ports; some have ocean views. Other amenities include a sauna and heated pool, complimentary newspaper, and continental breakfast delivered to your room.

MISSION RANCH RESORT

Long the traditional place to stay, just outside town, is the Mission Ranch (26270 Dolores at 15th, 831/624-6436 or 800/538-8221, www.missionranchcarmel.com, $100–250, some suites $265). Once a pastoral dairy farm and now a quiet, small ranch owned by Clint Eastwood, relaxed Mission Ranch overlooks the Carmel River and features views of the Carmel River wetlands and Point Lobos. And the mission *is* nearby. Under Eastwood ownership, the Victorian farmhouse and its outbuildings have had an expensive makeover and together now resemble a Western village. The 31 guestrooms are decorated here and there with props from Eastwood movies. Lodgings are available in the historic main house, the Hayloft, the Bunkhouse (which has its own living room and kitchen), and the

© JUSTIN MARLER

Mission Ranch Resort

Barn. The newer Meadow View Rooms feature, well, meadow views. Another attraction, inside the former creamery, is the casually Western yet sophisticated **Restaurant at Mission Ranch** (831/625-9040), which serves make-my-day American fare at dinner—steaks, chops, fresh local salmon and such—complete with checkered tablecloths and a wood-burning stove that starred in *The Unforgiven*. There's an outdoor patio, too, grand cove views, and even a children's menu. Best yet, local jazz artists often perform in the piano bar here. Sunday champagne brunch, another live jazz event, is legendary.

CARMEL HIGHLANDS

The swank and well-known 1916 **Highlands Inn** (along Highway 1 four miles south of Carmel, 831/620-1234 or 800/233-1234 for Hyatt central reservations, www.hyatt.com, $250 and up) is indeed beautiful, though most people would have to default on their house payment to stay for long. That the Highlands Inn is now beginning to sell off its luxurious rooms and suites

as timeshares—a reality not too popular with long-time guests—makes rooms that much more precious. Offering some of the world's most spectacular views, some Highlands Inn suites feature wood-burning fireplaces, double spa baths, fully equipped kitchens, and all the comforts, down to the handmade local soaps. Even those of more plebeian means can enjoy a stroll through the Grand Lodge to appreciate the oak woodwork, twin yellow granite fireplaces, gorgeous earth-toned carpet, leather sofas and chairs, and granite tables. Or stay for a meal—the exceptional **Pacific's Edge** features stunning sunset views and is locally beloved, not to mention a consistent award-winner. Open for lunch, dinner, and Sunday brunch. The more casual **California Market** (7 A.M.–10 P.M. daily) is another option.

The nearby **Tickle Pink Inn** (155 Highlands Dr., just south of Highlands Inn, 831/624-1244 or 800/635-4774, www.ticklepink.com, $250 and up, two-night minimum on weekends) offers equally spectacular views and 35 inviting rooms and suites, an oceanview hot tub, continental breakfast, and wine and cheese at sunset.

CARMEL VALLEY

The historic **Los Laureles Country Inn** (313 W. Carmel Valley Rd., 831/659-2233, www.los laureles.com, rooms $100–200 or $75 and up in off-season, suites $150 and up) was once part of the Boronda Spanish land grant, and later a Del Monte ranch. Rooms here once stabled Muriel Vanderbilt's well-bred thoroughbreds. The inn has an excellent restaurant (American regional), saloon, pool, and conference facilities. Golf packages are available. And if it ever opens again—recent word is, expect a reopening by late 2005—another intriguing local tradition is the 1928 **Robles del Rio Lodge** (200 Punta Del Monte, www.roblesdelriolodge.com). Perched atop a hill overlooking Carmel Valley and reached via winding back roads, Robles del Rio has been closed since 1999, yet at last report was still destined to become a 59-room "luxury boutique spa."

Dog-friendly **Carmel Valley Lodge** (Carmel Valley Road at Ford, 831/659-2261 or 800/641-4646 for reservations only, www.valleylodge.com,

Carmel Valley

$150–250) offers nice little extras, like Barista French roast coffee, phones with data ports, cable TVs with VCRs (free video library), and original art on the walls. The lodge features rooms fronting the lovely gardens, plus one- and two-bedroom cottages with wood-burning fireplaces, kitchens, and private patios or decks. Other amenities include a pool, sauna, hot tub, and fitness center. Two-bedroom, two-bath cottages are $250 and up.

To see how the other 1 percent lives, head for the five-star **Quail Lodge Resort & Golf Club** (Carmel Valley Golf and Country Club, 8205 Valley Greens Dr., 831/624-2888, www.quaillodge.com, $250 and up). The lodge features elegant contemporary rooms and suites, some with fireplaces, plus access to private tennis and golf facilities and fine dining at **The Covey** restaurant. In the same vein and just as pricey is Wyndham Hotels' **Carmel Valley Ranch Resort** (1 Old Ranch Rd. off Robinson Canyon Rd., 831/625-9500, www.wyndham.com, $250 and up), a gated resort with 100 suites, all individually decorated, with wood-burning fireplaces and private decks. Some suites feature a private outdoor hot tub. Recreation facilities include a private golf course, 12 tennis courts, pools, saunas, and whirlpools.

Luxurious but still something of a new concept in Carmel Valley accommodations is the **Bernardus Lodge** (831/659-3247 or 888/648-9463, www.bernardus.com, $250 and up), a luxury resort affiliated with the Bernardus Winery and open since August 1999. Crafted from limestone, logs, ceramic tiles, and rich interior woods, the nine village-style buildings feature 57 suites for "discriminating travelers" and offer endless luxury amenities, including a different wine-and-cheese tasting every night at turn-down and a full-service spa. Definitely unique are special educational forums on gardening, the culinary arts, and viticulture, not to mention the onsite ballroom, celebrated **Marinus** restaurant, and more casual **Wickets** bistro. Outdoor recreation options include tennis and bocce ball, croquet, swimming, hiking and horseback riding on adjacent mountain trails, and golfing at neighboring resorts.

For a super-luxury stay—and to avoid the country clubs and other "too new" places—the choice is the 330-acre **Stonepine Estate Resort** (150 E. Carmel Valley Rd., 831/659-2245, www.stonepinecalifornia.com). Once the Crocker family's summer estate, this is now a thoroughbred horse ranch, complete with polo grounds, hunter and cross-country jumper courses, sulky track, and dressage arenas. Rates are truly astronomical.

Food

BREAKFAST

For a perfect omelette with home fries and home-made valley pork sausage, try **The Cottage** (on Lincoln between Ocean and Seventh, 831/625-6260). Another good choice for breakfast is **Katy's Place** (on the west side of Mission between Fifth and Sixth, 831/624-0199, open daily), another quaint cottage, this one boasting the largest breakfast and lunch menu on the West Coast. Great eggs Benedict—10 different varieties to choose from! Also cozy and crowded is **Em Le's** (Dolores and Fifth, 831/625-6780). Try the buttermilk waffles, available for lunch or dinner. The **Tuck Box** tearoom (on Dolores near Seventh, 831/624-6365) inspires you to stop just to take a photograph. It was once famous for its pecan pie, shepherd's pie, and Welsh rarebit, as well as great cheap breakfasts, but new owners have changed the menu—and the prices.

For good value and elegant ambience at breakfast, not to mention an abundant Sunday brunch, try the **Terrace Grill** at the historic La Playa Hotel (Camino Real at Eighth, 831/624-6476). A local classic is the landmark **Village Corner** (Sixth and Dolores, 831/624-3588, breakfast, lunch, and dinner daily), a California-Mediterranean bistro beloved for its heated patio dining and pastas, seafood, fish, and all-Monterey wine list. Kid-friendly, but on the expensive side.

DOG- AND KID-FRIENDLY

Ready to get down with the dogs? A Carmel pooch pleaser is eclectic, employee-owned ⋈ **The Forge in the Forest** (Fifth and Junipero, 831/624-2233, lunch and dinner daily, Sun. brunch), a onetime blacksmith shop where eight tables are reserved for dogs and their people. Favorites here include Reuben egg rolls with Russian dressing (really, they're good), baked onion soup, and, for dessert, the chocolate chip cookie dream. For Fido or Fifi, ask for the Dog Pound Menu, which includes the Quarter Hounder. Also notably dog-friendly is the

charming, quintessentially Carmel ⋈ **Porta-Bella** (Ocean Avenue between Lincoln and Monte Verde, 831/624-4395, lunch and dinner daily), serving wonderful Mediterranean food, such as fresh goat cheese ravioli, porcini-crusted dayboat scallops, Dungeness crab cakes, and the signature roasted corn and Dungeness crab bisque. Very reasonable. And if you're traveling with the kids (and/or canine), they can all sit with you out on the flagstone patio. Canine kiddos get the white-linen water dish treatment.

The equally kid-friendly **Rio Grill** (in the

⋈ Carmel

Crossroads Shopping Village, 101 Crossroads Blvd., Highway 1 at Rio Road, 831/625-5436, lunch and dinner daily, great Sun. brunch) is a long-running favorite for innovative, southwestern-style American fare. Everything is fresh or made from scratch; many entrées are served straight from the oakwood smoker, like the chipotle chicken. Don't miss the Rio's famous ice-cream sandwich.

Inexpensive **From Scratch** restaurant (at The Barnyard Shopping Center, 831/625-2448, breakfast and lunch daily, Sun. brunch, dinner Tues.–Sat.) is a casual and eclectic place with local art on the walls. From Scratch serves up an abundant, ambitious, and very "local" breakfast menu, from fresh-squeezed orange and grapefruit juice to smoothies, pancakes, and huevos rancheros. Look for soups, salads, pastas, and sandwiches at lunch, and such things as seafood pasta with shrimp, crab, and scallops or pork chops glazed in honeymustard sauce at dinner. A great bet in Carmel for sushi is The Barnyard's been-there-forever, familyfriendly **Robata Grill & Sake Bar** (831/624-2643, lunch Mon.–Fri., dinner nightly).

Popular Carmel Valley newcomer is American M **The New Summer House** (6 Pilot Rd., 831/659-5020, lunch and dinner daily in summer, closed Tues. in winter), specializing in updated renditions of comfort-food classics, from Chinese chicken salad, meatloaf, and chicken pot pie to prawn risotto and "every day, all day turkey dinner." Open for brunch, too—Monterey omelettes, blueberry pancakes, even vegetarian eggs Benedict—from 9 A.M. on weekends. Dogs are welcome on the patio.

LUNCH AND DINNER

A local favorite in Carmel Valley is friendly, quite reasonable M **Café Rustica** (10 Delfino Place, 831/659-4444), brought to you by the same people who launched the Taste Café & Bistro in Pacific Grove. The fare here covers vast continental territory, so at lunch you can enjoy an egg salad sandwich on a baguette, a small pizza, or a grilled vegetable salad with creamy balsamic vinaigrette. Try the Pasta Rustica at dinner. Also beloved in Carmel Valley is the **Corkscrew Café** (55 W.

Carmel Valley Rd., 831/659-8888), sibling to Carmel's Casanova, serving up local wines, the café's own organic garden produce, and great things at lunch—from the grilled portabella mushroom sandwich and black-bean chicken and cheese enchiladas to salmon salad niçoise. And check out the Corkscrew Museum.

Back in Carmel proper, for rustic yet romantic Italian, the place is **Tutto Mondo Trattoria** (Dolores between Ocean and Seventh, 831/624-8977, lunch and dinner daily), where bruschetta, soups, and salads could make a meal, though pastas, pizzas, and other heftier fare is available. Wonderful desserts, plus Italian, French, and California wines.

Great for Chinese at lunch, dinner, and even takeout is **Tommy's Wok** (on Mission between Ocean and Seventh, 831/624-8518), beloved for its pot-stickers, pine nut or paper-wrapped chicken, and pu pu platter. Organic veggie choices, too. Fine for takeout pastries and desserts or a light French-country lunch is **Patisserie Boissiere** (on Mission between Ocean and Seventh, 831/624-5008). If excellent cheese and an apple would suffice for lunch, head for **The Cheese Shop** (Carmel Plaza, Ocean and Junipero, 831/625-2272), which features an awesome selection, foreign and domestic. If you're not packing your own two-buck Chuck, stop into sophisticated **Bouchee** (on Mission near Ocean, 831/626-7880), a wine shop by day and an impressive wine bar and French restaurant by night.

FINE DINING

Sophisticated yet simple is excellent M **La Bohême** (Dolores and Seventh, 831/624-7500, www.laboheme.com, dinner daily), a tiny, familystyle place serving French country cuisine at dinner. The three-course, prix fixe meal is served family-style, starting with salad and soups, continuing through the evening's entrée, and finishing with a homemade dessert. No reservations; call for the day's menu, see the website, or pick up the monthly calendar when you get to town.

M **Casanova** (on Fifth between Mission and San Carlos, 831/625-0501, lunch and dinner daily) is a Carmel classic, from its renowned, hand-dug wine cellar to its romantic, Old World–cottage dining rooms and stellar food. Casanova serves both Southern French and Northern Italian cuisine in a landmark Mediterranean-style house featuring several provincial-style dining rooms, plus a heated garden for temperature-sensitive romantics. Homemade pastas here are exceptional, as are the desserts.

Immensely popular **Grasing's** (in the Jordan Center at the corner of Sixth and Mission, 831/624-6562) serves colorful "coastal cuisine." At lunch, this translates into some coastal options, yet also includes sandwiches—grilled eggplant with roasted peppers, onions, and mushrooms, perhaps, or the "bistro burger," with apple-wood smoked bacon, avocado, and cheddar cheese. At dinner, fish and seafood star, starting with the crab risotto. Try the paella; dig into bronzed salmon with portabella mushrooms, roasted garlic, and Yukon golds; or choose the petite filet mignon, with shallot marmalade, baby carrots, asparagus, and potato cakes. Vegetarians won't starve, with choices such as lasagna with artichokes, tomatoes, spinach, Asiago cheese, and lemon vinaigrette. Somewhat less "fishy" is Kurt Grasing's upbeat

Carmel Chop House (Fifth and San Carlos, 831/625-1199), a true steakhouse featuring the Chop House Caesar salad and corn-fed meat (beef and lamb) and Maine lobster. Every entrée is served with potatoes and veggies.

Even if you can't afford to stay there, you can probably afford to eat at the Highlands Inn, on Highway 1 south of Carmel. The inn's **California Market** restaurant (831/622-5450, breakfast, lunch, and dinner daily) serves California regional dishes with fresh local ingredients. You'll enjoy oceanview and deck dining, plus fabulous scenery. Yet the locals' favorite for fine dining is the innovative **M Pacific's Edge Restaurant** (at the Highlands Inn, 831/622-5445), which showcases local ingredients. If you can't swing an exquisite five-course meal, how about a smashing cocktail with a still more smashing view?

More marvelous hotel dining is offered at the resort-casual, California-French **M Marinus** (at Bernardus Lodge, 415 Carmel Valley Rd., 831/658-3400), a well-heeled foodie destination, worthy recipient of *Wine Spectator's* Grand Award; and at **Covey** (at Quail Lodge Resort, 8205 Valley Greens Dr., 831/620-8860).

Entertainment and Events

Sunsets from the beach or from craggy Point Lobos are entertainment enough. But the **Sierra Club** folks (above the shoe store on Ocean near Dolores, 831/624-8032, 12:30–4:30 P.M. Mon.–Sat.) provide helpful information on hikes, sights, and occasional bike rides.

Carmel proper has laws prohibiting live music and leg-shaking inside the city limits. **Mission Ranch Resort** (26270 Dolores, 831/625-9040), in the county 11 blocks out of town, has a piano bar. Otherwise, you'll have to head into rowdy Monterey for dancing and prancing. But you can always go bar-hopping locally.

PERFORMING ARTS

For live drama, the outdoor **Forest Theater** (on the north side of Mountain View between Santa Rita and Guadalupe, 831/626-1681) hosts light

drama and musicals, Shakespeare, and concerts staged by the Pacific Repertory Theatre (see below). It's general seating, so arrive early. Come from mid-May through July for the theater's **Films in the Forest,** screened every Wednesday night. There's also the *indoor* **Forest Theater** (at the corner of Mountain View Avenue and Santa Rita Street, 831/624-1531, www.cetstaffplayers.org), with performances staged by the **Children's Experimental Theatre & Staff Players Repertory Company.** The **Pacific Repertory Theatre Company** (831/622-0700, http://pacrep.org or http://ticketguys.com/pacrep to reserve tickets) presents a variety of live stage productions in the outdoor Forest Theater; at the **Golden Bough Theatre** (on Monte Verde between Eighth and Ninth); and at the **Circle Theatre of the Golden Bough** (on the east side of Cassanova between Eighth and Ninth). Pacific

Carmel

Rep also sponsors the annual **Carmel Shakespeare Festival.**

EVENTS

Come on New Year's Day for the annual **Rio Grill Resolution Run** and in February for the annual **Masters of Food & Wine** at the Highlands Inn in May for the **Jeffers Tor House Garden Party,** the annual fundraiser; and June for the Carmel Valley **California Cowboy Show,** where you can put your boots up and enjoy cowboy music, cowboy poetry, and a cowboy-friendly glass of wine. June also kicks off the theater season in Carmel. Right around the first of the month (or slightly before), the Pacific Repertory Theatre troupe opens its performance season, part of which is devoted to the **Carmel Shakespeare Festival,** with plays presented from August into October. Plays are presented at the outdoor Forest Theater, the Golden Bough Playhouse, and other venues. The summer **Films in the Forest** at the outdoor Forest Theater begins in mid-May.

Johann Sebastian Bach never knew a place like Carmel, but his spirit lives on here nonetheless. From mid-July to early August, Carmel sponsors its traditionally understated **Bach Festival** (831/624-2046 for tickets, www.bachfestival.org), honoring J. S. and other composers of his era with daily concerts, recitals, and lectures at the mission and elsewhere, sometimes including the Hotel Del Monte at the Naval Postgraduate School in Monterey. If you're going, get your tickets *early.* Closer to actual performance dates, stop by the festival office at the Sunset Cultural Center (San Carlos at Ninth) to check on ticket availability.

At Carmel Beach, usually on a Sunday in late September or early October, the **Great Sandcastle Building Contest** gets underway. Events include Novice and Advanced Sandbox. (Get the date from the Monterey Chamber of Commerce, as Carmel locals generally "don't know," just to keep the tourists away.) Also in October, check out the **Tor House Festival,** the annual **Carmel Performing Arts Festival,** and both the annual **Taste of Carmel** and the **Carmel Valley Wine Festival.** In December, the **Music for Christmas** series at the Carmel Mission is quite nice.

WINE-TASTING

Not surprising in such a moderate Mediterranean climate, vineyards do well near Monterey and Carmel—particularly with chardonnay and pinot noir, yet also with cabernet sauvignon, merlot, syrah, and sauvignon blanc. Wineries and wines, quickly rising in stature, are recognized as eight distinct appellations. To keep up with them all, pick up the free *Monterey Wine Country* brochure and map at area visitors centers, or contact the **Monterey County Vintners & Growers Association** (831/375-9400, www.montereywines.org). Wine-related events well worth showing up for include the **Annual Winemakers' Celebration** in August and the **Great Wine Escape Weekend** in November. If you're short on touring time this trip, many Monterey County wines are available for tasting at **A Taste of Monterey** (700 Cannery Row in Monterey, 831/646-5446, www.tastemonterey.com, 11 A.M.–6 P.M. daily).

The very small **Chateau Julien Winery** (8940 Carmel Valley Rd., 831/624-2600, www.chateaujulien.com) is housed in a French-style château and is open daily for tasting, and for tours by reservation. The winery's chardonnay and merlot have both been honored as the best in the United States at the American Wine Championships in New York. Southwest of Carmel Valley and bordering Los Padres National Forest is the remote, spring-fed "boutique" **Heller Estate Vineyards** (831/659-6220 or 800/625-8466, www.hellerestate.com), was originally owned by the late William Durney and his wife, screenwriter Dorothy Kingsley, and is still noted for its award-winning organic wines. The winery is not open to the public, but the organic wines—chenin blanc, chardonnay, pinot noir, cabernet sauvignon, and merlot—may be tasted at Carmel Valley Village (69 W. Carmel Valley Rd.), and are also widely available in Carmel, Monterey, and vicinity.

At posh **Bernardus Winery** (5 W. Carmel Valley Rd., 831/659-1900 or 800/223-2533, www.bernardus.com), centerpiece of the notable foodie empire, wine is an art. You can sample that art, traditionally aged Bordeaux varietals, at the tasting room (11 A.M.–5 P.M. daily). Also look around for other premium, small-production wineries, such as **Joullian Vineyards** (831/659-8100 or 866/659-8101, www.joullian.com), with cabernet sauvignon, sauvignon blanc, merlot, zinfandel, and chardonnay. Joullian has a new tasting room in Carmel Valley (2 Village Dr., Ste. A, tasting and sales 11 A.M.–5 P.M. daily, excluding holidays). The winery is occasionally open for special Saturday open house or members-only events; call for details.

Between Greenfield and Soledad, along the inland Highway 101 corridor, is a handful of good wineries. The 1978 private reserve cabernet sauvignon of **Jekel Vineyards** (40155 Walnut Ave., Greenfield, 831/674-5522, tastings 11 A.M.–4 P.M. daily, tours by appointment) washed out Lafite-Rothschild and other international competitors in France in 1982. **Hahn Estates/Smith & Hook Winery** (37700 Foothill Rd., Soledad, 831/678-2132, www.hahnestates.com, 11 A.M.–4 P.M. daily, tours by appointment) is known for its cabernet sauvignon—and also for the amazing view across the Salinas Val-

ley to the Gabilan Mountains. Also in the area: **Chalone Vineyard** (on Stonewall Canyon Road at Hwy. 146 E., 831/678-1717, www.chalonewinegroup.com), the county's oldest vineyard and winery, known for its estate-bottled varietals; and noted **Paraiso Vineyards** (38060 Paraiso Springs Rd., 831/678-0300, www.paraisovineyards.com).

Not open to the public (no tasting room), but well worth visiting during special events, is **Morgan Winery** (Salinas, 831/751-7777, www.morganwinery.com), which has garnered a glut of gold medals and other recognition for its chardonnays. Winners here, too, are the syrah, pinot noir, and sauvignon blanc.

True wine fanatics must make one more stop: America's most award-winning vineyard, **Ventana Vineyards/Meador Estate** (2999 Monterey-Salinas Hwy., near the Monterey Airport just outside Monterey on Hwy. 68, 831/372-7415, www.ventanawines.com, 11 A.M.–5 P.M. daily, until 6 P.M. in summer).

Shopping and Information

For current shopping information and more suggestions, contact the **Carmel Chamber of Commerce** (on San Carlos between Fifth and Sixth, 831/624-2522 or 800/550-4333, www.carmelcalifornia.org).

HOUSEWARES

For something different to tote home as a souvenir, **It's Cactus** (on Mission between Ocean & Seventh, 831/626-4213, www.itscactus.com) offers colorful indigenous folk art from Guatemala, Indonesia, and other places around the globe. For candles, candlesticks, and oil lamps, try **Wicks & Wax** (in the Doud Arcade, Ocean at San Carlos, 831/624-6044). For fine soaps, other bath products, and home scents, head for the **Rainbow Scent Company** (on Lincoln between Ocean and Seventh, 831/624-6506).

Locals say the best home furnishings store around is **Homescapes** (on the southeast corner of Seventh and Dolores in Carmel proper,

831/624-6499, www.homescapescarmel.com), offering an impressive import selection, including many personally selected antiques from China, Korea, Japan, England, and Europe. (There's also a Homescapes outlet in Carmel Valley Village, 13766 Center St., 831/659-9990, 11 A.M.– 5 P.M. Fri.–Sat. and by appointment.)

ANTIQUES

You'll find plenty of antique shops in and around Carmel. For old toys and memorable memorabilia, try **Life In The Past Lane** (San Carlos and Fifth, 831/625-2121). **Sabine Adamson Antiques & Interiors** (on Dolores between Fifth and Sixth, 831/626-7464) specializes in fine European antiques and accessories. **Conway of Asia,** (Seventh and Dolores, 831/624-3643) offers antiques and oriental rugs from Myanmar (Burma), India, Tibet, and Thailand. **Vermillion** (in the Crossroads Shopping Center at Rio Road and Highway 1, 831/620-1502, www.vermillionasianarts.com) emphasizes museum-quality Japanese items, both antique and contemporary.

ART

For all its antique finery, Carmel has even more art galleries—dozens of them. A great place to start is the **Carmel Art Association Gallery** (on Dolores between Fifth and Sixth, 831/624-6176), founded here in 1927. The art association features more than 120 local artists and regularly presents an impressive selection of their painting, sculpture, and graphic arts. The **Weston Gallery, Inc.** (on Sixth between Dolores and Lincoln, 831/624-4453, www.westongallery.com) offers 19th- and 20th-century photographs by namesake local photographers Edward Weston and Brett Weston, as well as Ansel Adams, Michael Kenna, Jeffrey Becom, and Jerry Uelsmann.

Wonderful for local art is **Savage Stephens Contemporary Fine Art** (at Su Vecino Court, on Dolores between Fifth and Sixth, 831/626-0800). The bronze and stone sculptures by Sharon Spencer are standouts. The impressive **Highlands Sculpture Gallery** (on Dolores between Fifth and Sixth, 831/624-0535) is Carmel's oldest contemporary art gallery.

CLOTHES AND JEWELRY

Carmel's also no slouch when it comes to personal fashion, most of it on the pricey side. Definitely upscale is **Girl Boy Girl** (at the Court of the Fountains, Mission and Seventh, 831/626-3368), featuring contemporary women's fashions from more than 50 designers. Worth exploring at Carmel Plaza (Ocean and Mission) is classic **Ann Taylor** (831/626-9565). Always fun for something more exotic is **Exotica** (at the Crossroads Shopping Center, 831/622-0757), where you'll find handpainted and batiked natural fiber fashions, along with Laurel Burch, other interesting jewelry, and folk art.

PETS

Carmel being a pet-pampering town, Fido generally fares well here. **Diggidy Dog** (at Mission and Ocean, across from the Carmel Plaza, 831/625-1585) offers all the essential mutt merchandise, from toys and treats to well-stuffed beds. (Token cat items available, too.) At more upscale **Mackie's Parlour** (at Ocean and Monte Verde, 831/626-0600)—formerly another dog store, Fideaux—you can even get doggie feather beds. To help less fortunate creatures, buy gently used clothing, jewelry, art, books, collectibles, and antiques at the **SPCA Benefit Shop** (Society for the Prevention of Cruelty to Animals, Su Vecino Court between Fifth and Sixth, 831/624-4211).

INFORMATION

The weekly *Carmel Pine Cone* newspaper (www.carmelpinecone.com) covers local events and politics. The **Carmel Chamber of Commerce** and visitors center is in the Eastwood Building (on San Carlos between Fifth and Sixth, 831/624-2522 or 800/550-4333, www.carmel-california.org). Its annual *Guide to Carmel* includes information on just about everything, from shopping hot spots to accommodations and eateries. The **Carmel Valley Chamber of Commerce** is in the Oak Building (at 71 W. Carmel Valley Rd., Carmel Valley, 831/659-4000, www.carmelvalleychamber.com).

To get to Carmel from Monterey without a car or bike, take Monterey-Salinas Transit bus 52 (24 hours, 831/899-2555, www.mst.org).

Big Sur

The poet Robinson Jeffers described this redwood and rock coast as "that jagged country which nothing but a falling meteor will ever plow." It's only fitting, then, that this area was called Jeffers Country long before it became known as Big Sur. Sienna-colored sandstone and granite, surly waves, and sundown dance together in a never-ending celebration of the ancient and the newly born. Writer Henry Miller said Big Sur was "the face of the earth as the creator intended it to look," a point hard to argue. Still, Big Sur as a specific *place* is difficult to locate. It's not only a town, a valley, and a river. The entire coastline from just south of Carmel Highlands to somewhere north of San Simeon (some suggest the southern limit is the Monterey County line) is considered Big Sur country.

Once "in" Big Sur, wherever that might be, visitors notice some genuine oddities—odd by California standards, at least. Until recently, most people here didn't have much money and didn't seem to care. (This situation is changing as the truly wealthy move in.) They built simple or unusual dwellings—redwood cabins, glass tepees, geodesic domes, even round redwood houses with the look of wine barrels ready to roll into the sea—both to fit the limited space available and to express that elusive Big Sur sense of *style*.

Because the terrain itself is so tormented and twisted, broadcast signals rarely arrive in Big Sur. In the days before satellite dishes, there was virtually no TV; electricity and telephones with dial service have been available in Big Sur only since the 1950s, and some people along

Must-Sees

Look for **M** to find the sights and activities you can't miss and **N** for the best dining and lodging.

Neptune pool at Hearst Castle

M Point Sur State Historic Park: Listed on the National Register of Historic Places, the 1889 Point Sur Light Station overlooks a shipwreck site once known as the Graveyard of the Pacific (page 86).

M Andrew Molera State Park: Follow the short, winding trail to the two-mile beach and adjacent seabird sanctuary, or take the trail to Garnet Beach. Horseback tours are also available (page 86).

M Pfeiffer–Big Sur State Park: Redwoods, sycamores, big-leaf maples, cottonwoods, and willows hug the river here, a perfect place for family camping (page 87).

M Nepenthe: About a mile south of the Ventana Inn, built on the spot where the cabin Orson Welles bought for Rita Hayworth once stood, is Nepenthe—the restaurant almost as legendary as Big Sur itself (page 88).

M Julia Pfeiffer Burns State Park: The short walk along McWay Creek leads through the tunnel under the road to Saddle Rock and the cliffs above Waterfall Cove, where you'll see the only California waterfall that plunges directly into the sea (page 89).

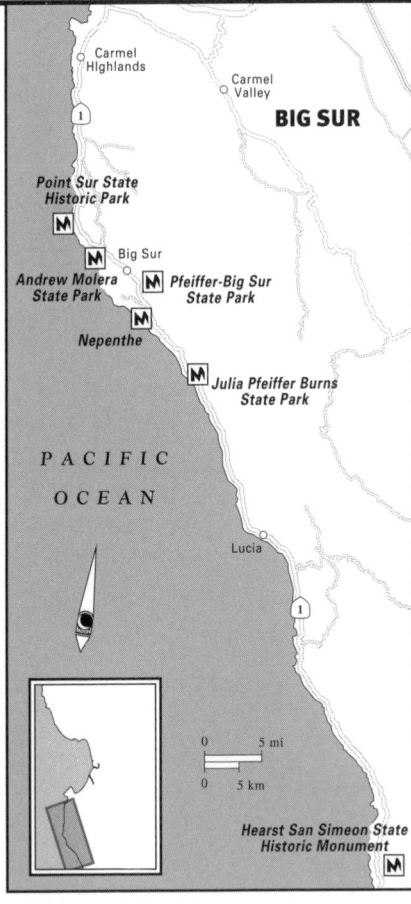

M Hearst San Simeon State Historic Monument: Once media magnate William Randolph Hearst's castle, this oceanview, Spanish Renaissance–style palace was designed by Julia Morgan, then filled with European art and finery (page 98).

the south coast and in more remote areas still have neither.

Social life in Big Sur consists of bowling at the naval station, attending a poetry reading or the annual Big Sur Potluck Revue at the Grange Hall in the valley, driving into "town" (Monterey) for a few movie cassettes, or—for a really wild night—drinks on the deck at sunset and dancing cheek to cheek at Nepenthe. Big Sur is a very *different* California, where even the chamber of commerce has been known to urge visitors "to slow down, meditate," and "catch up with your soul."

It's almost impossible to catch up with your soul, however, when traffic is bumper-to-bumper. Appreciating Big Sur while driving or, only for the brave, bicycling in a mile-long coastline convoy is akin to honeymooning in Hades—a universal impulse, but entirely the wrong ambience. As it snakes through Big Sur, California's Coast Highway (Highway 1), the state's first scenic highway and one of the world's most spectacular roadways, slips around the prominent ribs of the Santa Lucia Mountains, slides into dark wooded canyons, and soars across graceful bridges spanning the void. Though its existence means that a trip into Monterey no longer takes an entire day, people here nonetheless resent the highway that brings the flamed-out and frantic.

To show some respect, come to Big Sur during the week—in balmy April or early May, when wildflowers burst forth; or in late September or October, to avoid the thick summer fog. Though winter is generally rainy, weeks of sparkling warm weather aren't uncommon. In April, Big Sur hosts the renowned annual **Big Sur International Marathon** (BSIM, www.bsim.org), when the views include thousands of runners hugging the highway curves from the village to Carmel—one of the world's best. Since 2003, a BSIM-sponsored half marathon has been held along the shores of Monterey Bay in October.

HISTORY

The earliest Big Sur inhabitants, the Esselen people, once occupied a 25-mile-long and 10-mile-wide stretch of coast, from Point Sur to near Lucia in the south. A small group of Ohlone,

© KIM WEIR

"That same prehistoric look. The look of always," Henry Miller said of Big Sur. "Nature smiling at herself in the mirror of eternity."

the Sargenta-Ruc, lived from south of the Palo Colorado Canyon to the Big Sur River's mouth. Though most of the area's Salinan peoples lived inland in the Salinas Valley, near what is now Fort Hunter-Liggett, villages were also scattered along the Big Sur coast south of Lucia. Little is known about area natives, since mission-forced intertribal marriages and introduced diseases soon obliterated them. It is known, though, that the number of Esselens in Big Sur was estimated between 900 and 1,300 after the Spanish arrived in 1770, and that the Esselen people lived in the Big Sur valley at least 3,000 years ago.

The Esselen people were long gone by the time the first area settlers arrived. Grizzly bears were the greatest 18th-century threat to settlement, since the terrain discouraged any type of travel and the usual wildlife predation that came with it. The name Big Sur (Sur is "South" in Spanish, a reference point from the Monterey perspective) comes from Rio Grande del Sur, or the Big Sur River, which flows to the sea at Point

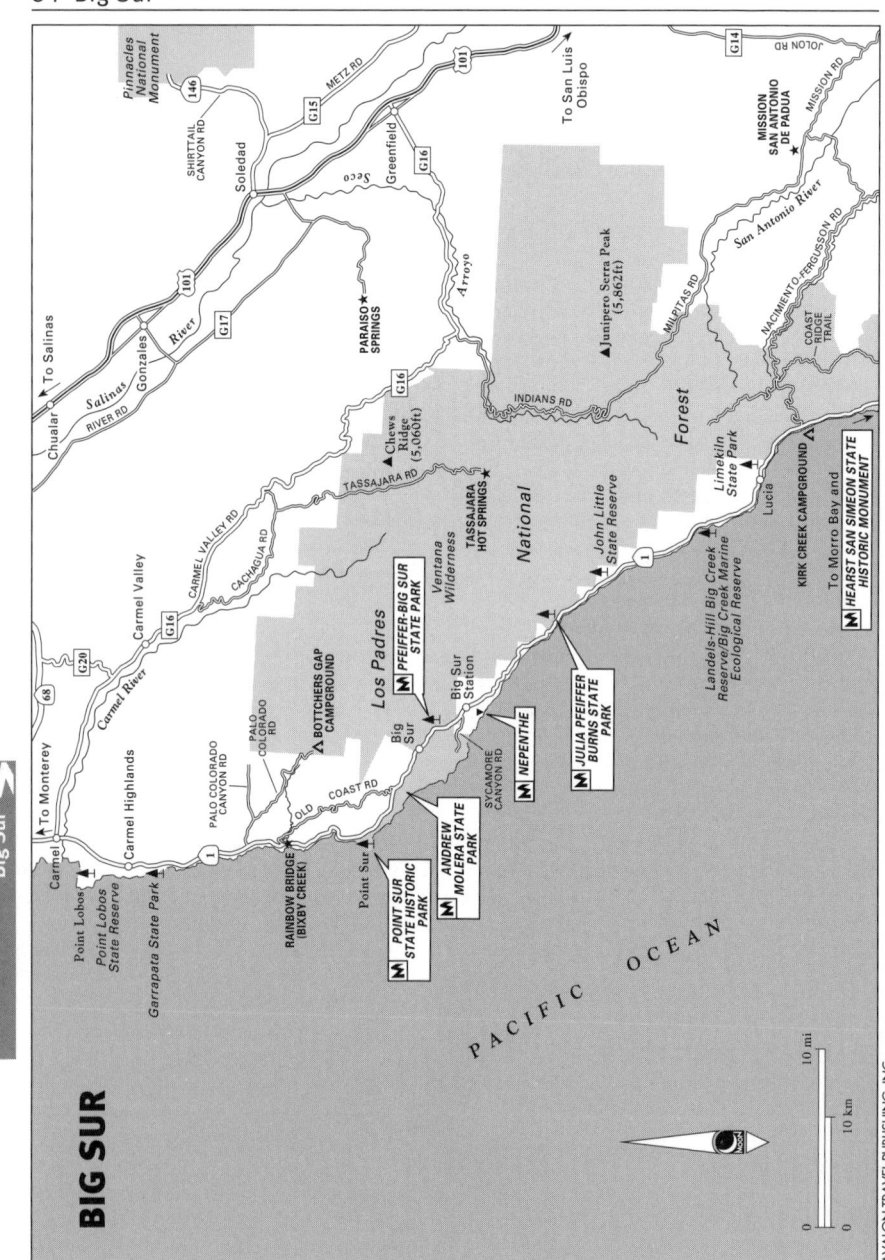

BIG SUR

PACIFIC OCEAN

Pinnacles National Monument

To Salinas

To Monterey

To San Luis Obispo

To Morro Bay and

MISSION SAN ANTONIO DE PADUA

HEARST SAN SIMEON STATE HISTORIC MONUMENT

KIRK CREEK CAMPGROUND

Limekiln State Park

Lucia

John Little State Reserve

Landels-Hill Big Creek Reserve/Big Creek Marine Ecological Reserve

JULIA PFEIFFER BURNS STATE PARK

NEPENTHE

SYCAMORE CANYON RD

ANDREW MOLERA STATE PARK

POINT SUR STATE HISTORIC PARK

Point Sur

RAINBOW BRIDGE (BIXBY CREEK)

OLD COAST RD

PALO COLORADO RD

BOTTCHERS GAP CAMPGROUND

PFEIFFER-BIG SUR STATE PARK

Big Sur Station

Big Sur

Ventana Wilderness

TASSAJARA HOT SPRINGS

National

Los Padres

Forest

TASSAJARA RD

INDIANS RD

Chews Ridge (5,060ft)

CACHAGUA RD

Carmel Valley

CARMEL VALLEY RD

Carmel River

Carmel Highlands

Carmel

Point Lobos

Point Lobos State Reserve

Garrapata State Park

PALO COLORADO CANYON RD

G20

68

G16

Junipero Serra Peak (5,862ft)

San Antonio River

MILPITAS RD

NACIMIENTO-FERGUSSON RD

COAST RIDGE TRAIL

MISSION RD

JOLON RD

G14

Arroyo Seco

PARAISO SPRINGS

G16

G17

Salinas River

RIVER RD

Gonzales

Chualar

To Salinas

G15

METZ RD

146

SHIRTTAIL CANYON RD

Soledad

101

Seco

Greenfield

G16

0   10 mi

0   10 km

© AVALON TRAVEL PUBLISHING, INC.

Sur. The river itself was the focal point of the 1834 Mexican land grant and the Cooper family's Rancho El Sur until 1965.

In the early 1900s came the highway, a hazardous 15-year construction project between Big Sur proper and San Simeon. Hardworking Chinese laborers were recruited for the job, along with less willing workers from the state's prisons. The highway was completed in 1937, though many lives and much equipment were lost to the sea in the process. Maintaining this remote ribbon of highway and its 29 bridges is still a treacherous year-round task. Following the wild winter storms of 1982–1983, for example, 42 landslides blocked the highway; the "big one" near Julia Pfeiffer Burns State Park took 19 bulldozers and more than a year to clear.

Today, around 4,000 people live in Big Sur country—just 3,000 more than in the early 1900s. "Big Surbanization" is well underway. Land not included in Los Padres National Forest and the Ventana Wilderness is largely privately owned. Plans for more hotels, restaurants, and civilized comforts for frazzled travelers continue to come up, and the eternal, wild peace Robinson Jeffers predicted would reign here forever has at last been touched by ripples of civilization. Nobody wants the character of Big Sur to change, but people can't agree on how best to save it.

As elsewhere in California, some Big Sur landowners believe that private property rights are sacrosanct, beyond the regulation of God or the government. Others argue that state and local land-use controls are adequate. Still others contend that federal intervention is necessary, possibly by granting the region scenic area or national park status—an idea fought sawtooth and nail by most residents. The reason Big Sur is still ruggedly beautiful, they say, is because local people have kept it that way. A favorite response to the suggestion of more government involvement: "Don't Yosemitecate Big Sur." In March 1986, both of California's senators proposed that the U.S. Forest Service take primary responsibility for safeguarding Big Sur's scenic beauty, with no new logging, mining claims, or grazing privileges allowed. The final plan, which limits but doesn't eliminate new development, seems to please almost everyone . . . except when new controversies arise.

Some proposed changes create no controversy, such as the late 2000 acquisition by Los Padres National Forest of 784 acres along San Carpoforo Creek and the 2001 purchase of the 1,226-acre Bixby Ocean Ranch by the Trust for Public Land for eventual inclusion in the national forest. The Bixby Ranch, once owned by the late Allen Funt, host of TV's *Candid Camera,* was prime Big Sur property otherwise slated for development. In May 2002, The Nature Conservancy and The Big Sur Land Trust bought the 10,000-acre Palo Corona Ranch, the "gateway to Big Sur" beginning a block south of Carmel. That property, most of which will be managed as county and state park land and accessible to the public, connects 13 other parks and preserves. These include Point Lobos Ranch, just south and west of Palo Corona, now managed as state park lands, and the Mitteldorf Preserve bordering Palo Corona's eastern edge.

Sights

GARRAPATA STATE PARK

Garrapata State Park (831/624-4909) stretches north along the coast for more than four miles from Soberanes Point, where the Santa Lucia Mountains first dive into the sea. Southward, the at first unimpressive **Point Sur** and its lighthouse beacon stand out beyond 2,879-acre Garrapata State Park and beach, the latter named after the noble wood tick and featuring a two-mile-long crescent of creek-veined white sand, granite arches, caves and grottos, and sea otters. Ticks or no ticks, the unofficial nude beach here is one of the best in Northern California. Winter whale-watching is usually good from high ground. On weekends in January, ranger-led whale-watch programs are held at Granite Canyon. Or, if it's not foggy, take the two-mile loop trail from the turnout for the view.

For more information, call the park directly, or contact the **Big Sur Station** joint State Parks/U.S. Forest Service office (831/667-2315).

South of Garrapata and inland is private **Palo Colorado Canyon,** reached via the road of the same name. Dark and secluded even in summer, the canyon is often cut off from the rest of the world when winter storms stomp through. The name itself is Spanish for "tall redwood." About eight miles in, at the end of the road, is isolated **Bottchers Gap Campground,** complete with restrooms, picnic tables, and multiple trailheads into the Ventana Wilderness. A few miles farther south on the highway is the famous **Rainbow Bridge,** now called **Bixby Creek Bridge**—260 feet high and 700 feet long, the highest single-arch bridge in the world when constructed in 1932, and still the most photographed of all Big Sur bridges.

◪ POINT SUR STATE HISTORIC PARK

Up atop Point Sur stands the Point Sur Light Station, an 1889 sandstone affair still standing guard at this shipwreck site, once known as the Graveyard of the Pacific. Listed on the National Register of Historic Places, this is the only complete turn-of-the-20th-century light station in California that's open to the public. In the days when the only way to get here was on horseback, 395 wooden steps led to the lighthouse, originally a giant, multiwick kerosene lantern surrounded by a Fresnel lens with a 16-panel prism. The Point Sur Light Station is now computer-operated and features an electrical aero-beacon, radio-beacon, and fog "diaphone." This 34-acre area, with its central rocky mound (good views and whale-watching), is now a state park, though the Coast Guard still maintains the lighthouse. Guided three-hour lighthouse walking tours are offered five or six times a week in summer, three times weekly in winter. Full-moon tours are also offered monthly spring through fall. Tours are $5 adults, $3 teens, $2 children. No reservations are accepted, and no picnics or pets are allowed, even if the latter are left in your vehicle. Current tour information is posted throughout Big Sur. For details, contact Point Sur Historic State Park (831/625-4419, www.pointsur.org). For information about winter whale-watching programs here and at both Garrapata and Julia Pfeiffer Burns State Parks, call 831/667-2315.

◪ ANDREW MOLERA STATE PARK

Inland and up, past what remains of the pioneering Molera Ranch (part of the original Rancho El Sur), is marvelous Andrew Molera State Park (831/667-2315, day-use fee $8), 2,100 acres first donated to The Nature Conservancy by Frances Molera in honor of her brother, then deeded to the state for management. There's no pavement here, just the pioneer family's home, now the Molera Cultural and Natural History Center; a dirt parking lot; and a short trail winding through sycamores, maples, and a few redwoods along the east fork of the Big Sur River to the two-mile beach and adjacent seabird sanctuary/lagoon below. (The big breakers cresting

© CALIFORNIA DEPARTMENT OF PARKS AND RECREATION

Andrew Molera State Park

along the coast here are created by the Sur Break-
ers Reef.) The trail north of the river's mouth
leads up a steep promontory to Garnet Beach,
noted for its colorful pebbles.

The new, improved Andrew Molera Trail
Camp opened in April 2003—a primitive yet
peaceful walk-in campground with 24 environmental campsites (first-come, first-camped; three-
night limit, no RVs, four people maximum per
site, $10, new restrooms). Dogs allowed only
with a leash and proof of current rabies vacci-
nation—and not beyond the picnic area.

Also at the park: **Molera Horseback Tours**
(831/625-5486 or 800/942-5486, www.moler-
ahorsebacktours.com, $25–35 per hour), which
offers regularly scheduled one- to three-hour
rides along the beach and through meadows and
redwood groves. Guides explain the history, flora,
and fauna of the area. Private rides are also available by appointment.

N PFEIFFER–BIG SUR STATE PARK

Inland, on the other side of the ridge from Andrew Molera State Park, is protected, sunny Big
Sur Valley, a visitor-oriented settlement adjoining

the Ventana Wilderness and surrounding picnic, camping, and lodge facilities at 821-acre
Pfeiffer–Big Sur State Park (831/667-2315, day-
use fee $8 for short hikes and picnicking). Take
the one-mile nature trail or meander up through
the redwoods to **Pfeiffer Falls,** a verdant, fern-
lined canyon at its best in spring and early summer, then to **Valley View** for a look at the
precipitous Big Sur River gorge below. Redwoods,
sycamores, big-leaf maples, cottonwoods, and
willows hug the river, giving way to oaks, chaparral, and Santa Lucia bristlecone fir at higher
elevations. There's abundant poison oak, and
raccoons can be particularly pesky here, like the
begging birds, so keep food out of harm's way.

To hike within the Ventana Wilderness, head
south on the highway a half mile to the U.S.
Forest Service office (831/667-2315) for a permit
and current information (trails begin here). About
a mile south of the entrance to Pfeiffer–Big Sur is
the road to Los Padres National Forest's **Pfeiffer
Beach** (take the second right-hand turnoff after
the park, open to the public 6 A.M.–sunset; day-
use fee $5) and its cypresses, craggy caves, and
mauve and white sands streaked with black. It's
heaven here on a clear, calm day, but the hiss-
ing sand stings mercilessly when the weather is

Big Sur

up. On any day, forget the idea of an ocean swim. The water's cold, the surf capricious, and the currents tricky; even expert divers need to register with rangers before jumping in.

The outdoor amphitheater at Pfeiffer–Big Sur State Park (which hosts many of the park's educational summer campfires and interpretive programs) and lagoons were built by the Civilian Conservation Corps during the depression. The large, developed, year-round campground features 214 family campsites with picnic tables and hot showers. To make camping reservations—essential in summer, when the park is particularly crowded, and on good-weather weekends—contact ReserveAmerica (800/444-7275, www.reserveamerica.com, sites $20–25, premium sites $30–35, group sites $75).

URBAN BIG SUR

Nowhere in Big Sur country are visitors really diverted from the land, because there are no big-time boutiques, gaudy gift shops, or even movie theaters. But urban Big Sur starts at Big Sur Valley and stretches south past the post office and U.S. Forest Service office to the vicinity of Deetjen's Big Sur Inn. This "big city" part of Big Sur includes the area's most famous and fabulous inns and restaurants: the Ventana Inn, the Post Ranch Inn, Nepenthe, and Deetjen's. A fascinating fact about Nepenthe: Although cinematographer Orson Welles was persona non grata just down the coast at San Simeon (for his too faithful portrayal of William Randolph Hearst in *Citizen Kane*), when he bought what was then the Trails Club Log Cabin in Big Sur for his wife, Rita Hayworth, in 1944, he was able to haunt Hearst from the north. Welles's place became Nepenthe ("surcease from sorrows" in the *Odyssey*) shortly after he sold it in 1947. More or less across the street from Nepenthe is the **Hawthorne Gallery** (48485 Hwy. 1, 831/667-3200, www.hawthornegallery.com), something of a Hawthorne family enterprise, offering Albert Paley forged metal sculptures, Max DeMoss bronze castings, Jesus Bautista Moroles granite sculp-

tures, and the landscape creations of Frederick L. Gregory, among others.

North of Deetjen's is the **Henry Miller Memorial Library** (831/667-2574, www.henrymiller.org, typically open 11 A.M.–6 P.M. Wed.–Mon. and for special events, closed Tues., but often open daily in summer) a collection of friendly clutter about the writer and his life's work, located on the highway about one mile south of the Ventana Inn, but almost hidden behind redwoods and an unassuming double gate. Henry Miller lived, wrote, and painted in Big Sur from 1944 to 1962. The library is housed not in Henry Miller's former home, but in that of the late Emil White. A good friend of Miller's, White said he started the library "because I missed him." Now a community cultural arts center operated by The Big Sur Land Trust, the library sponsors exhibits, poetry readings, concerts—including 2004's benefit concert by Patti Smith—and special events throughout the year. Original art and prints, posters, and postcards are available in the gallery, as are Miller's books, including rare editions.

South of Deetjen's is the noted **Coast Gallery** (at Lafler Canyon, 800/797-6869, www.coastgalleries.com), named for editor Henry Lafler, a friend of Jack London. Treasures here include rare Chagall prints and lithographs. Coast also has galleries in Carmel, Pebble Beach, and Hana, Hawaii.

Ⓜ NEPENTHE

Nepenthe (831/667-2345, www.nepenthebigsur.com), about a mile south of the Ventana Inn, was built almost exactly on the site of the cabin Orson Welles bought for Rita Hayworth. So, it's not too surprising that the restaurant is almost as legendary as Big Sur itself. A striking multilevel structure complete with an arts and crafts center, the restaurant was named for an ancient drug mentioned in Homer's *The Odyssey*, and taken to help people forget their grief. Naturally enough, the bar here does a brisk business.

As is traditional at Nepenthe, relax on the upper deck (the "gay pavilion," presided over by a sculpted bronze and redwood phoenix) with drink in hand to salute the sea and setting sun—surreal views. The open-beamed restaurant and its outdoor above-ocean terrace isn't nearly as rowdy as all those bohemian celebrity stories would suggest. Nonetheless, thrill-seekers insist on sitting on the top deck, though there's often more room available downstairs at the Café Kevah health food deli and deck (831/667-2344, brunch and lunch Mar.–Dec.). The fare at Nepenthe is good, but not as spectacular as the views on a clear day. Try the homemade soups, the hefty chef's salad, any of the vegetarian selections, Lolly's roasted chicken, or the world-famous Ambrosia burger (an excellent cheeseburger on a French roll with pickles and a salad for a fairly hefty price) accompanied by a Basket o' Fries. Good pies and cakes for dessert.

To avoid the worst of the tourist traffic and to appreciate Nepenthe at its best, come later in September or October. And although Nepenthe is casual any time of year, it's not *that* casual. Local lore has it that John F. Kennedy was once turned away because he showed up barefoot. Nepenthe is open for lunch and dinner daily, with music and dancing around the hearth at night.

And, if you can't be here in person, you can be here in spirit much more easily now that Nepenthe has an online weather camera pointing south over the back deck. To see what's happening along Nepenthe's coastline, visit the restaurant's website.

ⓜ JULIA PFEIFFER BURNS STATE PARK

Partington Cove is about one mile south of Partington Ridge, the impressive northern boundary of Julia Pfeiffer Burns State Park (831/667-2315). To get to the cove, park on the east side of the highway and head down the steep trail that starts near the fence (by the black mailbox) on the west side of the road. The branching trail leads back into the redwoods to the tiny beach at the stream's mouth; or across a wooden footbridge, through a rock tunnel hewn in the 1880s by pioneer John Partington, and on to the old dock where tan bark was once loaded onto seagoing freighters. A fine place for a smidgen of inspirational solitude.

There's a stone marker farther south at the park's official entrance, about seven miles south of Nepenthe. These spectacular 4,000 acres straddling the highway also include a large underwater park offshore. Picnic in the coast redwoods by McWay Creek (almost the southern limit of their range), or hike up into the chaparral and the Los Padres National Forest. After picnicking, take the short walk along McWay Creek (watch for poison oak), then through the tunnel under the road to **Saddle Rock** and the cliffs above **Waterfall Cove,** the only California waterfall that plunges directly into the sea. The cliffs are rugged here; it's a good place to view whales and otters. Only experienced scuba divers, by permit, are allowed to dive offshore.

The park also features limited year-round camping at walk-in environmental sites and group campgrounds. The two hike-in environmental campsites (up to eight people each, $15–20) offer spectacular views. For more information, including details on winter whale-watching programs on weekends, contact the park.

A 1,400-foot-wide slash of earth just north of Julia Pfeiffer Burns State Park, which stopped traffic through Big Sur for more than a year, has earned the area's landslide-of-all-time award—so far. Heading south from the park, the highway crosses Anderson Creek and rugged Anderson Canyon, where an old collection of highway construction cabins for convicts sheltered such bohemians as Henry Miller and his friend Emil White in the 1940s. A few human residents and a new population of bald eagles now call Anderson Canyon home.

THE ESALEN INSTITUTE

The Esselen and Salinan peoples frequented the hot springs here, supposedly called *tok-i-tok,* or "hot healing water." In 1939, Dr. H. C. Murphy (who officiated at John Steinbeck's birth in Salinas) opened Slate's Hot Springs resort on the site. The hot springs were transformed by grandson Michael Murphy into the famed Esalen Institute, where human-potential practitioners and participants, including Joan Baez, Gregory Bateson, the Beatles, Jerry

Brown, Carlos Castaneda, Buckminster Fuller, Aldous Huxley, Linus Pauling, B. F. Skinner, Hunter S. Thompson, and Alan Watts, taught or learned in residential workshops.

Esalen is the Cadillac of New Age retreats, according to absurdist/comedian/editor Paul Krassner. Even writer Alice Kahn, who, before arriving at Esalen, considered herself the "last psycho-virgin in California" and "hard-core un-evolved," eventually admitted that there was something about the Esalen Institute that defied all cynicism.

Esalen's magic doesn't necessarily come cheap. The introductory "Experiencing Esalen" weekend workshop runs $405–595 or so, including simple but pleasant accommodations and wonderful meals ($260–310, if a sleeping bag is all you'll need). Five- to seven-day workshops are substantially more: in the $745–1,060 and $1,200–1,655 ranges, respectively. But Esalen tries to accommodate the less affluent with scholarships, a work-study program, senior citizen discounts, family rates, and sleeping bag options. You can also arrange just an overnight or weekend stay (sans enlightenment), assuming space is available.

Esalen offers more than 400 workshops each year about "relating to our greater human capacity." Topics cover everything from the arts and creative expression to "intellectual play," from dreams to spiritual healing, and from martial arts to shamanism. Moving in a more intellectual and philosophical direction these days, Esalen increasingly offers such programs as "Psyche and Cosmos in the 21st Century: The Return of Soul to the World"; "Sure Enough: Getting Comfortable with Irreducible Uncertainty"; and "Applied Wisdom: Enduring Truths of the World's Wisdom Traditions."

Equally elevated are Esalen's baths. In February 1998, a mudslide roared down the hill to demolish the previous bathhouse facilities. The new, improved Esalen baths now open, include a geothermally heated swimming pool and a handicapped-accessible hot tub and massage area—at a cost of $5.3 million. Designed by architect Mickey Muennig, the new baths "float" above the ocean, thanks to an engineer-ing feat that required driving 34 piers and horizontal anchors into 25 feet of rock. Note the outdoor massage deck, tile work, fountain, and the "living roof," planted in native coastal grasses. Esalen satisfies the California Coastal Commission's public access requirement by allowing the general public access to the hot tubs (at the fairly unappealing hours of 1–3 A.M. daily). Call for details. The massages at Esalen are world-renowned ($50 and up per hour). Nudity is big at Esalen (though not required), particularly in the hot tubs, swimming pool, and massage area.

Entrance to Esalen and its facilities is strictly by reservation only. For information on workshops and lodgings or to request a copy of Esalen's current catalog ($15), contact the institute (831/667-3000, 831/667-3005 for workshop reservations or fax completed registration form to 831/667-2724, www.esalen.org, info @esalen.org). You can also download a current catalog from the website. The website's online *In the Air* magazine offers a good sense of what Esalen is all about.

NATURE RESERVES

Just south of the Esalen Institute is the **John Little State Reserve,** 21 acres of coast open to the public for day use (frequently foggy). For information, call the Big Sur Station (831/667-2315). About five miles south of Esalen, beyond the Dolan Creek and dramatic Big Creek bridges, is the entrance to **Landels-Hill Big Creek Reserve,** more than 4,200 acres owned by the University of California. Adjacent is the 1,200-acre **Big Creek Marine Ecological Reserve** (831/667-2543, www.redshift.com/-bigcreek). The two are co-managed as the Big Creek Reserve. Safe behind these rusted cast-iron gates are 11 different plant communities, at least 350 plant species, 100 varieties of birds, and 50 types of mammals. A 10-acre area is open as a public educational center; groups are welcome. Access is by permit only (in advance or sign in at the entrance) for educational field trips and research. Camping is available.

LUCIA AND THE NEW CAMALDOLI HERMITAGE

The tiny "town" of Lucia is privately owned, with a gas station and a good down-home restaurant (7 A.M. until dark, when they shut off the generator). Try the homemade split pea soup. Different, too, is a stay in one of the 10 rustic coastal cabins at **Lucia Lodge** (831/667-2391 or 866/424-4787 in the U.S. only, www.lucialodge.com, $175 and up mid-July–October, less in winter and spring). Come nightfall, kerosene lanterns provide the ambience. A simple yet spectacular spot. Online reservations available.

South of Lucia (at the white cross), the road to the left leads to the New Camaldoli Hermitage (831/667-2456, www.contemplation.com), a small Benedictine monastery at the former Lucia Ranch. The sign says that the monks "regret we cannot invite you to camp, hunt, or enjoy a walk on our property" due to their customary solitude and avoidance of "unnecessary speaking." But visitors *can* come to buy crafts and homemade fruitcake and to attend daily mass.

In addition, the hermitage is available for very serene individual retreats of up to two weeks, though few outsiders can stand the no-talk rules for much longer than a few days. Simple meals are included. The suggested offering is $60 per day for the retreat rooms, $70 per day for trailer hermitages (single occupancy).

LIMEKILN STATE PARK

About two miles south of Lucia is the newest Big Sur state park, open since 1995. It encompasses 716 acres in an isolated and steep coastal canyon, preserving some of the oldest, largest, and most vigorous redwoods in Monterey County. Named for the towering wood-fired kilns that smelted quarried limestone into powdered lime—essential for mixing cement—here in the late 1800s, Limekiln State Park (63025 Hwy. 1, Big Sur, 831/667-2403) offers a steep, one-mile (round-trip), creekside hike through redwoods to the four kilns, passing a waterfall (to the right at the first fork), pools, and cascades along the way. The park includes a day-use area for picnicking ($6 fee) and a very appealing 33-site family campground with minimal amenities but abundant ambience. Campsites are $15–20; extras include hot showers and laundry facilities. To get there, take the signed turnoff (on the inland or landward side of the highway) just south of the Limekiln Canyon Bridge. For more information, contact the park or see *Public Camping in Big Sur,* below.

Recreation

The ultimate activity in Big Sur is just bumming around, scrambling down to beaches to hunt for jade, peer into tidepools, or scuba dive or surf wherever possible. Cycling, sightseeing, and watching the sunset are other forms or entertainment. Along the coastline proper, there are few long hiking trails, since much of the terrain is treacherous, and most of the rest privately owned, but the Big Sur backcountry offers good hiking and backpacking.

VENTANA WILDERNESS

Local lore has it that a natural land bridge once connected two mountain peaks at Bottchers Gap, creating a window (or *ventana* in Spanish) until the 1906 San Francisco earthquake brought it all tumbling down. The Big Sur, Little Sur, Arroyo Seco, and Carmel Rivers all cut through this 236,145-acre area, creating dramatic gorges and wild land well worth exploring. Steep, sharp-crested ridges and serrated V-shaped valleys are clothed mostly in oaks, madrones, and dense chaparral. Redwoods grow on north-facing slopes near the fog-cooled coast; pines at higher elevations. The gnarly, spiral-shaped bristlecone firs found only here are in the rockiest, most remote areas, their total range only about 12 miles wide and 55 miles long.

Most of all, the Ventana Wilderness provides a great escape from the creeping coastal traffic (a free visitor permit is required to enter) and offers

FIGHTING OAK FUNGUS AMONG US

California's newest plant plague is **sudden oak death,** or *Phytophthora ramorum,* a shockingly sudden, fast-moving, fungus-like primitive brown alga that afflicts native California oak, madrone, and bay trees, as well as rhododendrons, camellias, and other ornamental plants. First identified in the mid-1990s near Mt. Tamalpais in Marin County, and now found as far south as Big Sur, as far north as southern Oregon, and in 13 other states, the disease is most prevalent along California's central coast regions. Trees in their death throes have large, weeping cankers that "bleed" dark red, viscous fluid; they also host swarms of beetles and the *Hypoxylon* fungus, evidence that tree tissues are dying. (There was some confusion about this fungal infection when sudden oak death was first identified. It's now believed that the fungus is a symptom, rather than a cause—already harmlessly present in trees, then breaking out and growing rapidly only where sapwood is dying.) Sudden oak death is similar to a pathogen that has afflicted forests in the Pacific Northwest since the 1960s. Perhaps ominously, it has also been found in redwood trees. There is no known cure, though in 2003, a breakthrough phosphite product proved successful in protecting oak trees from infection and in helping infected oaks fight off the disease. In 2004, the disease's genome was mapped, raising hopes that a universal cure will be developed.

So far, sudden oak death has been spreading within the coastal "fog belt." The disease spreads through soil and root systems, and probably also through water. The cooperation of hikers, mountain bikers, and even casual visitors is required to avoid spreading sudden oak death. Preventive steps include thoroughly washing one's shoes and tires before leaving infected areas, as well as prohibiting the export of wood products and plants. Complicating the problem further is the fact that a variety of other plants serve as "hosts" and distributors of sudden oak death. These include coffeeberry, huckleberry, and California buckeye, though the two dominant sources of ongoing infection are rhododendrons and California bay laurels.

For current information about sudden oak death, including quarantines and preventive measures, see the California Oak Mortality website (www.suddenoakdeath.org).

great backpacking and hiking when the Sierra Nevada, Klamath Mountains, and Cascades are still snowbound—though roads here are sometimes impassible during the rainy season. Hunting, fishing, and horseback riding are also permitted. Crisscrossing Ventana Wilderness are nearly 400 miles of backcountry trails and 82 vehicle-accessible campgrounds (trailside camping possible with a permit).

The wilderness trailheads are at Big Sur Station, Carmel River, China Camp, Arroyo Seco, Memorial Park, Bottchers Gap, and Cone Peak Road. The Ventana Wilderness recreation map, available for $4 from ranger district offices, shows all roads, trails, and campgrounds. Fire-hazardous areas, routinely closed to the public after July 1 (or earlier), are coded yellow on maps.

Trail and campground traffic fluctuates from year to year, so solitude-seekers should ask rangers about more remote routes and destinations. Since the devastating Marble Cone fire of 1978 (and other more recent fires), much of what once was forest is now chaparral and brush. As natural succession progresses, dense undergrowth obliterates trails not already erased by erosion. Despite dedicated volunteer trail work, lack of federal trail maintenance has also taken its toll.

Backcountry travelers should also heed fire regulations. Because of the high fire danger in peak tourist season, using a camp stove or building a fire outside designated campgrounds require a fire permit. Also, bring water—but think twice before bringing Fido, since flea-transmitted plague is a possibility. Other bothersome realities include ticks (especially in winter and early spring), rattlesnakes, poison oak, and fast-rising rivers and streams following rainstorms.

For more Ventana Wilderness information, contact the Big Sur Station office (831/667-2315) or **Los Padres National Forest** headquarters (6755 Hollister Ave., Ste. 150, Goleta, 805/968-6640, www.fs.fed.us/r5/lospadres).

For detailed backpacking information and current trail conditions, contact the ranger district office closest to your intended trailhead. If you'll be parking in the forest, Adventure Pass or Golden Passport required (see website). Additional information is available from the **Ventana Wilderness Society** (831/455-9514, www.ventanaws.org) and the **Ventana Wilderness Alliance** (831/423-3191, www.ventana wild.org). For guided trips on horseback, contact **Ventana Wilderness Guides and Expeditions** (38655 Tassajara Rd., Carmel Valley, 831/659-2153, www.nativeguides.com), operated by members of the Esselen tribe.

Other federal wildernesses in Los Padres National Forest, the third largest in California, include the Chumash, Sespe, Matilija, Dick Smith, San Rafael, Santa Lucia, Garcia, and Silver Peak Wilderness Areas.

HIKING

The grandest views of Big Sur come from the ridges just back from the coast. A great companion is *Hiking the Big Sur Country,* by Jeffrey P. Schaffer (Wilderness Press). The short but steep **Valley View Trail** from Pfeiffer–Big Sur State Park is usually uncrowded, especially midweek; there are benches up top for sitting and staring off the edge of the world. Those *serious* about coastal hiking should walk all the way from Pfeiffer–Big Sur to Salmon Creek, near the southern Monterey County line. The trip from Bottchers Gap to Ventana Double Cone via **Skinner Ridge Trail** is about 16 miles one way and challenging, with a variety of possible campsites, dazzling spring wildflowers, and oak and pine forests.

Otherwise, take either the nine-mile **Pine Ridge Trail** from Big Sur or the 15-mile trail from China Camp on Chews Ridge to undeveloped Sykes Hot Springs, just 400 yards from Sykes Camp (very popular these days). Another good, fairly short hike is the trip to nearby Mount Manuel, a nine-mile round trip. The two-mile walk to **Pfeiffer Beach** is also worth it: miles from the highway, fringed by forest, with a wading cove and meditative monolith.

BACK ROADS

For an unforgettable dry-season side trip and a true joyride, take the **Old Coast Road** from just north of the Bixby Bridge inland to the Big Sur Valley. You'll encounter barren granite, a thickly forested gorge, and good views of sea and sky before the road loops back to Highway 1 south of Point Sur, near the entrance to Andrew Molera State Park. **Palo Colorado Road,** mostly unpaved and narrow, winds through a canyon of redwoods, ferns, and summer homes, up onto hot and dry Las Piedras Ridge, then down into the Little Sur watershed.

Marvelous for the sense of adventure and the views is a drive along the **Nacimiento-Fergusson Road,** from the coast inland to what's left of old Jolon and the fabulous nearby mission, both located within the Fort Hunter-Liggett Military Reservation. (Taking this route is always somewhat risky, particularly on weekends, since all roads through Hunter-Liggett are closed when military exercises are underway.) Even more thrilling is driving rough-and-ready **Los Burros Road** farther south, an unmarked turnoff just south of Willow Creek and Cape San Martin that leads to the long-gone town of Manchester in the Los Burros gold mining district. An indestructible vehicle and plenty of time are required for this route, and it's often closed to traffic after winter storms.

Big Sur back roads leading to the sea are rarer and easy to miss. About one mile south of the entrance to Pfeiffer–Big Sur State Park is **Sycamore Canyon Road,** which winds its way downhill for two exciting miles before the parking lot near Pfeiffer Beach. At Willow Creek, there's a road curling down from the vista point to the rocky beach below; and just south of Willow Creek, a dirt road leads to Cape San Martin—good for views any day, but especially fine for whale-watching.

Big Sur

Accommodations and Food

PUBLIC CAMPING

In the accommodations category, nothing but camping is truly inexpensive in Big Sur, so to travel on the cheap, make campground reservations *early* (where applicable) and stock up on groceries and sundries in Monterey up north, or in San Luis Obispo to the south. All the following options are under $50. The U.S. Forest Service **Bottchers Gap Campground** on Palo Colorado Canyon Road has primitive, walk-in tent sites ($12, first-come, first-camped). Rough road, no drinking water, campground closed only during wet weather. The Forest Service **Kirk Creek Campground** is far south of urban Big Sur and just north of the intersection with Nacimiento-Fergusson Road. It consists of 33 first-come, first-camped sites ($18, walk-in/bike-in sites $5), picnic tables, and grills, all situated on a grassy seaside bluff. Inland, halfway to Jolon, are two small creekside campgrounds managed by Los Padres National Forest. They are free, since there's no reliable drinking water, and are popular with deer hunters. Also run by the Forest Service and even farther south, north of Gorda, is the 43-site **Plaskett Creek Campground** ($18, walk-in/bike-in sites $5).

For more information on the area's national forest campgrounds and for free visitor permits, fire permits, maps, and other information about Los Padres National Forest and the Ventana Wilderness, stop by the **Big Sur Station** State Parks/U.S. Forest Service office at Pfeiffer–Big Sur State Park (831/667-2315, 8 A.M.–4:30 P.M. daily), or the **Monterey Ranger District** office (406 S. Mildred Ave., King City, 831/385-5434).

At state park facilities, try **Andrew Molera State Park** for secluded camping, with walk-in tent sites not far from the dusty parking lot, three-night maximum; or **Julia Pfeiffer Burns State Park,** with two separate environmental campsites (far from RVs). More comforts (including flush toilets and hot showers) are available at the attractive family campground at **Pfeiffer–Big Sur State Park.** It has 214 campsites

and some group campgrounds, plus a regular summer schedule of educational and informational programs. There are no hookups. Another possibility, just south of Lucia, is the postcard-pretty **Limekiln State Park** (63025 Hwy. 1, 831/667-2403), which takes up most of the steep canyon and offers some good hiking in addition to attractive tent and RV sites (no hookups, but water, hot showers, and flush toilets are available). For information about any of the area's state park campgrounds, stop by the office at Pfeiffer–Big Sur State Park or call 831/667-2315. For reservations at Pfeiffer–Big Sur and Limekiln, contact ReserveAmerica (800/444-7275, www.reserveamerica.com, usually necessary May–early Sept. and on warm-weather weekends).

PRIVATE CAMPING

Not far from the state campgrounds at Pfeiffer–Big Sur State Park is the private riverside **Big Sur Campground and Cabins** (Hwy. 1, 831/667-2322), with tent sites and RV sites, including hookups. Tent cabins and cabins are also available, as well as hot showers, laundry facilities, a store, telephone access, and a playground. Also on the Big Sur River, with similar facilities and prices, is the **Riverside Campground and Cabins** (Hwy. 1, 831/667-2414), with tent or RV sites, plus cabins. The private **Ventana Campgrounds** (Hwy. 1, 831/667-2712, www.ventanawildernesscampground.com), managed by the Ventana Inn, has 80 very private, pretty sites in a scenic 40-acre redwood setting along Post Creek. There are some RV hookups, hot showers (three bathhouses), fireplaces, and picnic tables. Rates for all private camping optionsare under $50 (cabins are higher).

MOTELS AND HOTELS

Always a fine bet for cabins and affordable for just plain folks is the charming **𝕹 Ripplewood Resort** (about a mile north of Pfeiffer–Big Sur, 831/667-2242, www.ripplewoodresort.com).

The primo units, most with fireplaces and kitchens (bring your own cookware), are down by the Big Sur River and booked months in advance for summer. Rates for most are are $100–150; several are under $100. Convenient onsite café, too (breakfast and lunch). For something dramatically different, why not camp out in a yurt? **Treebones Resort** (877/424-4787, www.treebonesresort.com), south of Big Sur proper and just a mile north of Gorda, is scheduled to open in fall 2004. Offerings include 16 "view" yurts, five campsites, a pool and spa, and all the comforts in its large guest-services building.

Other Big Sur options include the adobe **Glen Oaks Motel** (831/667-2105, www.glenoaks-bigsur.com, $50 and up) and the **Fernwood Resort** (831/667-2422, $50 and up), both on Highway 1. The historic **Big Sur River Inn** (Hwy. 1, Big Sur Valley, 831/625-5255 or 800/548-3610, www.bigsurriverinn.com) is a motel-restaurant-bar popular with locals and featuring views of the river and live music most weekends. Nearby, the 61-room 🅽 **Big Sur Lodge** (47225 Hwy. 1, 831/667-3100 or 800/424-4787, www.bigsurlodge.com, $100 and up), just inside the park's entrance, is quiet, with a pool, a sauna, a restaurant, and a circle of comfy cabins, each with its own porch or deck. Some rooms—the remodeled ones are quite charming—feature wood-burning fireplaces or fully stocked kitchens. A lodge stay includes a complimentary pass to all area state parks.

DEETJEN'S BIG SUR INN

Just south of the noted Nepenthe restaurant and the Henry Miller Library is the landward Norwegian-style Deetjen's Big Sur Inn in Castro Canyon (831/667-2377, www.deetjens.com, $100 and up, under $100 with shared bath), a rambling, ever-blooming inn with redwood rooms. It's now listed on the National Register of Historic Places and operated as a nonprofit venture by the Deetjen's Big Sur Inn Preservation Foundation. *Very* Big Sur. The 20 eccentric, rustic rooms and cabins—one's named Chateau Fiasco, after the Bay of Pigs invasion—are chock-full of bric-a-brac and feature thin walls,

front doors that don't lock, fireplaces, books, and reasonably functional plumbing. No TVs, no telephones. Forget about trendy creature comforts. People love this place—and have ever since it opened in the 1930s—because it has *soul*. Private or shared baths. Reservations advised, because rooms are usually booked up many months in advance. Eating at Deetjen's (breakfast 8–11:30 A.M., dinner from 6:15 P.M.) is as big a treat as an overnight. Wonderfully hearty, wholesome breakfasts and dinners are served. Reservations are also taken for meals.

VENTANA INN & SPA

Perhaps tuned into the same philosophical frequency as Henry Miller—"There being nothing to improve on in the surroundings, the tendency is to set about improving oneself"—the Ventana Inn (831/667-2331 or 800/628-6500, www.ventanainn.com, $250 and up, two-night minimum on weekends) didn't provide distractions like TV or tennis courts when writer Lawrence A. Spector first built the place in 1975. Though it's still a hip, high-priced resort, and there are still no tennis courts, things have changed. Now the desperately undiverted *can* phone home, if need be, or watch in-room TV or videos. But the woodsy, world-class Ventana, high up on the hill in Big Sur, still offers luxurious and relaxed contemporary lodgings on 240 acres overlooking the sea, with outdoor Japanese hot baths and heated pools.

This rough-hewn and hand-built hostelry comprises 12 separate buildings, with rooms featuring unfinished cedar interiors, parquet floors, and down-home luxuries like queen- or king-sized beds with hand-painted headboards, handmade quilted spreads, and lots of pillows. All rooms are reasonably large and have in-room refrigerators; most have fireplaces. Rooms and suites with both fireplaces and hot tubs are at the top of the inn's price range. The Ventana Inn also has a library, not to mention hiking trails and hammocks. Complimentary group classes—so very *California*—include Native American tai chi, Chi Gong, guided meditation, yoga, and hiking. Complimentary continental breakfast is served (delivered to your room by request), and in the afternoon (4–5:30 P.M.), you can enjoy the complimentary wine and cheese buffet in the main lodge. Reservations are usually essential. Children are discouraged at Ventana, which is not set up to entertain or otherwise look after them.

Ranked number two of the 25 "Best Small Hotels in the World" in the 1998 *Travel & Leisure* reader survey, the Ventana Inn became the Ventana Inn & Spa with the 1999 debut of its full-service spa. For a price, expect world-class massages, wraps, facials, scrubs, and other body therapies.

If a stay here or a self-pampering spa session seems just *too rich,* take a pleasant stroll through the woods and try drinks with a view or a bite of enticing California cuisine at the inn's lovely, two-tiered **Cielo** restaurant, overlooking the ocean—it's one of the region's best, most beloved restaurants. The Ventana Inn is located 0.8 mile south of Pfeiffer–Big Sur State Park; look for the sign on the left.

POST RANCH INN

For good reason, new Big Sur commercial development was rare in the 1990s. If further coastal development must come in this decade, the environmentally conscious Post Ranch Inn (831/667-2200 or 800/527-2200 for inn reservations, 831/667-2800 for restaurant reservations, www.postranchinn.com, $250 and up—substantially up) offers the style—if not the price range—most Californians would cheer. All the upscale travel mags rave about the place, open since 1992, calling it "the most spectacular hotel on the Pacific Coast" *(Travel & Leisure).* According to *Condé Nast Traveler's* Readers' Choice Awards, in 2003 it was the number one hotel in North America and tied for "best of the best" in the world; and in the magazine's 2004 Gold List, Post Ranch tied again for first place, this time in the Best Places to Stay category. So, yes, this place is something special. Developer Myles Williams, of New Christy Minstrels folk-singing fame, and architect Mickey Muennig took the Big Sur region's rugged love of the land to heart when they built the very contemporary Post Ranch Inn. They also acknowledged the community's increasing economic

stratification and took other real-world problems into account, adding 24 housing units for workers (affordable housing is now scarce in these parts) and donating land for Big Sur's first fire station.

Perched on a ridge overlooking the grand Pacific Ocean, the Post Ranch Inn is a carefully executed, aesthetic study in nature awareness. The 30 redwood-and-glass "guesthouses" are designed and built to harmonize with—almost disappear into—the hilltop landscape. The triangular "treehouses" are built on stilts, to avoid damaging the roots of the oaks with which they intertwine; the spectacular sod-roofed "ocean houses" seems to blend into the ocean views; and the gracious "coast house" duplexes impersonate stand-tall coastal redwoods. Absolute privacy and understated, earth-toned luxury are the main points here. Each house includes a wood-burning fireplace, a two-person spa tub in the stunning slate bathroom, a good sound system, in-room refrigerators stocked with complimentary snacks, a private deck, a king-sized bed—and views. Extra amenities include plush robes, in-room coffeemakers and hair dryers, and even walking sticks. Priced for Hollywood entertainment execs and Silicon Valley survivors, continental breakfast included.

Guests can also enjoy the **Post Ranch Spa**—offering massage, wraps, and facials—and the exceptional California-style **Sierra Mar** restaurant, where the views are every bit as inviting as the daily changing menu. Full bar, excellent wine list. Open for lunch and dinner. Prime-time seatings are reserved for inn guests, but nonguests can dine earlier or later.

The Post Ranch Inn is located 30 miles south of Carmel on Highway 1, on the west (seaward) side of the road. As at Ventana, children are discouraged here.

FOOD

Look for fairly inexpensive fare in and around the Big Sur Valley. Good for breakfast is the **Ripplewood Resort** (831/667-2242), just north of Pfeiffer–Big Sur near the tiny Big Sur Library, where favorites include homemade baked goods and French toast. Another local find is the **Big Sur Bakery & Restaurant** (831/667-0520), near the post office. Legendary ⚲ **Deetjen's** (831/667-2377) is special for breakfast—wholesome and hearty fare served in the open-beamed, hobbit-style dining rooms. Dinner is more formal (fireplace blazing to ward off the chill mist, classical music, and two seatings by reservation only), with entrées such as steak, fish, California country cuisine, and vegetarian dishes. Tasty home-baked pies are an after-meal specialty at the casual and cheery **Big Sur Lodge Restaurant** (831/667-3111) at the Big Sur Lodge, overlooking the river and known for red snapper and California-style fare. Beer and wine available. Another draw is the lodge's **Espresso House,** perfect for coffee, tea, or a quick snack.

Everyone should sample the view from famed ⚲ **Nepenthe** (831/667-2345) at least once in a lifetime; just below Nepenthe is **Café Kevah** (831/667-2344, brunch and lunch Mar.–Dec.) For more information, see the listing for Nepenthe under *Accommodations,* above. A quarter mile north of Palo Colorado Road on Highway 1 is the **Rocky Point Restaurant** (831/624-2933, lunch, dinner, and cocktails daily), a reasonably well-heeled steak and seafood place overlooking the ocean.

The finest of local fine dining is served at the area's luxury-hotel restaurants: ⚲ **Cielo,** at the Ventana Inn & Spa, and ⚲ **Sierra Mar,** at the Post Ranch Inn. Both serve lunch and dinner daily. For information, see the listings for both inns.

Information and Services

For general information about the area, contact the **Big Sur Chamber of Commerce** (831/667-2100, www.bigsurcalifornia.org, information@bigsurcalifornia.org; send a stamped, self-addressed, legal-sized envelope for a free guide to Big Sur, or download it from the website.) At last report, the office was staffed only 9 A.M.–1 P.M. on Monday, Wednesday, and Friday, but you can also send an email or leave a phone message, and someone will contact you. Combined headquarters for area state parks and the U.S. Forest Service is **Big Sur Station** (Hwy. 1, 831/667-2315, 8 A.M.–4:30 P.M. daily), on the south side of Pfeiffer–Big Sur. This is the place to go in search of forest and wilderness maps, permits, and backcountry camping and recreation information. There's a **launderette** at

⚲ Big Sur

EYEING E-SEALS

Everyone knows that massive northern elephant seals lumber ashore every winter at Año Nuevo, north of Santa Cruz, much as the swallows come back to Capistrano. Yet most people don't know that if you can't get reservations to see the "e-seals" at the Año Nuevo preserve, you can come observe them from a vista point just south of Piedra Blancas, about 4.5 miles north of Hearst Castle.

The northern elephant seal colony here began in November 1990, when a handful of seals hauled ashore at the small cove just south of the Piedras Blancas lighthouse; the following spring, almost 400 seals came ashore to molt; and in 1992, the first pup was born. By 2002, the total Piedras Blancas population of northern elephant seals was estimated at 8,500, including 2,150 new pups. More than 2,600 pups were born during the 2002–2003 pupping season. The seals' breeding and pupping season begins in December and lasts into March. (Keep your distance at all times, and never come between an e-seal and the ocean, their natural escape route. These are wild animals that will react to provocation and perceived threats.) From April to August, the e-seals molt, a natural phenomenon that looks like an outbreak of disease, as old fur is shed and shiny new skin emerges. Docents at the designated viewing area explain the natural history and habits and life cycles of the northern elephant seal. Tours can be arranged.

For more information, stop by the **Friends of the Elephant Seals** office in the Plaza del Cavalier in San Simeon (250 San Simeon Ave., Ste. 3B, 805/924-1628, www.elephantseal.org).

Pfeiffer–Big Sur State Park in the Big Sur Lodge complex.

Bicycling Big Sur can be marvelous, except when you're fighting RVs and weekend speedsters for road space. Forewarned, fearless cyclists should plan to ride from north to south to take advantage of the tailwind. (Driving south makes sense, too, since most vistas and turnouts are seaward.) It takes *at least* five hours by car to drive the 150 miles of Highway 1 between Monterey and San Luis Obispo.

Hitchhiking is almost as difficult as safely riding a bicycle along this stretch of road, so don't count on thumbs for transportation. More reliable is **Monterey-Salinas Transit** (831/899-2555, www.mst.org) Bus 22, which runs to and from Big Sur daily from mid-April to October, stopping at Point Lobos, Garrapata State Park, the Bixby Creek Bridge, Point Sur Light Station, Pfeiffer–Big Sur and the River Inn, Pfeiffer Beach, the Ventana Inn, and Nepenthe.

San Simeon and Vicinity

M HEARST SAN SIMEON STATE HISTORIC MONUMENT

The Hearst San Simeon State Historic Monument, just south of Big Sur, ranks right up there with Disneyland as one of California's premier tourist attractions. Somehow, this fact alone puts the place into proper perspective. Media magnate William Randolph Hearst's castle is a rich man's playground, filled to overflowing with artistic diversions and other expensive toys, a monument to one man's monumental ego and equally impressive poor taste.

In real life, of course, Hearst was quite a wealthy and powerful man, the man many people still believe was the subject of the greatest American movie ever made, Orson Welles's 1941 *Citizen Kane*. (These days, even Welles's biographers say the movie was about the filmmaker himself.) Yet there's something to be said for popular opinion. "Pleasure," Hearst once wrote, "is worth what you can afford to pay for it." And that attitude showed itself quite early; for his 10th birthday, little William asked for the Louvre as a present. One scene in the movie, in which Charles Foster Kane shouts across the cavernous living room at Xanadu to attract the attention of his bored young mistress, endlessly working jigsaw puzzles while she sits before a fireplace as big as the mouth of Jonah's whale, won't seem so surreal once you see San Simeon.

Designed by Berkeley architect Julia Morgan, the buildings themselves are odd yet hand-

© ROBERT HOLMES/CALTOUR

Hearst Castle, San Simeon

some hallmarks of Spanish Renaissance architecture. The centerpiece, La Casa Grande, has 100 rooms (including a movie theater, a billiards room, two libraries, and 31 bathrooms) adorned with silk banners, fine Belgian and French tapestries, Norman fireplaces, European choir stalls, and ornately carved ceilings

Big Sur

the Neptune Pool at Hearst Castle

virtually stolen from continental monasteries. The furnishings and art Hearst collected from around the world complete the picture, one that includes everything but humor, grace, warmth, and understanding.

The notably self-negating nature of this rich but richly disappointed man's life is somehow fully expressed here in the country's most ostentatious and theatrical temple to obscene wealth. In contrast to Orson Welles's authentic artistic interpretation of either his own or Hearst's life, William Randolph's idea of hearth, home, and humanity was full-flown fantasy, sadly separated from heart and vision.

Tours

In spring, when the hills are emerald green, Hearst Castle appears as if by magic up on the hill from the faraway highway. (Before the place opened for public tours in the 1950s, the closest view commoners could get was from the road, with the assistance of coin-operated telescopes.) One thing visitors *don't* see on the tour shuttle up to the enchanted hill is William Randolph Hearst's 2,000-acre zoo—"the largest private zoo since Noah," as Charles Foster Kane might put it, and once the country's largest. The inmates have long since been dispersed, though survivors of Hearst's exotic elk, zebra, Barbary sheep, and Himalayan goat herds still roam the grounds.

The four separate tours of the Hearst San Simeon State Historic Monument take approximately two hours each. Theoretically, you could take all the San Simeon tours in a day, but don't try it. So much Hearst in the short span of a day could be detrimental to one's well-being. A dosage of two tours per day makes the trip here worthwhile, yet not overwhelming. Visitors obsessed with seeing it all should plan a two-day stay in the area, or come back again some other time. Whichever tour, or combination of tours, you select, be sure to wear comfortable walking shoes. Lots of stairs.

The **Experience Tour,** or Tour One, is the recommended first-time visit, taking in the castle's main floor, one guesthouse, and some of the gardens—a total of 150 steps and a half mile of walking. Included on the tour is a short showing in the theater of some of

Big Sur

Hearst's "home movies." Particularly impressive in a gloomy Gothic way is the dining room, where silk Siennese banners hang over the lord's table. The poolroom and mammoth great hall, with Canova's *Venus,* are also unforgettable. All the tours include both the Greco-Roman Neptune Pool and statuary and the indoor Roman Pool, with its mosaics of lapis lazuli and gold leaf. It's hard to imagine Churchill, cigar in mouth, cavorting here in an inner tube. The Experience Tour also includes the National Geographic movie, *Hearst Castle: Building the Dream.*

Tour Two requires more walking, covering the mansion's upper floors, the kitchen, the libraries, and Hearst's Gothic Suite, with its frescoes and rose-tinted Venetian glass windows (he ran his 94 separate business enterprises from here). The delightfully lit Celestial Suite was the nonetheless depressing extramarital playground of Hearst and Marion Davies. **Tour Three** covers one of the guesthouses, plus the "new wing," with 36 luxurious bedrooms, sitting rooms, and marble bathrooms furnished with fine art.

HEARST RANCH ACQUIRED

Thanks to $34.5 million in California parks funds, in September 2004 the state acquired development rights for the 13 miles of coastline and portions of 83,000-acre **Piedra Blanca Ranch,** the Hearst Corp. lands surrounding Hearst San Simeon State Historical Monument—thus guaranteeing the land's protection. Other portions of the ranch were purchased for $95 million. Cattle ranching is still allowed on part of the historic ranch, and the company may yet build a 100-room hotel, 27 homes, and employee housing. A prod to the public land acquisition came in 1998, when the Hearst Corp. announced plans to build a 650-room hotel, 18-hole golf course, and luxury home development.

As a result of the 2004 acquisition, the public gained access to lands which were previously off limits. For current access information, contact area state parks and visitors bureaus.

Gardeners will be moved to tears by **Tour Four** (offered Apr.–Aug. only), which includes a long stroll through the San Simeon grounds, but does not go inside the castle itself. Realizing that all the rich topsoil here had to be manually carried up the hill makes the array of exotic plant life, including unusual camellias and about 6,000 rosebushes, all the more impressive—not to mention the fact that gardeners at San Simeon worked only at night, because Hearst couldn't stand watching them. Also included on the fourth tour is the lower level of the elegant, 17-room Casa del Mar guesthouse (where Hearst spent much of his time), the recently redone underground Neptune Pool dressing rooms, the never-finished bowling alley, and Hearst's wine cellar. David Niven once remarked that, with Hearst as host, the wine flowed "like glue." Subsequently, Niven was the only guest allowed free access to the castle's wine cellar.

Fairly new at San Simeon are the **Hearst Castle Evening Tours,** two-hour adventures featuring the highlights of other tours—with the added benefit of allowing you to pretend to be some Hollywood celebrity, just arrived and in need of orientation. (Hearst himself handed out tour maps, since newcomers often got lost.) Guides dress in period costume and show you around. It's worth it just to see the castle in lights. At last report, evening tours were offered on Friday and Saturday nights March–May and Sept.–Dec., but call or see the website for current details. December **Christmas at the Castle** tours are particularly festive.

To make reservations for **physically challenged/wheelchair-accessible tours,** call Hearst Castle directly (805/927-2070) at least 10 days in advance. Wheelchair-accessible tours, which explore the ground floor only, take about two hours and are offered at least three times daily. Wheelchairs are available for loan at no extra charge. Chairs brought by visitors need to be able to get through doorways 28 inches wide. Someone strong enough to maneuver an occupied chair up and down narrow ramps and steep inclines must accompany visitors requiring wheelchairs.

Practicalities

Hearst San Simeon State Historic Monument (750 Hearst Castle Rd., San Simeon, 805/927-2020—recorded info only or 805/927-2000, www.hearstcastle.org) is open daily except Thanksgiving, Christmas, and New Year's Day, with the regular two-hour tours leaving the visitors center area on the hour from early morning until around dusk. Tour schedules change by season and day of the week. Reservations aren't required, but the chance of getting tickets on a drop-in, last-minute basis is small. For current schedule information and to make reservations, call ReserveAmerica (800/444-4445) and have that credit card handy. You can also get current information and book online at www.hearstcastle.org. For cancellations and refunds, call 800/695-2269 in the U.S. (To make ticket reservations from outside the U.S., call 916/414-8400, ext. 4100, or reserve on the website.) Wheelchair-accessible tours of Hearst Castle are offered on a different schedule; call 805/927-2070 for reservations and information, or see the website. The TDD number is 800/274-7275.

At last report, there were two tiers of prices—one for the high season, May 15 through September 15, and another for the off season. In the summer high season, admission to any of the regular tours (Tour One through Tour 4) is $24 adult and $12 youth (aged 6–17). In the off season, from mid-September through mid-May, admission to any of the four regular tours is $20 adult and $10 youth (aged 6–17). Any time of year, evening tour rates are $30 adults, $15 children. A special brochure for international travelers (printed in Japanese, Korean, French, German, Hebrew, Italian, and Spanish) is available. With a little forethought—head for Cambria or the town of San Simeon—visitors can avoid eating the concession-style food here.

Adjacent to the visitors center is the Hearst Castle's giant-screened **National Geographic Theater** (805/927-6811), where, at last report, the larger-than-life *Hearst Castle: Building the Dream* and *Everest* were showing on the 70-by-52-foot screen. Call for current times and details (no reservations required).

SOUTH FROM SAN SIMEON

Once you're done with the display of pompous circumstance on the hill, sample San Simeon proper. The area's serene sandy beaches are heavenly for a long coast walk—just the thing to clear out all the clutter. Good ocean swimming and picnicking, too. Stop for picnic supplies and sandwiches at **Sebastian's General Store** (805/927-4217), a state historic monument in the red-roofed village of San Simeon, built by Hearst for his laborers. Another picnicking possibility, an area especially appealing for winter whale-watchers, is **Piedras Blancas Lighthouse** (888/804-8608, www.lighthousefriends.com), just up the coast. The light station is open for limited public tours. There's good tidepooling at nearby **Twin Creeks Beach** (805/924-1628, www.elephantseal.org), but public access may be restricted, as the area is now seasonal home for a northern elephant seal colony. Docent tours are available (see "Eyeing the E-seals" on the website).

Its borders blending into San Simeon Acres motel row, about eight miles south of Hearst castle, the artsy coastal town of **Cambria** now bears the Roman name for ancient Wales, but was previously called Rosaville, San Simeon, and (seriously) Slabtown. In some ways, Cambria is becoming the Carmel of southern Big Sur, with its galleries and come-hither shops—but so far, without the crowds. Several of the area's historic buildings remain, including the 1877 Squibb-Darke home, the Brambles restaurant (on Burton Drive in Old Town to the east), and the restored Santa Rosa Catholic Church on Bridge Street (across Main, past the library and post office). Just outside Cambria proper in Cambria Pines is Arthur Beal's beautifully bizarre **Nit Wit Ridge** (881 Hillcrest Dr., 805/927-2690), something of a middle-class San Simeon built from abalone shells, glass, discarded car parts, toilet seats, beer cans, and more, a state historical monument since 1981. Guided tours are available.

For more information about the area, including events, accommodations, and restaurants, contact the **San Simeon Chamber of Commerce** (9255 Hearst Dr., 805/927-3500), on the highway just south of the Sands Motel in

Big Sur

© KIM WEIR

Besides Morro Rock, the coastal town of Morro Bay is noted for its giant chess board.

the Cavalier Plaza, or the **Cambria Chamber of Commerce** (767 Main St., 805/927-3624, www.cambriachamber.org).

The biggest city immediately south from San Simeon is **San Luis Obispo,** a convenient stop halfway between L.A. and San Francisco along Highway 101 and most famous for creating both the word and the modern concept "motel," a contraction of "motor hotel." The town's (and the world's) first motel, the Motel Inn on Monterey Street, still stands, at last report slated for complete renovation. Agriculture is big business around here, a fact reflected in the prominent presence of the well-respected **California State Polytechnic University,** also known as Cal Poly or (snidely) "Cow Poly." Pick up an "Ag's My Bag" bumper sticker as a souvenir or—if you can time your trip appropriately—roll into town on a Thursday evening to enjoy the **Higuera Street Farmers Market,** one of the best anywhere (cancelled only in the event of rain). To get more of the San Luis Obispo story, stop by **Mission San Luis Obispo de Tolosa** (downtown on Mission

Plaza, 751 Palm St.) and the **Museum & History Center of San Luis Obispo County** in the old Carnegie library (696 Monterey Street). For current city and county information, stop by the **San Luis Obispo County Visitors & Conference Bureau** (downtown at 1037 Mill St., 805/781-2531 or 800/634-1414, www.sanluisobispocounty.com).

Speaking of missions and old California stories: Well worth going out of your way for—inland from the coast and north of San Luis Obispo—is **Mission San Antonio de Padua,** smack-dab in the middle of Fort Hunter-Liggett (expect a security check at the base gate), not the grandest or most spruced-up, but among the most evocative of all the California missions. From here, take narrow, unpaved Nacimiento-Fergusson Rd. back over the coastal mountains to Big Sur. Nearby **Lake San Antonio** is popular in winter for guided bald eagle–watching tours.

Off in the other direction, via Highway 58, is the new **Carrizo Plain National Monument,** earthquake territory once sacred to the Chumash people. The native grasses and scrub lands surrounding Soda Lake offer refuge to some of the state's most endangered animal species. And, if you head east from Paso Robles via Highway 46, you'll come to the shrine marking (almost) the spot where actor **James Dean** *(Rebel Without a Cause, Giant,* and *East of Eden)* died in a head-on car accident in 1955. **Paso Robles** itself and nearby **Templeton** are the center of an increasingly popular—and increasingly impressive—wine region. For area information, contact the **Paso Robles Visitor & Conference Bureau** (1225 Park St., 800/406-4040, www.pasorobleschamber.com).

Near San Luis Obispo along the coast is Morro Rock, California's own little Gibraltar, spotted by Cabrillo in 1542—the first thing people notice at **Morro Bay.** Worthy of a gaze downtown: the Morro Bay Chess Club's **giant outdoor chessboard,** though **Morro Bay State Park, Montaña de Oro State Park,** and area parks and beaches offer more varied scenery. For more area information, contact the **Morro Bay Visitors Center & Chamber of Commerce** (880 Main St., Morro Bay, 805/772-4467 or 800 231-0592, www.morrobay.org) and the **Cayucos Chamber of Commerce** (158 N. Ocean Ave. in nearby Cayucos, 805/995-1200 or 800/563-1878, www.cayucoschamber.com).

Still heading south, you'll find **Santa Maria,** most noted for its unique culinary heritage, preserved since the days of the vaqueros. This is the hometown of Santa Maria Barbecue, a complete meal that traditionally includes slabs of prime sirloin barbecued over a slow red-oak fire then sliced as thin as paper, served with *salsa cruda,* pinquito beans, salad, toasted garlic bread, and dessert. Near town is the **Guadalupe-Nipomo Dunes Preserve,** a coastal wildlife and plant preserve also protecting the remains of Cecil B. DeMille's *The Ten Commandments* movie set, buried under the sand here once filming was finished. **Lompoc** is noted for its blooming flower fields—this is a major seed-producing area—and is home to **Vandenberg Air Force Base,** as well as **Mission La Purisima State Historic Park,** California's only complete mission compound, four

miles east of town. For more detailed area information, contact the **Santa Maria Visitor & Convention Bureau** (614 S. Broadway, Santa Maria, 800/331-3779, www.santamaria.com) and the **Lompoc Valley Chamber of Commerce** (111 S. I St., Lompoc, 805/736-4567 or 800/240-0999).

Farther south, **Solvang** is an authentic Danish-style town founded in 1911 and now a well-trod tourist destination. If you've got time, worth exploring nearby are the towns of **Los Olivos** and **Los Alamos,** center of northern Santa Barbara County's impressive wine country. For area information, contact the **Solvang Visitors Bureau** (1639 Copenhagen Dr., 805/688-6144 or 800/468-6765, www.solvangusa.com).

Technically speaking, Point Conception, just below Vandenberg, marks the spot where California turns on itself—that pivotal geographical point where Northern California becomes Southern California. The subtle climatic and terrain changes are unmistakable by the time you arrive in **Santa Barbara,** a richly endowed city noted for its gracious, red-tile-roofed, California Spanish–style buildings—for the most part, an architectural affectation subsequent to the 1925 earthquake that was so devastating here. Even if you have time for nothing else, stop to see the **Santa Barbara County Courthouse,** one block up from State Street at Anapamu and Anacapa, an L-shaped, Spanish-Moorish castle that is quite possibly the most beautiful public building in all of California. Other attractions are abundant, from **Mission Santa Barbara,** "Queen of the Missions," to the **Santa Barbara Museum of Natural History** and the **Santa Barbara Botanic Gardens.** Despite the presence of offshore oil wells, public beaches in the area are sublime. In the harbor area, don't miss **Stern's Wharf,** for serene sunsets and other attractions, and the new **Santa Barbara Maritime Museum.** For more information about Santa Barbara and vicinity, contact the **Santa Barbara Conference & Visitors Bureau** (1601 Anacapa St., Santa Barbara, 805/966-9222 or 800/549-5133, www.santabarbaraca.com).

Big Sur

For less expensive yet equally satisfying coastal adventures, continue south from Santa Barbara to **Ventura** and **Oxnard.** From here, set off on whale-watching trips and guided boat tours of California's **Channel Islands,** a national park equally visible but often less accessible from Santa Barbara. For more area information, contact the **Ventura Visitors & Convention Bureau** (89 S. California St., Ste. C, 805/648-2075 or 800/333-2989, www.ventura-usa.com) and the **Oxnard Convention & Visitors Bureau** (200 W. Seventh St., 805/385-7545 or 800/269-6273, www.ox-nardtourism.com), inside Connelly House at Heritage Square.

Salinas and Vicinity

The sometimes bone-dry Salinas River starts in the mountains above San Luis Obispo and flows north through the Salinas Valley, much of the time underground, unseen. Named for the salt marshes, or *salinas,* near the river's mouth, the Salinas River is the longest underground waterway in the United States. The 100-mile-long Salinas Valley, with its fertile soil and lush lettuce fields, is sometimes referred to as the nation's Salad Bowl. To the west is the Santa Lucia Range; to the east are the Gabilan and Diablo Mountains. Cattle graze in the hills.

No longer such a small town—suddenly, and surprisingly, at least somewhat hip—Salinas was long known as the blue-collar birthplace of novelist John Steinbeck, who chronicled the lives and hard times of California's down-and-out. Some things don't change much. More than 60 years after the 1939 publication of Steinbeck's Pulitzer Prize–winning *The Grapes of Wrath,* the United Farm Workers (UFW) are still attempting to organize the primarily Hispanic farm laborers and migrant workers here. The idea of a unionized agricultural labor force has never been

Must-Sees

National Steinbeck Center

MELISSA SHEROWSKI

M **National Steinbeck Center:** The first American to win both the Pulitzer and Nobel Prizes for literature, John Steinbeck wasn't always appreciated in his hometown of Salinas. This high-tech museum is changing all that (page 109).

M **Steinbeck House:** A must-see for Steinbeck fans, this jewel-box Victorian, just two blocks from the National Steinbeck Center, is also a delicious destination for lunch (page 110).

M **Pinnacles National Monument:** Exploring these barren 24,000 acres of volcanic spires and ravines atop the San Andreas Fault is a little like rock climbing on the moon (page 112).

M **San Juan Bautista:** The historic plaza of this charming mission-era town served as the rallying point for two revolutions, the theatrical setting for David Belasco's *Rose of the Rancho,* and the actual setting for the mission scenes in Alfred Hitchcock's *Vertigo* (page 114).

M **Gilroy Garlic Festival:** It's chic to reek in Gilroy, where, on the last full weekend in July, you can sample garlic perfume, garlic chocolate, and all-you-can-eat garlic ice cream (page 117).

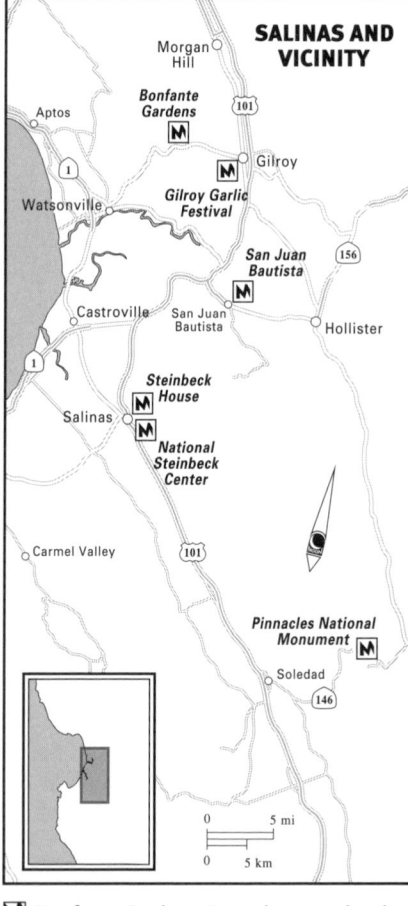

SALINAS AND VICINITY

M **Bonfante Gardens:** More than two decades were spent planning and developing this 75-acre park's unique landscape, where botanical oddities and themed gardens complement family-friendly rides and other theme-park traditions (page 118).

popular in the United States, and certainly not with Salinas Valley growers. In 1936, during a lettuce workers' strike, Salinas was at the center of national attention. Reports to the California Highway Patrol that communists were advancing on the town—an event "proven" by red flags planted along the highway, some of which were sent as evidence to politicians in Sacramento—led to tear gas and tussling between officers, growers, and strikers. The state highway commission later insisted that the construction warning banners be returned to the area's roadsides.

Sights

A Salinas tradition (since 1911) is the four-day **California Rodeo,** held on the third weekend in July. It is one of the world's largest rodeos, with bronco busting and bull riding, roping and tying, barrel racing, a kiddie parade, cowboy poetry, and a big western dance on Saturday night. The rowdiness here—cowboy-style, of course— rivals Mardi Gras. For information, contact the California Rodeo (1034 N. Main St., Salinas, 831/775-3100 or 800/771-8807 for the office or 800/549-4989 for advance ticket sales, www.carodeo.com). There's Western high art, too. See the massive triptych sculpture by Claes Oldenberg, titled *Hat in Three Stages of Landing,* on the lawn of the nearby Salinas Community Center (940 N. Main Street). The series of 3,500-pound yellow hats appears to have been tossed from the nearby rodeo grounds. Art-lovers, also note the **John Cerney agriculture-related art,** colossal cutout displays out standing in the fields surrounding Salinas.

The **Boronda Adobe** (333 Boronda Rd. at W. Laurel, 831/757-8085, open for tours 10 A.M.–2 P.M. Mon.–Fri., 1–4 P.M. Sun., donation requested), headquarters for the Monterey County Historical Society (www.mchsmuseum.com), is an outstanding example of a Mexican-era Monterey colonial adobe. Built between 1844 and 1848 by Jose Eusebio Boronda and virtually unaltered since, the tiny structure has been refurbished and now features museum displays and exhibits, including a few handsome original furnishings. Note the wood shingles, a considerable departure from traditional red-clay tiles. Also here is the one-room 1897 **Old Lagunita School House** that starred in the John Steinbeck story "The Red Pony," and a turn-of-the-20th-century home designed by architect William H. Weeks, currently being restored for use as a museum.

Toro Park (501 Monterey-Salinas Hwy./Hwy. 68, 831/755-4899 or 888/588-2267, 8 A.M.–dusk daily, day-use fee $4 weekdays, $6 weekends and holidays), a good picnic stop six miles out of town on the way to Monterey, is a pleasant, 4,756-acre regional park with good hiking, biking, and horseback trails. For an invigorating walk and views of both Monterey Bay and Salinas Valley, take the 2.5-mile trail to Eagle Peak.

THE NEW SALINAS

Forget all those cowpoke jokes. These days, Salinas is cowtown cool, continuing to find new ways to blend the old and the new. The arrival downtown of the National Steinbeck Center started something of a Salinas Valley cultural renaissance. Now, Old Town boasts some stylish coffee stops, restaurants—sometimes with a happy tip of the Stetson to Western heritage, as at Hullaballoo on Main and Smalley's (see below for details)—and shops, such as **Rooms in Bloom** (246 Main St., 831/753-7080); **This Or Die** (next door at 248 Main St., 831/751-6777); and **Lush** (345 Main St., 831/771-9002). In summer 2004, the 16-screen **Maya Cinemas** complex was under construction, thanks to movie producer Moctesuma Esparza, of *The Milagro Beanfield Wars* and *Selena* fame, creating yet another reason to come downtown. There are intriguing events, too, including **Vino, Vittles and Verse,** a Cowboy Poetry Wine Supper associated with A Taste of Monterey, staged in July in Old Town Salinas. In September comes **Taste of the Valley,** a food and wine festival serving as the centerpiece of the annual local

SALINAS AND VICINITY

Salute to Agriculture. Also part of the same general party is the **Farm Workers Challenge** at The Farm, an afternoon "inter-farm challenge" in which farm workers race to lay sprinkler pipes, back up an outhouse, and pack fresh lettuce. Afterward, there's complimentary corn on the cob all around.

STEINBECK'S LEGACY

The Grapes of Wrath didn't do much for John Steinbeck's local popularity. Started as a photojournalism project chronicling the "Okie" Dust Bowl migrations to California during the Depression, Steinbeck's *Grapes* instead became fiction. The entire book was a whirlwind, written between June and October 1938. After publication, it became a bestseller and remained one through 1940. Steinbeck was unhappy about the book's incredible commercial success; he believed there was something wrong with books that became so popular.

Vilified here as a left-winger and Salinas Valley traitor during his lifetime, Steinbeck never came back to Salinas. (The only way the town would ever take him back, he once said, was in a six-foot wooden box. And that's basically how it happened. His remains are at home at the local Garden of Memories Cemetery.) Most folks here have long ago forgiven their local literary light for his political views, so now you'll find his name and book titles at least mentioned, if not prominently displayed, all around town.

National Steinbeck Center

Some people have long been trying to make it up to Steinbeck. After all, he was the first American to win both the Pulitzer and Nobel Prizes for literature. Efforts to establish a permanent local Steinbeck Center finally succeeded, and in summer 1998, the doors of the $10.3 million National Steinbeck Center (1 Main St., 831/775-7240 or 831/796-3833, www.steinbeck.org, 10 A.M.–5 P.M. daily except Easter, Thanksgiving, Christmas, and New Year's Day, $10.95 adults, $8.95 seniors over age 62 and students with ID, $7.95 youths age 13–17, $5.95 children age 6–12, free for age 5 and under) opened

the National Steinbeck Center

to the public. Billed as a "multimedia experience of literature, history, and art," the Steinbeck Center provides at least one answer to the question of how to present literary accomplishment to an increasingly nonliterary culture. And that answer is—ta da!—high-tech interactivity. In addition to changing exhibits, seven themed permanent galleries—incorporating sights, sounds, and scents—introduce Steinbeck's life, work, and times in settings ranging from Doc Ricketts's lab on Cannery Row and the replica boxcar of "ice-packed" lettuce to the (climbable) red pony in the barn. Seven theaters show clips from films derived from Steinbeck's writings. But some appreciations are strictly literal, including John Steinbeck's trusty green truck and camper, Rocinante (named after Don Quixote's horse), in which the writer sojourned while researching *Travels with Charley.* The **Art of Writing Room,** with literary exhibits and all kinds of technical interactivity, explores the themes of Steinbeck's art and life. The 30,000-piece **Steinbeck Archives** here, open only to researchers by appointment, was originally housed in the local

John Steinbeck Library on Lincoln Avenue. The archival collection includes original letters, first editions, movie posters, and taped interviews with local people who remember Steinbeck. Some of the barbed remarks, made decades after the publication of *The Grapes of Wrath,* make it clear that local wrath runs at least as deep as the Salinas River. The relatively new, highly interactive **Valley of the World Gallery** showcases local agriculture, on its own terms more so than those Steinbeck represented. Nonetheless, it's a valuable contribution to public awareness, given California's increasing distance from its agricultural roots.

Other attractions include the sunny **One Main Street Café** and the **museum store,** which features a good selection of books in addition to gift items. To visit some of the actual places Steinbeck immortalized in his fiction, be sure to pick up the 24-page *Steinbeck Country: A Guide to Exploring John Steinbeck's Monterey County.* Also see if you can find a used copy of *The John Steinbeck Map of America,* now out of print.

Ⓜ Steinbeck House

Steinbeck described the family home—a jewel-box Victorian, located just two blocks from the National Steinbeck Center—as "an immaculate and friendly house, grand enough, but not pretentious." And so it still is, as both a dining and historic destination—a must-see for Steinbeck fans. The Salinas Valley Guild serves up gourmet lunches for Steinbeck fans and literary ghosts alike, featuring Salinas Valley produce and Monterey County wines and beer, at Steinbeck House (132 Central St., 831/424-2735, 11 A.M.–2:30 P.M. Mon.–Sat.), the author's birthplace and "a living museum." The menu changes weekly, served by volunteers dressed in period Victorian costumes. Reservations are suggested, but not required. The house is also open for guided tours (call for current information), and there's a "Best Cellar" book and gift shop in the basement (831/757-0508). All proceeds support the Steinbeck House and local charities.

Other Steinbeck Attractions

On the first weekend in August, come for the annual **Steinbeck Festival:** four days of films, lectures, tours, and social mixers. And in late February or early March, the town throws a Piscean **Steinbeck Birthday Party.** For information and tickets for these and other events, call 831/775-4721 or 831/796-3833. **The Western Stage** (156 Homestead Ave., 831/755-6816, www.western-stage.com) performs occasional Steinbeck works, other dramatic productions, and popular concerts on the Hartnell College campus.

Practicalities

CAMPING

Camp at the **Mazda Raceway at Laguna Seca** facility near Monterey (see under *Accommodations* in the *Monterey* chapter). **Fremont Peak State Park** (San Juan Canyon Road, 831/623-4255), southeast of San Juan Bautista, has some first-come, first-camped, primitive campsites that only make sense if you're heading that way, anyway.

In the Soledad and King City areas, **Arroyo Seco** features several U.S. Forest Service campgrounds; take Arroyo Seco Road west off Highway 101, just south of Soledad, or take Carmel Valley Road south to its end and turn right. Or camp at **Los Coches Wayside Camp,** just south of Soledad, or **Paraiso Hot Springs** (831/678-2882), nearby on Paraiso Springs Road. **San Lorenzo County Park** (831/385-5964 or 831/385-1484 for information and reservations), on the Salinas River near King City, boasts some 200 campsites with hot showers and picnic tables. The **Monterey County Agricultural & Rural Life Museum** (1160 Broadway in San Lorenzo Park, 831/385-8020) features Spreckels farmhouse, a barn with antique farm equipment, a cook wagon, a schoolhouse, and a historic railroad depot. Continuing south toward San Luis Obispo, both **Lake San Antonio** (north and south shore, 831/385-8399 for information) and

Lake Nacimiento have abundant campsites. All camping options are under $50.

MOTELS AND B&B

For budget travelers, Salinas has a nice array of inexpensive motels, including the usual Days Inn, Econo Lodge, Motel 6, and Super 8. Most other motels lining Highway 101 are a bit more upscale. Rooms at the **Comfort Inn** (144 Kern St., 831/758-8850 or 800/888-3839, $100–$150), just off the freeway, feature in-room coffeemakers; some have microwaves and refrigerators. Across the way, the fairly new, three-story **Best Western Hanns Inn** (175 Kern, 831/784-0176 or 888/829-0092 for central reservations, www.bestwesterncalifornia.com) has all the modern comforts and similar rates.

For something more rural, head for **Barlocker's Rustling Oaks Ranch Bed & Breakfast** (25252 Limekiln Rd. off River Rd., 831/675-9121, $100–250). There are five guestrooms. Extras include horseback rides and trails, swimming pool (in season), a pool table, and a genuine country breakfast.

FOOD

Get up to speed on the local politics of food production, then sample that famed Salinas Valley produce. Try the **Alisal Certified Farmers Market** (E. Alisal and Pearl, 831/757-1819, 9 A.M.–6 P.M. Thurs., until 8 P.M. in summer). If you're here on the weekend, head for the **Salinas Sunday Certified Farmers Market** at the Northridge Mall (796 Main St., 831/728-5060, 8 A.M.–noon Sun.). Another possible stop, any day, is **The Farm** (831/455-2575, www.thefarm-salinasvalley.com, 10 A.M.–6 P.M. Mon.–Sat.), on Highway 68 just west of Salinas, off the Spreckels exit—look for the giant, mural-like sculptures by John Cerney—featuring certified organic fruits and vegetables, specialty products, agricultural memorabilia, and the opportunity to get out in the fields and commune with the vegetables. Farm tours are available by reservation, and there's a little farm-animal zoo as well.

SUGAR TOWN AND A STAGE STOP

A satellite community southeast of Salinas, the town of **Spreckels** was developed by Claus Spreckels in the late 1890s to house employees of his sugar beet factory. This is a genuine "company town," down to the sugar beet architectural motifs in the roof gables of many historic homes.

Natividad is a onetime stage station about seven miles north of Salinas and the site of the 1846 **Battle of Natividad,** where Californios attacked Yankee invaders herding 300 horses to Frémont's troops in Monterey.

A wonderful coffee stop just a couple blocks from the Steinbeck Center is the **Cherry Bean Gourmet Coffee House & Roastery** (332 Main St., 831/424-1989). And if you're just passin' through in a hurry, Salinas has an **In-N-Out Burger** (151 Kern Street). For breakfast downtown, try the specialists at **First Awakenings** (171 Main St., 831/784-1125, 7 A.M.–2:30 P.M. daily), where the pancakes are reputedly the best in the county. Cheap and good is the locally popular **Rosita's Armory Cafe** (231 Salinas St., 831/424-7039). Best bet for burgers and a long-running Salinas tradition is the unassuming **Toro Place Café** (665 Monterey-Salinas Hwy., 831/484-1333). Weather permitting, take your burger out to the patio. And yes, that's a real bull's head on the wall.

The new Salinas hotspot, at last report, was unpretentious all-American ⚑ **Hullaballoo** (228 S. Main St., 831/757-3663), where you can covet the cheeseburgers and country-fried chicken, savor the backyard salmon, or go bonkers over the blackened prime rib. ⚑ **Smalley's Roundup** (700 W. Market, 831/758-0511, lunch Tues.–Fri., dinner Tues.–Sun., dinner reservations advised) is an icon, locally famous for its oakwood barbecue and other cowboy-style fine dining. Always the best bet for a literary lunch, especially for Steinbeck fans, is the historic ⚑ **Steinbeck House** (132 Center St., 831/424-2735, 11 A.M.–2:30 P.M. Mon.–Sat.), just two blocks from the National

Steinbeck Center; see the listing above for more information. The **Salinas Valley Fish House** (172 Main St., 831/775-0175) offers various "fresh catches," plus an oyster bar.

INFORMATION

The **Salinas Valley Chamber of Commerce** (119 E. Alisal St., 831/424-7611, www.salinaschamber.com) offers information on accommodations and sights, as well as a great little brochure: *Steinbeck Country Starts in Salinas.* The Salinas chamber is also an official Monterey County Convention & Visitor Bureau outpost—and headquarters for the **Old Town Salinas Association** (831/758-0725, www.oldtownsalinas.com, 8:30 A.M.–5 P.M. Mon.–Fri., 9 A.M.–3 P.M. Sat., closed Sun.)—so stop here for any downtown event and business information or general Monterey County visitor information. There's another in King City, the **King City Visitors Center** (1160 Broadway in San Lorenzo Park, 831/385-1484, 10 A.M.–4 P.M. daily).

Salinas has an **Amtrak** station (11 Station Place, 831/422-7458 or 800/872-7245, www.amtrak.com); call or visit the website for fare and schedule information. There's no train station in Monterey, but you can connect from here to there via **Monterey-Salinas Transit** (1 Ryan Ranch Rd., Monterey, 831/424-7695 or 831/899-2555, www.mst.org) bus 20 or 21, or via the Amtrak Thruway bus as part of your train fare. **Greyhound** (19 W. Gabilan St., 831/424-4418 or 800/231-2222, www.greyhound.com) is also here, and the **Salinas Municipal Airport** (831/758-7214) is on Airport Boulevard.

Vicinity of Salinas

SOLEDAD

Soledad, a sleepy town where no one hurries, is the oldest settlement in the Salinas Valley. Stop by the local bakery *(panaderia)* on Front Street for fresh Mexican pastries and hot tortillas. **Misión Nuestra Señora de la Soledad** (831/678-2586, 10 A.M.–4 P.M. daily) was founded here in 1791 to minister to the Salinas Valley natives. Our Lady of Solitude Mission, three miles southwest of town, was quite prosperous until 1825. But this, the 13th in California's mission chain, was beset by problems, ranging from raging Salinas River floods to disease epidemics, before it crumbled into ruin. The chapel was reconstructed and rededicated, and another wing has since been restored. The original 1799 mission bell still hangs in the courtyard of this active parish church. Outside is a lovely garden. The mission also offers a museum and gift shop. Just three miles south of Soledad (west at the Arroyo Seco interchange from Highway 101) is another historic survivor, the 1843 **Richardson Adobe**, at Los Coches Rancho Wayside Campground. For more information about the area, contact the **Soledad Mission Chamber of Commerce** (635 Front St., 831/678-2278).

PARAISO HOT SPRINGS

Nestled in a grove of lovely palm trees, with a sweeping valley view, this 240-acre old resort is a few miles southwest of Soledad. Paraiso Hot Springs (34358 Paraiso Springs Rd., 831/678-2882, day-use fee $25) has an indoor hot mineral bath (suits required), outdoor pools, picnic tables and barbecues, campgrounds, and Victorian cabins—all rarely crowded. Weekly and monthly rates are available, but most people fancy day use, which is a bit pricey.

⋈ PINNACLES NATIONAL MONUMENT

Exploring these barren 24,000 acres of volcanic spires and ravines is a little like rock climbing on the moon. The weird, dark red rocks are bizarrely eroded, unlike anywhere else in North America, forming gaping gorges, crumbling caverns, and terrifying terraces. Rock climbers' heaven (not for beginners), this stunning old volcano offers excellent trails, too, with pebbles the size of houses to stumble over. Visitors afraid of earthquakes should know that the Pinnacles sit

MELISSA SHEROWSKI

entrance to Pinnacles National Monument

atop an active section of the San Andreas Fault. Spring is the best time to visit, when wildflowers brighten up the chaparral, but sunlight on the rocks creates rainbows of color year-round. Rock climbing is the major attraction, for obvious reasons. Climbers come during the cool weather. But you can also hike, and watch the raptors in winter: golden eagles, red-shouldered hawks, kestrels, and prairie falcons.

Though it was Teddy Roosevelt who first utilized presidential decree on behalf on the Pinnacles—protecting it as a national monument in 1906—in early 2000, then-President Bill Clinton announced plans to expand the park by some 5,000 acres. Some of that acreage, when acquired, may encourage gentler, more family-oriented recreation.

Hiking

Of Pinnacles' existing (pre-expansion) 24,000-plus acres, nearly 16,000 are protected as wilderness. Only hiking trails connect the park's east and west sides. Some trails are fairly easy, while others are rugged. Pinnacles has four self-guided nature trails; the **Geology Hike** and **Balconies Trail** are quite fascinating. The short **Moses Spring Trail** is one of the best. Longest is the

trek up the **Chalone Peak Trail,** 11 miles round-trip, passing fantastic rock formations (quite a view of Salinas once you get to the top of North Chalone Peak). Less ambitious is the **Condor Gulch Trail,** an easy two-mile hike into Balconies Caves from the Chalone Creek picnic area. Various interconnecting trails encourage creativity on foot. The best caves, as well as the most fascinating rock formations and visitors center displays, are on the park's east side. The fit, fast, and willing can hike east to west and back in one (long) day. The easiest return trip is via the Old Pinnacles Trail, rather than the steep Juniper Canyon Trail. Pack plenty of water.

Practicalities

As lasting testament to the land's rugged nature, there are two districts in the Pinnacles National Monument (5000 Hwy. 146, Paicines, 831/389-4485, www.nps.gov/pinn)—west and east—and it's not possible to get from one to the other by road. Within the monument, bicycles and cars may only be used on paved roads. If coming from the west, get visitor information at the **Chaparral Ranger Station,** reached via Highway 146 heading east (exit Hwy. 101 just south of Soledad). For most visitors, Pinnacles is most

Salinas and Vicinity

accessible from this route, but it's a narrow road, not recommended for campers and trailers. If coming from the east, stop by the **Bear Gulch Visitor Center,** reached via Highway 25, then Highway 146 heading west. From Hollister, it's about 34 miles south, then about five miles west to the park entrance. Pinnacles is open for day use only; the vehicle entry fee is $5, the walk-in fee is $2; valid for seven days. An annual pass costs $15. Within the monument, bicycles and cars may only be used on paved roads.

Good rules of thumb in the Pinnacles: Carry water at all times, and watch out for poison oak, stinging nettles, and rattlesnakes. Spelunkers should bring good flashlights and helmets. Pick up guides to the area's plant life and natural history, and also topo maps, at the visitors centers. Rock climbers can thumb through old guides there for climbing routes.

No camping is offered (or allowed) within the park. The closest private camping is **Pinnacles Campground, Inc.** (2400 Hwy. 146, 831/389-4462, www.pinncamp.com, under $50), near the park's entrance on the east side. The campground is quite nice, featuring flush toilets, hot showers, fire rings, picnic tables, a swimming pool, some RV hookups, and group facilities. Basic supplies and some food are available at the campground's store. But you can also stay in considerable style, thanks to the **Inn at the Pinnacles** (831/678-2400, www.innatthepinnacles.com, $200–250), just a few miles west of the park's west entrance.

ⓜ SAN JUAN BAUTISTA AND VICINITY

The tiny town of San Juan Bautista is charming and charmed, as friendly as it is sunny. (People here say the weather in this pastoral valley is "salubrious." Take their word for it.) Named for John the Baptist, the 1797 Spanish mission of San Juan Bautista is central to this serene community at the foot of the Gabilan Mountains. But the historic plaza, still bordered by old adobes and now a state historic park, is the true center of San Juan—rallying point for two revolutions, onetime home of famed bandit Tiburcio Vasquez,

and the theatrical setting for David Belasco's *Rose of the Rancho.* Movie fans may remember Jimmy Stewart and Kim Novak in the mission scenes from Alfred Hitchcock's *Vertigo,* which were filmed here.

One of the most colorful characters ever to stumble off the stage in San Juan Bautista was one-eyed stagecoach driver Charley Parkhurst, a truculent, swaggering, tobacco-chewing tough. "He," however, was a woman, born Charlotte Parkhurst in New Hampshire. (Charley voted in Santa Cruz in 1866, more than 50 years before American women won the right to vote.)

In addition to history, San Juan Bautista has galleries, antique and craft shops, and an incredible local theater troupe. To get oriented, pick up a walking tour brochure around town or at the **San Juan Bautista Chamber of Commerce** (1 Polk St., 831/623-2454, www.sanjuanbautista.com, open Mon.–Fri.). In June, experience mid-1800s mission days at **Early Days in San Juan Bautista,** a traditional celebration complete with horse-drawn carriages, period dress, music, and fandango. The barroom at the Plaza Hotel is even open for card games. Also fun in June is the **Peddler's Faire and Street Rod Classic Car Show,** one of the biggest street fairs anywhere and the chamber's annual fundraiser. The **Flea Market** held here in August, with more than 200 vendors, is one of the country's best. Later that month, **San Juan Fiesta Day** is the most popular venue of the wandering **Cabrillo Music Festival.** But the event of the year is *La Virgen del Tepeyac,* or *La Pastorela* (they alternate yearly), traditional Christmas musicals that attract visitors from around the world—if they're still on. For more details and current information, contact El Teatro Campesino (831/623-2444, www.elteatrocampesino.com). Christmas chorale music is also offered at the mission.

History

Partly destroyed by earthquakes in 1800 and 1906 (the San Andreas Fault is just 40 feet away), **Mission San Juan Bautista** has been restored many times. The 15th and largest of the Franciscan settlements in California, the mission here is not as architecturally spectacular as others in the

Catholic chain. Visitors can tour sections of the mission—which still features an active parish church—though it's not really part of the adjacent state historic park. After visiting the small museum and gardens, note the old dirt road beyond the wall of the mission cemetery. This is an unspoiled, unchanged section of the 650-mile El Camino Real, the "royal road" that once connected all the California missions. Archaeological excavations at the mission by CSU Monterey, Hartnell College, and Cabrillo College students unearthed the foundations of the mission's original quadrangle, tower, well, and convent wing (which many historians previously believed had never existed). Students also cleared the 1799 Indian Chapel of debris and restored it; inside is an ornate altar built in the 1560s and moved to the chapel for the Pope's visit in 1987. Many of the students' other discoveries are on display in the mission's museum.

San Juan Bautista's oldest building is the **Plaza Hotel,** at Second and Mariposa Streets on the west side of the plaza, originally barracks built in 1813 for Spanish soldiers. In horse and buggy days, San Juan Bautista was a major stage stop between San Francisco and Los Angeles, and the hotel was famous statewide. (Note the two-story outhouse out back.) Also fascinating are the stable—with its herd of fine old horse-drawn vehicles and the "Instructions for Stagecoach Passengers" plaque out front—and the restored blacksmith shop. Also worth a peek: the jail, washhouse, and cabin. For information, contact San Juan Bautista State Historic Park (19 Franklin St., 831/623-4881, 10 A.M.–4:30 P.M. daily, in summer until 5 P.M., day-use fee $2).

Above the town of San Juan Bautista is **Pagan Hill.** Today, a giant concrete cross stands where mission fathers once put up a wooden one, intended to ward off evil spirits supposedly summoned by Indian neophytes secretly practicing their traditional earth religion.

El Teatro Campesino

Don't pass through San Juan Bautista without trying to attend a performance by San Juan Bautista's El Teatro Campesino (permanent playhouse at 705 Fourth St., 831/623-2444, www.elteatro-campesino.com). Chicano playwright Luis Valdez founded this small group as guerrilla theater on the United Farm Workers' picket lines more than two decades ago. But Valdez's smash hits *Zoot Suit* and *Corridos* have since brought highly acclaimed nationwide tours and the birth of other Chicano *teatros* throughout the American Southwest. El Teatro's Christmas-season *La Pastorella,* the shepherd's story that alternates with the miracle play *La Virgen del Tepeyac,* is a hilarious and deeply poetic spectacle, a musical folk pageant about shepherds trying to get past comic yet terrifying devils to reach the Christ child. Besides Spanish-language plays, concerts, and film festivals, the company also presents contemporary and traditional theater in English.

Practicalities

A few tent sites and 165 RV hookups are available at the private **Mission Farm Campground and RV Park** (400 San Juan–Hollister Rd., 831/623-4456), located in a walnut orchard. Or, for fishing and tent/RV camping, try private (stocked) **McAlpine Lake** (900 Anzar Rd., 831/623-4263, www.mcalpinelake.com). Both options are under $50. There are also a few cabins. Accommodations with the right ambience are available at the mission-style **Posada de San Juan Hotel** (310 Fourth St., 831/623-4030, $100–150), with a fireplace and whirlpool tubs in almost every room.

For farm-fresh produce, pick up a copy of the free guide to nearby family farms and ranches. Fresh cherries are available in June; apricots in July; and apples, walnuts, and kiwis in the fall. For good bread—at least 35 kinds—plus pastries and picnic fixings, stop by **San Juan Bakery & Grocery** (319 Third St., 831/623-4570).

The **Mission Cafe** (300 Third St., 831/623-2635) is good for families at breakfast and lunch. Try **Felipe's** (313 Third St., 831/623-2161) for Mexican and Salvadoran food. **Doña Esther** (25 Franklin, 831/623-2518) serves Mexican fare—and the best margaritas in town. More upscale is **Jardines de San Juan** (115 Third St., 831/623-4466, open daily), where you can get *pollos borachos* (drunken chickens) at lunch and dinner. Nice garden setting. For Italian, try either **Don Ciccio's** (107 The Alameda, 831/623-4667) or the **Inn at Tres Pinos,** south of Hollister (6991 Hwy. 25, Tres Pinos, 831/628-3320).

For steaks with plenty of giddy-up, locals single out very Western **The Cutting Horse** (307 Third St., 831/623-4549, dinner only). People say this is the best steakhouse around. Despite the ominously accurate name, well worth a stop for continental-style lunch and dinner (and the view of the San Juan Valley) is the nearby **Fault Line Restaurant** (11 Franklin, 831/623-2117).

FREMONT PEAK STATE PARK

In March 1846, Gen. John C. Frémont and Kit Carson built a "fort" here in defiance of the Mexican government, unfurled their flags on Gabilan Peak (now Fremont Peak), and waited for the supposedly imminent attack of Californio troops. When no battle came, they broke camp and took off for Oregon. Fremont Peak State Park (831/623-4255 or 831/623-2465 for recorded info, www.fpoa.net or www.parks.ca.gov, day-use fee $4), a long, narrow, isolated strip in the Gabilan Mountains northeast of Salinas, has rolling hills with oaks, madrones, Coulter pines, and spring wildflowers that attract hundreds of hummingbirds. The park offers good hiking in spring and good views from the top of Fremont Peak. Another attraction at Fremont Peak is an observatory with a 30-inch Challenger reflecting telescope, open to the public at least twice monthly for free programs including lectures and observation.

Camping is available in about 25 primitive campsites (some in the picnic area) and a group camp. To get to the park from Highway 156, head 11 miles south on San Juan Canyon Road (County Road G1)—paved, but very steep and winding (trailers definitely not recommended). For reservations, contact **ReserveAmerica** (800/444-7275, www.reserve america.com, $11–15).

HOLLISTER

If Gilroy is the garlic capital of the world, then Hollister is the earthquake capital. Because of the region's heavy faulting, some say this San Benito

County town moves every day, however imperceptibly. (A small 1985 quake shook loose a 20,000-gallon oak wine cask and flooded the Almaden Winery just south of town.) Agricultural Hollister is as historic as San Juan Bautista, but the "feel" here is straight out of the Old West. Stop by the **San Benito County Historical Society Museum** (498 Fifth St. at West, 831/635-0335, 1–3 P.M. Sat.–Sun. or by appointment), then wander through Old Town (particularly along Fifth) to appreciate Hollister's old Victorians.

Traditional cowboy events and some unique competitions are the name of the game during June's **San Benito County Rodeo,** an event dedicated to the vaquero. The **Fiesta-Rodeo** in July dates back to 1907, when it was first held to raise funds for rebuilding Mission San Juan Bautista after the big quake in 1906. The most memorable event here is the big **Hollister Independence Rally,** a motorcyclists' gathering on the **Fourth of July** weekend made famous by Marlon Brando in the movie *The Wild Ones.*

GILROY

Will Rogers supposedly described Gilroy as "the only town in America where you can marinate a steak just by hanging it out on the clothesline." But Gilroy, the "undisputed garlic capital of the world," dedicates very few acres to growing the stinking rose these days. The legendary local garlic farms have been declining due to soil disease since 1979—ironically, the first year of the now famous and phenomenally successful Gilroy Garlic Festival. Gilroy now grows housing subdivisions—former *San Francisco Chronicle* columnist Herb Caen defined modern Gilroy as the place "where the carpet ends and the linoleum begins"—and the San Joaquin Valley grows most of California's garlic. Nonetheless, that unmistakable oily aroma still permeates the air in summer, since more than 90 percent of the world's garlic is processed or packaged here.

Other attractions in Gilroy include Goldsmith Seeds' seasonal six-acre **Field of Dreams** experimental flower seed garden (408/847-7333 for tour information). Downtown Gilroy has its historic attractions, too. The best place to start ex-

It's chic to reek in Gilroy.

ploring is the **Gilroy Historical Museum** (Fifth and Church, 408/848-0470, 9 A.M.–5 P.M. Mon.–Fri.).

For more information about what's cookin' in and around Gilroy, contact the **Gilroy Visitor Bureau** (7780 Monterey St., 408/842-6436, www.gilroyvisitor.org) and the **Gilroy Chamber of Commerce** (7471 Monterey, 408/842-6437, www.gilroy.org).

Gilroy Garlic Festival

It's chic to reek in Gilroy. On the last full weekend in July, 150,000 or more garlic-lovers descend on the town for several dusty days of sampling garlic perfume, garlic chocolate, and all-you-can-eat garlic ice cream (for some reason, just a few gallons of the stuff takes care of the entire crowd). Who wouldn't pay the $10 admission for belly dancing, big bands, and the crowning of the Garlic Queen? For more information, contact the **Gilroy Garlic Festival Association** (7473 Monterey, 408/842-1625, www.gilroygarlicfestival.com). If you're looking for garlic gifts and accessories at other times, Gilroy boasts a number of garlic-themed shops; get a current listing from the city's website (www.gilroy.org).

Wine-Tasting

Besides sniffing out local Italian scallions, tour the Gilroy "wine country." Most of the area's wineries are tucked into the Santa Cruz Mountain foothills west of the city, seven of these along Highway 152's Hecker Pass—just beyond Goldsmith Seeds and the Bonfante Gardens theme park (see below). At the mountain's summit is 3,688-acre **Mt. Madonna County Park** (7850 Pole Line Rd., 408/842-2341, day-use fee $5, campsite reservations available), where 20 miles of hiking trails wind through redwoods and oak woodlands. Stop for a picnic, or a bite at the venerable **Mt. Madonna Inn Restaurant** (831/724-2275). The hearty, full-flavored red wines produced here are still made by hand. **Solis Winery** (3920 Hecker Pass Rd., 408/847-6306 or 888/411-6457, www.soliswinery.com, 11 A.M.–5 P.M. daily except major holidays, tours by appointment) offers tastings of its chardonnay, sangiovese, merlot, cabernet sauvignon, and syrah. Come by **Sarah's Vineyard** (4005 Hecker Pass Rd., 408/842-4278, http://sarahs-vineyard.com, noon–5 P.M. Fri., 11 A.M.–5 P.M. Sat.–Sun.) to taste its estate-grown chardonnays and pinot noirs. The **Fortino Winery** (4525 Hecker Pass Rd., 408/842-3305,

Salinas and Vicinity

www.fortinowinery.com) is run by the Fortino family and specializes in hearty, old-country red wines. Other Gilroy area wineries include the **Thomas Kruse Winery** (3200 Dryden Ave., 408/842-7016), with its eclectic collection of antique equipment, presided over by philosopher-winemaker Thomas Kruse. His Gilroy Red and other wines sport handwritten, offbeat labels.

Ⓜ Bonfante Gardens

The region's most amazing and newest visitor attraction, Gilroy's glorious, $100 million Bonfante Gardens Theme Park, is an inspired horticultural feat. That's right—*horticultural.* Trees and shrubs, in particular. Some 23 years were spent planning and developing the 75-acre park's unique landscape before Bonfante Gardens finally opened its gates in June 2001. Botanical oddities abound, from the five themed gardens to the 25 wonderful "circus trees" created by the late Axel Erlandson—wonders created by grafting and pleaching, feats that have never been successfully duplicated. Kids are equally impressed by the Monarch Garden's immense greenhouse, with a monorail, train, and river running through it.

Though the pace here is relaxed and the thrills understated, traditional theme-park activities haven't been neglected. Bonfante Gardens includes 40 family-friendly rides and attractions, from the cheerful 1927 Illions Supreme Carousel and the Quicksilver Express roller coaster to the very cool antique car ride. The latter allows you to "tour" either the 1920s or 1950s—dig those old gas stations—depending on where you climb on. Still, encouraging people to appreciate trees is the main point of Bonfante Gardens. All attractions are literally woven into the landscape. New in 2004: the **Wild Bird Adventure,** a 1,500-square-foot aviary where kids can feed and interact with the birds.

At last report, park admission was $31.99 adults, $22.99 seniors and children age 3–6 (age 2 and under free); parking is $7 per vehicle. Advance ticket prices on the website can go as low as $19.99 for adults, however, and at various times there may be other specials (such as "Bring a Friend for Free"). The park is open daily in summer, on weekends only during much of the rest of year. For current hours and days of operation, admission prices, special events, and other details, contact Bonfante Gardens (3050 Hecker Pass Hwy., west of Gilroy on Hwy. 152, 408/840-7100, www.bonfantegardens.com).

Casa de Fruta and Coyote Reservoir

"Unforgettable" is one word for Casa de Fruta (Pacheco Pass Hwy., 831/637-0051, www.casadefruta.com). The sprawl of neon-lit, truck stop–type buildings is complete with a trailer park and swimming pool, motel, petting zoo, merry-go-round, and miniature train and tunnel. Stop off at the Casa de Fruta Coffee Shop (open 24 hours) and read about the Casa de Fruta Country Store, Casa de Fruta Gift Shop, Casa de Fruta Fruit Stand, Casa de Burger, Casa de Sweets Bakery and Candy Factory, Casa de Choo-Choo, and Casa de Merry-Go-Round on the "mail me" souvenir paper placemats. (This being California, there's a Casa de Wine, too.) To see the coffee cups "flip," ask the coffee shop staff for a show.

Coyote Reservoir (8 A.M.–sunset year-round, day-use fee $5, camping $9–18, reserve one of 75 sites at www.gooutsideandplay.org), eight miles north of Gilroy, is great for sailboarding, sailing, and fishing. For information, contact **Coyote Lake County Park** (10840 Coyote Lake Rd., Gilroy, 408/842-7800, www.parkhere.org). To get to Coyote Lake, take the Leavesley Road/Highway 152 exit east from Highway 101; after two to three miles, head north on New Avenue, then east on Roop Road to Gilroy Hot Springs Road. The Coyote Reservoir Road turnoff is about a mile farther, the campground two miles more.

Santa Cruz

Still in tune with its gracefully aging boardwalk, Santa Cruz is a middle-class tourist town enlightened and enlivened by retirees and the local University of California campus. It's possible to live here without a lot of money, though that's getting harder, with the advent of Silicon Valley commuters. Still, Santa Cruz is quite a different world from the affluent and staid Monterey Peninsula.

The Santa Cruz attitude has little to do with its name, taken from a nearby stream called Arroyo de Santa Cruz ("Holy Cross Creek") by Portolá. No, the town's relaxed good cheer must be karmic compensation for the morose mission days and the brutishness of nearby Branciforte. The Gay Nineties—the 1890s, that is—were happier here than anywhere else in Northern California, with trainloads of Bay Area vacationers in their finest summer whites stepping out to enjoy the Santa Cruz waterfront, the Sea Beach Hotel, and the landmark boardwalk and amusement park. The young and young-at-heart headed straight for the Victorian amusement park, with its fine merry-go-round, classic wooden roller coaster, pleasure pier, natatorium (indoor pool), and dancehall casino. More decadent fun-lovers visited the ships anchored offshore to gamble or engage the services of prostitutes.

Santa Cruz still welcomes millions of visitors each year, yet it somehow manages to retain its dignity—except when embroiled in hot local political debates, or when inundated by college students during the annual rites of spring. A tourist town it may be, but some of the best things to do here are free: watching the sun set from East or West Cliff Drive, beachcombing, bike riding (excellent local bike lanes), swimming, surfing, and sunbathing.

Old-timers weren't ready for the changes in community consciousness that arrived in Santa Cruz along with the idyllic UC Santa Cruz campus in the 1960s. More outsiders came when back-to-the-landers fled San

Must-Sees

Look for **M** to find the sights and activities you can't miss and **M** for the best dining and lodging.

MELISSA SHEROWSKI

Santa Cruz Museum of Art and History

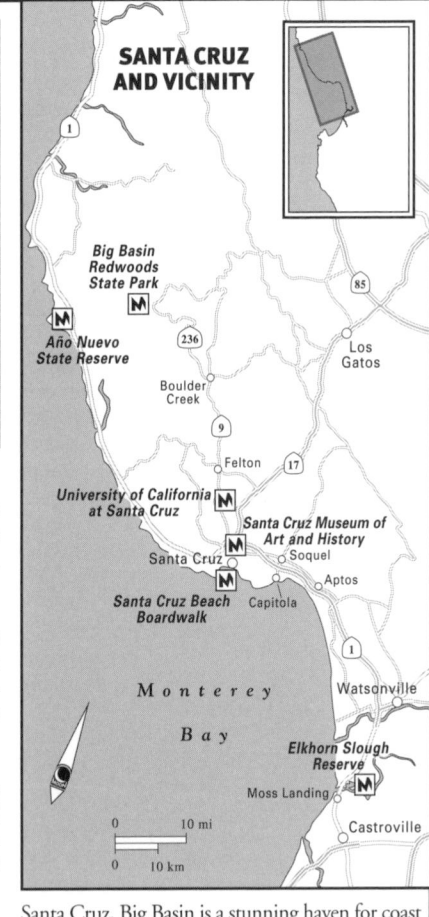

SANTA CRUZ AND VICINITY

Big Basin Redwoods State Park

Año Nuevo State Reserve

Boulder Creek

Los Gatos

Felton

University of California at Santa Cruz

Santa Cruz Museum of Art and History

Santa Cruz

Soquel

Aptos

Santa Cruz Beach Boardwalk

Capitola

Monterey

Bay

Watsonville

Elkhorn Slough Reserve

Moss Landing

Castroville

0   10 mi
0   10 km

M **Santa Cruz Beach Boardwalk:** This is the West Coast's answer to Atlantic City, an authentic amusement park complete with a classic wooden roller coaster (page 123).

M **Santa Cruz Museum of Art and History:** Leave it to Santa Cruz to come up with the most creative combinations—including the art of exhibiting history and the history of regional art (page 125).

M **University of California at Santa Cruz:** This redwood-cloistered city on the hill just beyond town, designed by noted architects, offers stunning views of Monterey Bay among its many other attractions (page 129).

M **Año Nuevo State Reserve:** This reserve is breeding ground and rookery for the unusual northern elephant seal. The guided winter tours require advance reservations (page 150).

M **Big Basin Redwoods State Park:** California's first state park, about 24 miles up canyon from

Santa Cruz, Big Basin is a stunning haven for coast redwoods and hikers alike (page 152).

M **Elkhorn Slough Reserve:** Among California's largest remaining coastal estuaries, Elkhorn Slough was once the mouth of the Salinas River. Now it's a protected estuarine wildlife sanctuary, prime for birding, kayaking, and nature walks (page 156).

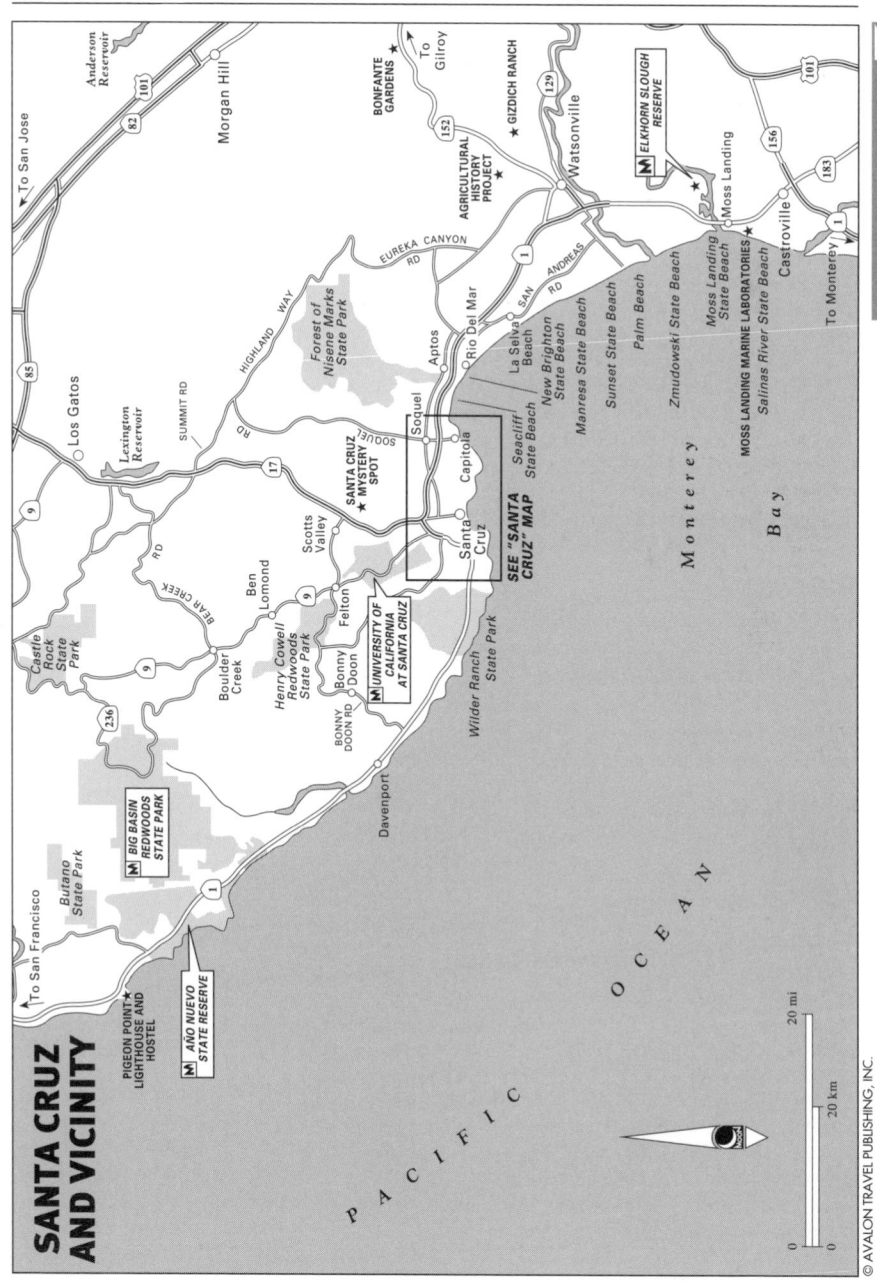

SANTA CRUZ
AND VICINITY

To San Francisco

To San Jose

Anderson Reservoir

101

82

Morgan Hill

85

Los Gatos

Lexington Reservoir

9

Castle Rock State Park

236

Butano State Park

Boulder Creek

Ben Lomond

9

BEAR CREEK RD

SUMMIT RD

17

HIGHLAND WAY

Forest of Nisene Marks State Park

EUREKA CANYON RD

BONFANTE GARDENS ★

To Gilroy

152

AGRICULTURAL HISTORY PROJECT ★

GIZDICH RANCH ★

129

Watsonville

M ELKHORN SLOUGH RESERVE

101

156

183

Moss Landing

Castroville

1

To Monterey

Aptos

Rio Del Mar

1

SAN ANDREAS RD

La Selva Beach

New Brighton State Beach

Manresa State Beach

Sunset State Beach

Palm Beach

Zmudowski State Beach

Moss Landing State Beach

MOSS LANDING MARINE LABORATORIES ★

Salinas River State Beach

SOQUEL DR

Soquel

Capitola

Santa Cruz

Seacliff State Beach

SEE "SANTA CRUZ" MAP

Scotts Valley

SANTA CRUZ MYSTERY SPOT ★

Felton

Henry Cowell Redwoods State Park

BONNY DOON RD

Bonny Doon

M UNIVERSITY OF CALIFORNIA AT SANTA CRUZ

Wilder Ranch State Park

M BIG BASIN REDWOODS STATE PARK

Davenport

1

PIGEON POINT ★ LIGHTHOUSE AND HOSTEL

M AÑO NUEVO STATE RESERVE

Monterey

Bay

PACIFIC   OCEAN

20 mi

0

20 km

0

© AVALON TRAVEL PUBLISHING, INC.

Francisco's Haight-Ashbury for the hills near here, and when Silicon Valley electronics wizards started moving in. The city's boardwalk-and-beach hedonism may be legendary, but so are the Santa Cruz City Council's foreign policy decisions opposing contra aid, proclaiming the city a "free port" for Nicaragua, and calling for divestiture of South African investments. In October 2000, Santa Cruz passed its own "living wage" law, mandating a minimum pay rate of $11 per hour ($12 without benefits) for city workers and companies that contract with the city.

Though there's always some argument, the city's progressive politics are now firmly entrenched, as are other "dancing-on-the-brink" attitudes. The "People's Republic of Santa Cruz" is also a way station for the spiritually weary, with its own unique evangelical crusade for higher consciousness. Dreams and dreamers run the show.

HISTORY

The charming Santa Cruz blend of innocence and sleaze has roots in local history. The area's earliest residents were the Ohlone people, who avoided the sacred redwood forests and subsisted on seafood, small game, acorns, and foods gathered in woodland areas. Then came the mission and missionaries, a Spanish military garrison, and the den-of-thieves culture of Branciforte; the latter community posed an active threat to the holy fathers' attempted good works among the heathens. Misión Exaltación de la Santa Cruz declined, was abandoned, then collapsed following an earthquake in 1857.

A small trading town, borrowing the mission's name, grew up around the old mission plaza in the 1840s. The town supplied whalers with fruits and vegetables. Nearby Branciforte became a smugglers' haven, hosting bullfight festivals and illicit activities until 1867. The "education" and excitement imported by foreigners proved to be too much for the Ohlone; the only traces of their culture today are burial grounds. Branciforte disappeared, too, absorbed as a suburb when loggers and "bark-strippers" (those who extracted tannin from tan oaks for processing leather) arrived to harvest the forests during the gold rush.

By the late 1800s, Santa Cruz was well established as a resort town. Logging continued, however. In the early 20th century, the local lumber industry was ready to log even majestic Big Basin. But those plans were thwarted by the active intervention of the Sempervirens Club, which successfully established California's first state park.

GREATER SANTA CRUZ

Just east of Santa Cruz, along the south-facing coast, are the towns of Soquel, Capitola, and Aptos—the Santa Cruz burbs. High-rent **Soquel,** once a booming lumber town and the place where Portolá and his men were all but stricken by their first sight of coastal redwoods, is now noted for antiques and oaks.

The wharf in **Capitola** has stood since 1857, when the area was known as Soquel Landing. The name "Camp Capitola" was an expression of Soquel locals' desire to be the state capital—the closest they ever came. The city was, however, the state's first seaside resort. Nowadays, Capitola is big on art galleries and fine craft shops—take a stroll along Capitola Avenue, from the trestle to the creek—but it's still most famous for its begonias. The year's big event is the **Begonia Festival,** usually held early in September. Stop by **Antonelli Bros. Begonia Gardens** (2545 Capitola Rd., 831/475-5222) to see a 10,000-square-foot greenhouse display of begonias, best in August and September.

Aptos, on the other side of the freeway, is more or less the same community as Capitola, but home to Cabrillo College and the **World's Shortest Parade,** usually held on July 4th weekend and sponsored by the Aptos Ladies' Tuesday Evening Society.

Heading north on Highway 9 from Santa Cruz, you'll pass through the Santa Cruz Mountains and the towns of Felton, Ben Lomond, and Boulder Creek before winding down the other side of the mountains into Saratoga, on the flank of Silicon Valley. This route is the gateway to several beautiful redwood state parks, including Henry Cowell, Fall Creek, Big Basin, and Castle Rock.

Sights

ⓜ SANTA CRUZ BEACH BOARDWALK

The Santa Cruz Beach Boardwalk (831/423-5590 for activities info and 831/426-7433 for current hours, generally open daily Memorial Day–Labor Day, weekends only the rest of the year) may be old, but it's certainly lively, with a million visitors per year. This is the West Coast's answer to Atlantic City. The original wood planking is now paved over with asphalt, stretching from 400 Beach Street for a half mile along one of Northern California's finest swimming beaches. A relatively recent multimillion-dollar facelift didn't diminish the boardwalk's charms one iota. The boardwalk is an authentic amusement park, with dozens of carnival rides, odd shops and eateries, good-time arcades, and even a big-band ballroom. Ride the **Sky Glider** to get a good aerial view of the boardwalk and beach scene—and, across the street, check out the **Boardwalk Bowl** (115 Cliff St. at Beach, 831/426-3324) bowling alley.

None other than the *New York Times* has declared the 1924 **Giant Dipper** roller coaster here one of the nation's 10 best. A gleaming white wooden rocker 'n' roller, the Dipper is quite a sight anytime, but it's truly impressive when lit up at night. The 1911 **Charles Looff carousel**, one of a handful of Looff creations still operating in the United States, has 70 handcrafted horses, two chariots, and a circa-1894 Ruth Band pipe organ—all lovingly restored to their original glory. (Both the Dipper and the carousel are National Historic Landmarks.)

Newer rides feature more terror, of course. The **Cliff Hanger** offers spins and hang gliding–like thrills, and the pendulum-like **Fireball** serves up fiery upside-down spins. The bright lights and unusual views offered by the Italian-made **Typhoon** are just part of the joys of being suspended upside down in midair. The **Hurricane** is the boardwalk's modern high-tech roller coaster, providing a two-minute thrill ride with a maximum gravitational force of 4.7 Gs and a

banking angle of 80 degrees. Also state of the art in adrenaline inducement at the boardwalk is the **Wave Jammer**—not to mention **Chaos, Crazy Surf, Tsunami,** and **Whirl Wind.** For a scary changeup, try the new **Fright Walk** dungeon (separate admission).

The antique devices in the penny arcades at the boardwalk's west end cost a bit more these days, but it's worth it to Measure the Thrill of Your Kisses or Find Your Ideal Mate. Playing miniature golf at the **Neptune's Kingdom** amusement center—housed in the boardwalk's original "plunge" building, or natatorium—is a nautical-themed adventure in special effects, with an erupting volcano, firing cannons, and talking pirates. It's the perfect diversion for the video-game generation and their awestruck parents. Though the rest of the boardwalk's attractions are seasonal, Neptune's Kingdom and the arcade are open daily year-round. Nearby is the esteemed **Cocoanut Grove** (831/423-2053) casino and ballroom, a dignified old dancehall that still swings with nostalgic tunes from the 1930s and '40s at special shindigs. Sunday brunch in the Grove's Sun Room, with its Victorian-modern decor and galleria-style, retracting glass roof, is a big event.

To fully appreciate the boardwalk then and now, pick up the ***Walking Tour of the Historical Santa Cruz Boardwalk*** brochure, as well as a current attractions listing/map. Both will help you locate yourself, then and now. Annual events held at the boardwalk include the **Clam Chowder Cook-Off and Festival** in late February; the **Central Coast Home & Garden Expo** in early April; the **Santa Cruz Band Review** in October, a fundraiser for local high school bands; and the **Santa Cruz Christmas Craft and Gift Festival,** held at the Cocoanut Grove during Thanksgiving weekend. On Friday nights in summer, starting in June, come for free concerts.

Admission to the boardwalk is free, though enjoying its amusements is not. If you'll be staying all day, the best deal is usually the all-day ride ticket, $25.95 at last report, or Unlimited Rides Plus for $29.95, which offers unlimited rides plus two other attractions. During **65-Cent Nights,** on certain Monday and Tuesday evenings in summer, ride prices revert to olden-days equivalents: $.65 per ride, and also $.65 for hot dogs, cotton candy, and Pepsis. Season passes are available. Height, age, and chaperone requirements are enforced. For current complete information, contact the **Santa Cruz Seaside Company** (400 Beach St. in Santa Cruz, 831/423-5590, www.beachboardwalk.com). While you're at it, inquire about special vacation packages.

THE WHARF

The pier at the western end of Santa Cruz Beach, once a good place to buy cheap, fresh fish, did booming business during the state's steamship heyday. Today, the place is packed instead with tourists, and most fish markets, restaurants, and shops here charge a pretty penny. Still, the wharf's worth a sunset stroll. (Peer down into the fenced-off "holes" to watch the sea lions.) A few commercial fishing boats still haul their catches of salmon and cod ashore in summer, doubling as whale-watching tour boats in winter. Worth a look, too, are the kiosk displays on wharf and fishing history.

HISTORIC SIGHTS

If you're over- or underwhelmed by the boardwalk, take the Santa Cruz **walking tour.** This expedition is a lot quicker than it used to be, since many of the city's unusual Victorians—with frilly wedding-cake furbelows and "witch's hat" towers on the Queen Annes—departed to that great Historical Register in the Sky during the 1989 earthquake. But some grandes dames remain. To find them, stop by the visitors center and pick up the *Historic Santa Cruz Walking Tours and Museum Guide* brochure. Most houses are private homes or businesses, so don't trespass. **Ocean View Avenue** is so perfect in terms of period authenticity that it took

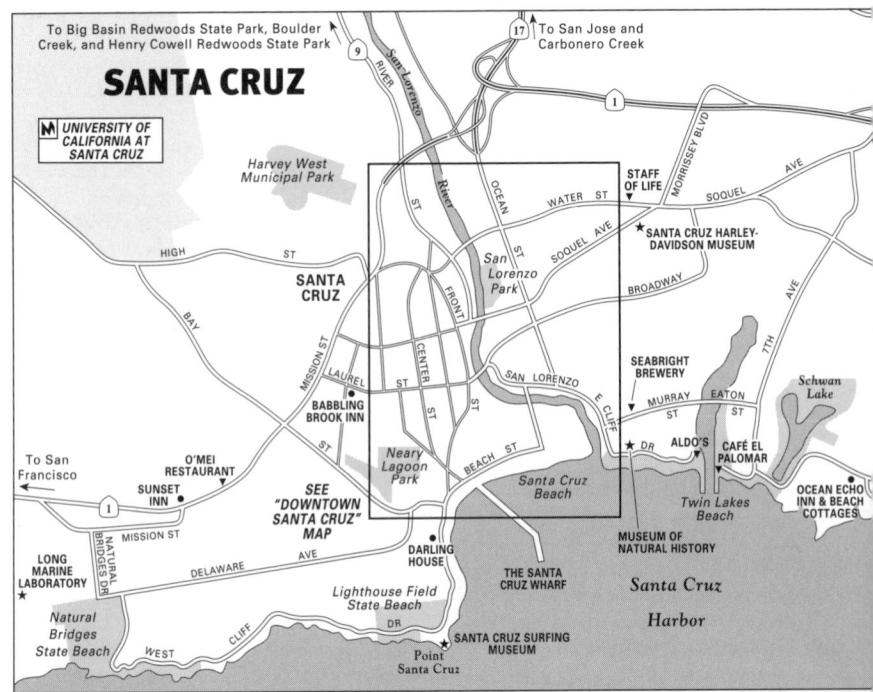

only a few loads of topsoil (covering the asphalt street with dirt) to successfully transform the neighborhood into the cinematic setting for the film version of John Steinbeck's *East of Eden.* A good example of the colonial revival style is **Villa Perla,** at the head of Ocean View. Near the Santa Cruz Mission are other notables, including the **Stick Villa** (207 Mission St.); the **Schwartz Mansion** (222 Mission St.); and the saltbox-style **Willey House,** on the corner of Mission and Sylvar.

To find out more about area history, stop by the Santa Cruz Museum of Art and History (see below for information). In particular, the museum staff can fill you in on regional historical sites under their care, including the Davenport Jail (1917), up the coast in Davenport, though no longer open to the public, and the Evergreen Cemetery (established 1850) at Evergreen and Coral Streets, one of the oldest Protestant cemeteries in California. Next door to the museum is the visitors center.

SANTA CRUZ MUSEUM OF ART AND HISTORY

A sure sign that downtown Santa Cruz is almost done digging out from the rubble of the devastating 1989 earthquake is the Museum of Art and History at the McPherson Center (705 Front St. at Cooper, 831/429-1964, www.santacruzmah.org, 11 A.M.–5 P.M. Tues.–Sun., $5, free first Fri. of the month). Traveling exhibits and local artists get prominent play. Memorable shows have included 2001's **Art Undercover: Tom Killion, Gay Schy, Peter and Donna Thomas,** an examination of "small press art"; 2002's **Simply Scene: The California Paintings of Herman Struck (1887–1954)**; and 2003's **El Rio/The River: Artists Impressions.** Up on the roof is the new **Mary and Harry Blanchard Sculpture Garden,** a showcase for intriguing works from the museum's permanent collection. Come for **After Hours** ($1, 5–7 P.M. first Thurs. of the

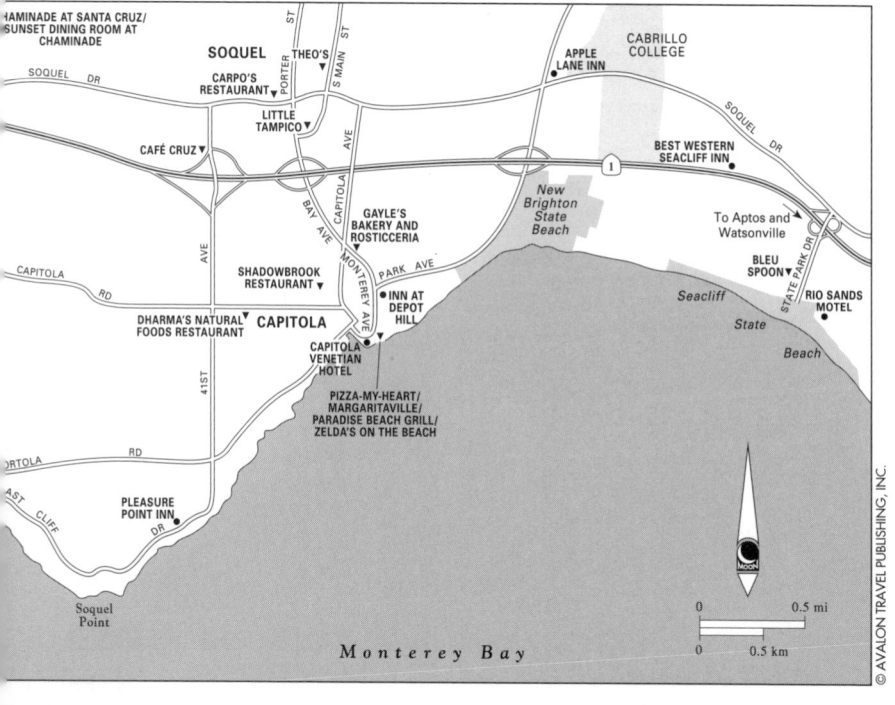

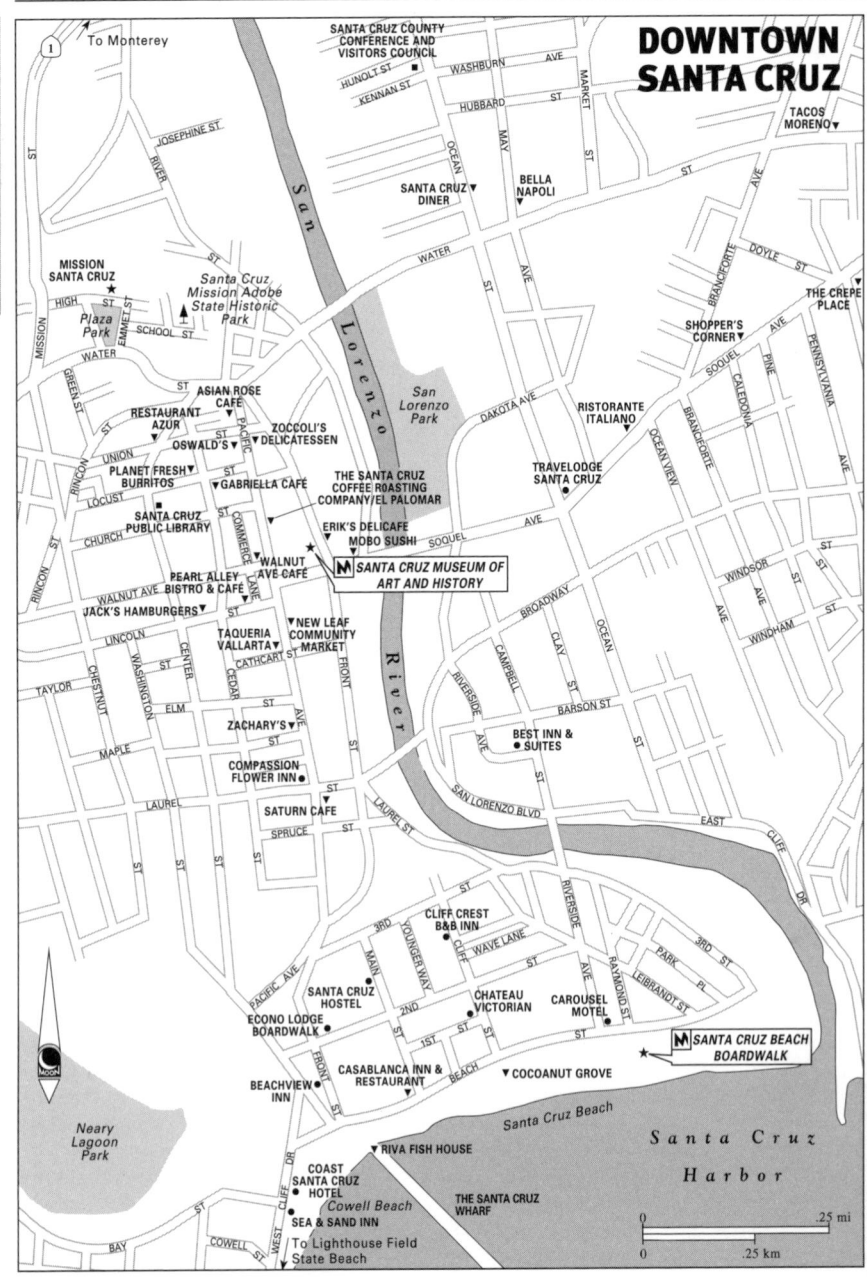

DOWNTOWN SANTA CRUZ

To Monterey

SANTA CRUZ COUNTY CONFERENCE AND VISITORS COUNCIL

HUNOLT ST
KENNAN ST
WASHBURN AVE
HUBBARD ST
MARKET ST

TACOS MORENO

JOSEPHINE ST
RIVER ST
OCEAN AVE
MAY ST

SANTA CRUZ DINER
BELLA NAPOLI

WATER ST

San Lorenzo River

BRANCIFORTE
DOYLE ST

THE CREPE PLACE

MISSION SANTA CRUZ
Santa Cruz Mission Adobe State Historic Park

SHOPPER'S CORNER

SOQUEL AVE
PINE ST
CALEDONIA

HIGH ST
EMMETT ST
SCHOOL ST

Plaza Park
WATER

San Lorenzo Park

DAKOTA AVE

RISTORANTE ITALIANO

BRANCIFORTE
OCEAN VIEW

PENNSYLVANIA

GREEN ST
RINCON ST

ST
ASIAN ROSE CAFÉ
RESTAURANT AZUR
ZOCCOLI'S DELICATESSEN
OSWALD'S
PACIFIC

TRAVELODGE SANTA CRUZ

UNION ST
PLANET FRESH BURRITOS
GABRIELLA CAFE
LOCUST ST

THE SANTA CRUZ COFFEE ROASTING COMPANY/EL PALOMAR

CHURCH ST
SANTA CRUZ PUBLIC LIBRARY
COMMERCE

ERIK'S DELICAFE
MOBO SUSHI
SOQUEL AVE

WINDSOR

RINCON ST
PEARL ALLEY BISTRO & CAFÉ
WALNUT AVE CAFE
WALNUT AVE
JACK'S HAMBURGERS

M SANTA CRUZ MUSEUM OF ART AND HISTORY

BROADWAY
CLAY ST
OCEAN ST

WINDHAM

LINCOLN ST
TAQUERIA VALLARTA
NEW LEAF COMMUNITY MARKET
CATHCART ST
CEDAR ST

CAMPBELL

CHESTNUT
WASHINGTON ST
CENTER ST
ELM ST
FRONT ST

RIVERSIDE AVE
BARSON ST

TAYLOR

ZACHARY'S

MAPLE

COMPASSION FLOWER INN

BEST INN & SUITES

LAUREL ST

SATURN CAFE
SPRUCE ST

SAN LORENZO BLVD

EAST

CLIFF DR

CLIFF CREST B&B INN

3RD ST

RIVERSIDE

YOUNGER WAY
WAVE LANE

PARK
3RD ST
RAYMOND ST
LEIBRANDT ST

MOON

SANTA CRUZ HOSTEL
ECONO LODGE BOARDWALK
PACIFIC AVE
MAIN ST
2ND ST

CHATEAU VICTORIAN
1ST ST
BEACH ST

CAROUSEL MOTEL

AVE

M SANTA CRUZ BEACH BOARDWALK

Neary Lagoon Park

BEACHVIEW INN

CASABLANCA INN & RESTAURANT

COCOANUT GROVE

Santa Cruz Beach

Santa Cruz Harbor

RIVA FISH HOUSE

COAST SANTA CRUZ HOTEL
SEA & SAND INN

COWELL ST
BAY ST
WEST CLIFF DR

Cowell Beach

THE SANTA CRUZ WHARF

To Lighthouse Field State Beach

0   .25 mi
0   .25 km

© AVALON TRAVEL PUBLISHING, INC.

month) for wine, appetizers, live music, and a leisurely look at current exhibits. Adjacent to the museum is The Octagon, an eight-sided, 1882 brick building relocated here and now the museum store. Inside is an intriguing collection of gift and art items, including—at least sometimes—the marvelously whimsical work (such as greeting cards) of Santa Cruz artist James Carl Aschbacher.

SANTA CRUZ MISSION ADOBE STATE HISTORIC PARK

Restored and open to the public is the Santa Cruz Mission Adobe (144 School St., 831/425-5849 or 831/429-2850, 10 A.M.–4 P.M. Thurs.–Sun., small admission fee), a state historical park just off Mission Plaza. This is one of the county's last remaining original adobes, built by and for Native Americans "employed" at Mission Santa Cruz. It was later a 17-unit "home for new citizens." Only seven units remain, these now comprising a California history museum circa the 1840s. Restored rooms illustrate how Native American, Californio, and Irish American families once lived. Call for current information about guided tours and "living history" demonstrations (usually offered Sun., the latter just in Mar.). School groups are welcome on Thursdays and Fridays by advance reservation only. Come in September for **Mission Adobe Day.** Plan a picnic here anytime (bring your own water).

MISSION SANTA CRUZ

Nearby is what's left of the original mission: Just a memory, really. The original site of the **Misión de Exaltación de la Santa Cruz** (126 High St., 831/426-5686, 10 A.M.–4 P.M. Tues.–Sat., 10 A.M.–2 P.M. Sun.) was at High and Emmet Streets, too close to the San Lorenzo River, as it turned out. The move to higher ground left only the garden at the lower level. The original Santa Cruz mission complex was finished in 1794 but was completely destroyed by earthquakes in the mid-19th century. The replica church, scaled down by half

Mission Santa Cruz

MELISSA SHEROWSKI

and built in 1931 on the upper level, seems to have lost more than just stature.

SANTA CRUZ CITY MUSEUM OF NATURAL HISTORY

At least for now, the city's Museum of Natural History (1305 E. Cliff Drive, 831/420-6115, www.santacruzmuseums.org, 10 A.M.–5 P.M. Tues.–Sun., small admission fee) is at home in Tyrell Park above Seabright/Castle Beach, east of the boardwalk. The onetime 1915 Carnegie Library that anchors the park's southern edge, overlooking Monterey Bay, features exhibits and displays on the Santa Cruz area's natural and cultural history. There's a Tidepool Touch Tank and a Fossil Sand Dollar Dig—and the kids also dig that big cement gray whale on the lawn. The museum also sponsors a year-round schedule of classes and events.

SANTA CRUZ HARLEY-DAVIDSON MUSEUM

The local Harley-Davidson shop (1148 Soquel Ave., 831/421-9600, www.santacruzharley.com) is something of a "destination dealership." Among the exquisitely restored Harleys on display are an H-D bicycle first introduced in 1917, a 1929 JDH two-cam twin, and a stylish 1930 VL. Historical photos, posters, and memorabilia round out the collection (available Tues.–Sun. for public viewing). The website offers a grand tour, too.

SANTA CRUZ MYSTERY SPOT

The much bumper-stickered, ballyhooed Mystery Spot (465 Mystery Spot Rd., 831/423-8897, www.mysteryspot.com, 9 A.M.–7 P.M. daily in summer, last tour at 7; 9 A.M.–5 P.M. daily the rest of the year, last tour at 5, $5) is a place where "every law of gravitation has gone haywire." Or has it? Trees, people, even the Spot's rustic shack and furnishings seem spellbound by "the force" (though people wearing slick-soled shoes seem to have the hardest time staying with the mysterious program). Hard-core tourists tend to love this place—Mom, Dad, and the kids can *literally* climb the walls—but others leave wondering why they spent the money to get in.

To get to the Mystery Spot, follow Market Street north from Water Street for a few miles. Market becomes Branciforte; Mystery Spot Road branches left off Branciforte—you can't miss it.

SANTA CRUZ SURFING MUSEUM

Cowabunga! Instead of cutting a ribbon, they snipped a hot pink surfer's leash when they opened the world's first surfing museum (831/420-6289, www.santacruzsurfingmuseum.org, noon–4 P.M. Wed.–Mon. in summer, same hours Thurs.–Mon. in winter, $1 requested donation) here at **Lighthouse Field State Beach** (831/420-5270) in May 1986. This historical exhibit reaches back to the 1930s, with displays on the evolution of surfboards and equipment—

The Santa Cruz Surfing Museum was once a lighthouse.

including the Model T of boards, a 15-foot redwood plank weighing 100 pounds, and an experimental Jack O'Neill wetsuit made of nylon and foam, the forerunner to the Neoprene "short john." Some say two Polynesian princes introduced surfing to Santa Cruz in 1885. True or not, by 1912, local posters announced the surfing exploits of Olympic swimmer and "Father of Surfing" Duke Kahanamoku. Come at Christmas for the popular **Caroling under the Stars** annual event.

The museum's location, on the ground floor of the brick lighthouse on West Cliff Drive, northwest of town near Steamer's Lane—prime surf turf—seems the most fitting place for official homage to life in pursuit of the perfect wave. The lighthouse was built by the family of Mark Abbott, a surfer killed nearby. The museum's gift shop is a great place to get one-of-a-kind T-shirts and other emblems of California cool.

Santa Cruz now has two functioning lighthouses. The **Santa Cruz Harbor Light,** on the

SURF'S UP AT O'NEILL'S

A Santa Cruz phenomenon with considerable worldwide renown, **O'Neill Surf Shop** (831/475-4151, www.oneill.com) is the legendary business legacy of Jack O'Neill, a local surfer who, in the 1950s, created a wetsuit that protected surfers from Northern California's chilling waters. The business grew and flourished, becoming the world's number one wetsuit manufacturer. O'Neill also sells popular surfing-styled sportswear. There are four O'Neill shops in Santa Cruz County, including one at the beach (222 E. Cliff Dr.), one at the boardwalk (400 Beach St.), and one downtown (110 Cooper St., Ste. 100-D). The fourth is in Capitola (1115 41st Ave.).

O'Neill's legacy is broader and deeper, however, especially since the O'Neill children are now fully involved in the company's enterprises. The company's slogan, "It's always summer on the inside," is not just a marketing tagline, but a life philosophy. Come to Santa Cruz in February for a literal test of the summer-inside lifestyle at the famed **O'Neill Cold Water Classic,** a contest that attracts top surfers from around the world. The **O'Neill Sea Odyssey** (www.oneillseaodyssey.org) is an ocean-going environmental education program offered free for grammar school children onboard the 65-foot Team O'Neill catamaran.

rock jetty at the entrance to the Santa Cruz harbor, also known as Walton's Lighthouse (in honor of Derek Walton), was officially dedicated in June 2002.

SANTA CRUZ MEMORIAL PARK & FUNERAL HOME

Perhaps more interesting even than the Mystery Spot are two other oddball attractions, located at the Santa Cruz Memorial Park & Funeral Home (3301 Paul Sweet Rd., 831/426-1601, Mon.–Fri. by appointment, donations appreciated). Here you'll find a wax interpretation of *The Last Supper,* plus displays attempting to rekindle the controversy over the **Shroud of Turin**—that renowned piece of linen purported to show Christ's after-death visage—by chal-

lenging the conclusions of carbon tests declaring the shroud a fake.

An interpretation of Da Vinci's famous painting in life-sized wax figures, *The Last Supper* is the original work of two Katherine Struberghs (mother and daughter) from Los Angeles. The women spared themselves no trial or trouble in this endeavor. (Each hair on every wax head was implanted by hand—that task alone requiring eight months.) But after some 40 years' residence at the Santa Cruz Art League, Jesus and his disciples were in a sad state of disrepair. That was before the funeral home and local Oddfellows Lodge took on the task of financing something of a resurrection. The job involved patching the cracks in the figures' heads, washing and setting their hair and beards, replacing fingers (and fingernails and toenails), and polishing their glass eyeballs.

UNIVERSITY OF CALIFORNIA AT SANTA CRUZ

The city on the hill just beyond town is the UC Santa Cruz campus, planned by architect John Carl Warnecke and landscape architect Thomas Church—a total of 10 clustered colleges and associated buildings overlooking the Pacific Ocean. Campus buildings were designed by noted architects, including Charles Moore, William Wurster, Joseph Esherick, Ernest Kump, Antoine Predock, Hugh Stubbins, Ralph Rapson, William Turnbull, and Kathy Simon. When the doors of UC Santa Cruz opened in the 1960s, few California students could gain admission to the close-knit, redwood-cloistered campus. The selection process (complete with essay) was weighted in favor of students with unusual abilities, aptitudes, and attitudes—those not likely to thrive within the traditional university structure. So many children of movie stars and other members of California's moneyed upper classes have attended UC Santa Cruz that it has been playfully dubbed "California's public finishing school." The university's student body has so far remained relatively small (more than 12,000 currently), though growth is on the agenda. A sign that the times they are a-changin' at Santa Cruz came in February 2000, when the faculty voted

ALL HAIL THE SANTA CRUZ SLUGS

Refreshingly out of step with the period's hyperactive corporate careerism, the UC Santa Cruz student body convinced then-Chancellor Robert Sinsheimer in 1986 to declare as their school mascot the noble banana slug—a common on-campus companion—instead of the more socially acceptable sea lion, after a hard-fought, five-year campaign. When the chancellor declared the Santa Cruz Sea Lions the official choice in 1981, students protested that the banana slug would more appropriately be "a statement about the ideology of Santa Cruz," a philosophy with no room for football teams, cheerleaders, fraternities, and sororities.

Finally acceding to the students' preference for a slimy, spineless, sluggish, yellow gastropod—defended as "flexible, golden, and deliberate" by one professor—Sinsheimer said that students should have a school mascot "with which they can empathize." He also proposed genetic engineering research on slugs to "improve the breed," because "the potential seems endless."

overwhelmingly to eliminate the university's founding "no required grading" policy.

The University of California regents set about transforming the redwood-forested rangeland here, once the Henry Cowell Ranch, into California's educational Camelot in 1961. Designs ranged from modern Mediterranean to "Italian hill village" (Kresge College). The official explanation for the Santa Cruz "college cluster" concept was to avoid the depersonalization common to large UC campuses, but another reason was alluded to when then-Governor Ronald Reagan declared the campus "riot-proof."

To truly appreciate this place, wander the campus hiking trails and paths (but not alone). Some of the old converted ranch buildings are worth noting: the lime kilns, blacksmith's shop, cookhouse, horse barn, bull barn, slaughterhouse, cookhouse, workers' cabins, and cooperage. On a clear day, the view of Monterey Bay (and of whales passing offshore in winter and spring) from the top of the hill on the 2,000-

acre campus is marvelous. For information and guided campus tours, stop by the wood-and-stone Cook House (831/459-4008, www.ucsc.edu, slugvisits@cats.ucsc.edu) near the entrance.

LONG MARINE LABORATORY

Well worth a stop for nature-lovers, the Joseph M. Long Marine Laboratory is just off Delaware Avenue, near Natural Bridges State Beach on the western edge of town. A university research and education facility, the lab is affiliated with the on-campus Institute of Marine Sciences, established in 1972. Research conducted here ranges from marine biology and marine geophysics to paleo-oceanography and coastal processes—from plankton to blue whales, cold water ecology to tropical coral reefs. Associated facilities include an 18,000-square-foot California Department of Fish and Game Marine Wildlife Veterinary Care and Research Center, the nation's largest and most advanced, and a state-of-the-art National Marine Fisheries Service laboratory, which conducts fisheries research and houses the nation's first National Science Center for Marine Protected Areas. Under construction, at last report: the UC Santa Cruz Center for Ocean Health and a seabird/raptor facility.

To help interpret the lab's work and to educate future generations of marine biologists, the new **Seymour Marine Discovery Center** is open to the public (831/459-3800, www2.ucsc.edu/seymourcenter, 10 A.M.–5 P.M. Tues.–Sat., noon–5 P.M. Sun., $5 adults, $3 students, seniors, and youths age 6–16, free for children 5 and under). Docent-led tours of the lab's other marine research facilities are available. Lab tours are offered at 1, 2, and 3 P.M., on a first-come, first-escorted-around basis (sign up an hour in advance). For additional information about Long Marine Lab programs and facilities, see www.natsci.ucsc.edu.

To get here from Santa Cruz, take Highway 1 (Mission Street) north, turn left on Swift Street, and then right on Delaware Avenue. Continue on Delaware to the Long Marine Lab entrance at the end of the road.

Recreation

Most of the outdoor action in Santa Cruz proper happens at local beaches; swimming, surfing, and fishing are all big, as are tamer pastimes like beachcombing, sandcastle-building, and sunbathing. The in-town **Santa Cruz Beach** at the boardwalk, with fine white sand and towel-to-towel baking bodies in summer, is "the scene"—especially for outsiders from San Jose, locals say. For more privacy, head east to the mouth of the San Lorenzo River. Southwest of the pier, **Cowell Beach** is a surfing beach where Huey Lewis and the News filmed one of their music videos. Just before **Lighthouse Field State Beach** on West Cliff is the Santa Cruz Surfing Museum (see information under *Sights,* above), an eclectic lighthouse collection of surf's-up memorabilia keeping watch over the hotdoggers in churning Steamer Lane.

NATURAL BRIDGES STATE BEACH

Located farther southwest, at the end of West Cliff Drive, Natural Bridges State Beach (831/423-4609, www.santacruzstateparks.org or www.sc-parkfriends.org, 8 A.M.–sunset daily, parking fee $6 per car, walk-ins and bike-ins free) attracts mythic monarch butterflies each year from October to May. Though Pacific Grove, near Monterey, proudly proclaims itself the destination of choice for these regal insects, Santa Cruz claims to get the most monarchs. This is the only state-owned monarch butterfly preserve in California. One of the sandstone "natural bridges" here collapsed in 1980, under assault from a winter storm. The other still stands, though. To the north are some great tidepools, available for exploration (but don't touch) at low tide. Leathery green fields of brussels sprouts fringe the fragile sandy cliffs.

Monarch butterfly tours (wheelchair-accessible) are offered on weekends from mid-October through February. For information on guided butterfly walks and tidepool tours, call or stop by the visitors center. Come in October for **Welcome Back Monarch Day,** and again in February for the annual **Migration Festival** sendoff, a park fundraiser cosponsored by Friends of Santa Cruz State Parks. (The monarchs may be leaving, but the gray whales offshore are just arriving in February; migrants come and go all year.)

Natural Bridges State Beach

Santa Cruz

BEACHES AND SURFING

Along East Cliff Drive are **Tyrell Park** and more inaccessible sandy beaches. **Twin Lakes State Beach,** near the Santa Cruz Yacht Harbor on the eastern extension of East Cliff before it becomes Portolá, is a popular locals' beach, usually quite warm. Beyond the Santa Cruz Yacht Harbor, various small, locally popular beaches line East Cliff Drive. The unofficially named **26th Street Beach** (at the end of 26th Street, naturally enough) is probably tops among them. Hot for local surfing is the **Pleasure Point,** East Cliff at Pleasure Point Drive.

Davenport Beach, at Davenport Landing up the coast toward Año Nuevo, is a hotspot for sailboarders and is often relatively uncrowded. **Red White and Blue Beach** ((5021 Coast Rd., 831/423-6332, day-use fee $10, children $1, camping $15), at the red, white, and blue mailbox just south of Davenport, is a popular, privately operated nude beach (too popular, some say; women shouldn't go alone). Nearby is **Bonny Doon Beach,** up the coast from Santa Cruz at the intersection of Highway 1 and Bonny Doon Road, south of Davenport. It's free, and even wilder for sunbathing sans swimsuit. It's also popular with surfers.

About six miles down the coast from Santa Cruz City Beach and just south of the Capitola suburbs is immensely popular **New Brighton State Beach** (1500 Park Ave., 831/464-6330, day-use fee $6, campsites $20–35). Its 93 often sunny acres are protected by wooded headlands that offer a great family campground, nature trails, good bird-watching, and a dazzling nighttime view of Monterey Bay. A coming attraction at New Bright, once adequate funding is secured, will be the snazzy new **Pacific Migrations** visitors center.

Several miles farther south, two-mile-long **Seacliff State Beach** (Park Drive, Aptos, 831/685-6500, 831/685-6442 for recorded info, or 831/685-6444 for visitors center, day-use fee $6, RV campsites $35) is so popular, you may not be able to stop. It's nice for hiking, pelican-watching, fossil-spotting, swimming, and sunbathing. The wheelchair-accessible pier reaches out to the

ENCHANTED CIRCLE

Tour the eclectic scenery of Santa Cruz greenbelt areas on the area's **Circle of Enchantment Trail,** also known as the Circle Trail. The 23-mile trail is actually two separate loops; each segment can be hiked in a half day.

Begin either loop in downtown Santa Cruz at the San Lorenzo River pedestrian bridge, just off Front Street.

The circle's western loop, about a 12-mile hike, follows the river down to the boardwalk. It then climbs to the bayside recreation trail along W. Cliff Drive and continues on to Natural Bridges State Park and the Long Marine Lab before angling inland. The route then follows Delaware Avenue into wooded Arroyo Seco Canyon, then up the hill to the UC Santa Cruz campus—redwoods and fabulous views—and the Pogonip grasslands before circling back to the river levee.

The eastern loop is more urban, yet it eventually leads to the "Top of the World" lookout, Arana City Park, Santa Cruz Yacht Harbor, and along E. Cliff Drive and the Pleasure Point area before returning to Lorenzo Park downtown.

A general route map and detailed directions are available at www.ecotopia.org.

concrete carcass of the doomed World War I–vintage *Palo Alto,* sunk here after seeing no wartime action, and now a long-abandoned amusement pier (not open to the public). Birds live in the prow these days. People enjoy the adjacent pier's more mundane pleasures: people-watching, fishing (no license required), and strolling. Guided walks are occasionally offered; call the visitors center for schedules and reservations.

As the name suggests, **Rio del Mar State Beach** (free) is where Aptos Creek meets the sea. Here you'll find restrooms, miles of sand, and limited parking.

To reserve state beach campsites—absolutely essential in summer—contact **ReserveAmerica** (800/444-7275, www.reserveamerica.com). For more information on regional state beaches and parks, see www.santacruzstateparks.org and www.scparkfriends.org. For beaches farther south, see *Watsonville and Vicinity,* below.

SAILING

For an unusual view of the boardwalk and the bay, take a boat ride. One of the best going—definitely not just any boat—is the *Chardonnay II,* a 70-foot, ultralight sailing yacht offering special-emphasis cruises: Choose from astronomy, fireworks, "gourmet on the bay," marine ecology, wine-tasting, and whale-watching (winter and spring). There's even a Wednesday night Boat Race Cruise in the company of almost every other boat from the Santa Cruz Yacht Harbor. This sleek albino seal of a sailboat can hold up to 49 passengers and features every imaginable amenity, including a CD player, TV/VCR, built-in bar, cellular phones, and plenty of below-deck space, making it fun as a private group charter for personally designed adventures. There's a two-hour minimum rental for departures from Santa Cruz, a three-hour minimum from Monterey. For more information and to make reservations (required), contact **Chardonnay Sailing Charters** (831/423-1213, www.chardonnay.com, $39.50 per person for scheduled rides, $550–800/hour for private charters).

Other boat and charter companies at or near the city's yacht harbor include **Pacific Yachting** (790 Mariner Park Way, 831/423-7245 or 800/374-2626, www.pacificsail.com), which offers similar boat rides on smaller yachts, as well as sailing lessons and a six-day seagoing instruction vacation. Probably the best deal going, though, is through the **University of California at Santa Cruz Boating Club** (831/425-1164, ucscboat@cats.ucsc.edu, www.ucsc.edu/opers/boating). In summer, UCSC sailing and boating courses are open to the public. If you qualify for membership—as a student or alumnus—you can use the boats all year. The local **Coast Guard Auxiliary** (432 Oxford Way, 831/423-7119) also offers sailing, boating skills, seamanship, and coastal navigation courses.

OTHER WATER SPORTS

For more traditional boat tours, whale-watching trips (winter and summer), and fishing charters, contact **Stagnaro's Sportfishing** (at the municipal wharf, 831/427-2334, www.stagnaros.com) or **Scurfield's Landing/Shamrock Charters** (at the yacht harbor, 831/476-2648, www.scurfslanding.com).

Kayaking is great sport in these parts. **Venture Quest** (125 Beach St., 831/427-2267; and at the municipal wharf, 831/425-8445; www.kayaksantacruz.com) sells kayaks and accessories and offers lessons and guided tours. **Kayak Connection,** at the Santa Cruz Yacht Harbor (413 Lake Ave., 831/479-1121) and at Elkhorn Slough (2370 Hwy. 1., Moss Landing, 831/724-5692, www.kayakconnection.com), also rents and sells equipment, in addition to offering guided bird-watching, fishing, and moonlight tours.

Several full-service dive shops in town can provide complete information on local diving conditions, as well as instruction, rentals, and sales. Try **Aqua Safaris Scuba Center** (6896-A Soquel Ave., 831/479-4386, www.aquasafaris.com) or **Adventure Sports Unlimited** (303 Potrero St., 831/458-3648 or 888/839-4286, www.asudoit.com).

Club Ed (831/464-0177 or 800/287-7873, www.club-ed.com), on Cowell Beach on the right side of Santa Cruz Wharf, in front of the WestCoast Santa Cruz Hotel, rents surfboards, boogie boards, skim boards, and sailboards, and offers lessons in riding all of the above.

Accommodations

Private campgrounds and trailer parks are always a possibility; a fairly complete current listing is available at the local chamber of commerce, or see Tom Stienstra's guide, *California Camping.* Area possibilities include **Cotillion Gardens** (300 Old Big Trees Rd., Felton, 831/335-7669); **Carbonero Creek** (917 Disc Dr., Scotts Valley, 831/438-1288 or 800/546-1288); and the **Santa Cruz KOA** (1186 San Andreas Rd., Watsonville, 831/722-0551 or 800/562-7701, www.koa.com).

BEACH CAMPING

Best for nearby tent camping is **New Brighton State Beach** (1500 Park Ave., Capitola, 831/464-6330 or 831/464-6329, $20–35). "New Bright" features 115 developed campsites (especially nice ones on the cliffs), some sheltered picnic tables, and a small beach. It's a good base camp for the entire Santa Cruz area. You can get here via local bus—take number 58 or the Park Avenue route. This area was once called China Beach, or China Cove, after the Chinese fishermen who built a village here in the 1870s. The campground is popular, so

reserve (see below) for summer at least six months ahead.

Near Aptos, **Seacliff State Beach** (831/685-6500 or 831/685-6444, $35, less for overflow campsites) has a better beach than New Brighton, but camping is a disappointment. Strictly an RV setup, the park has 26 sites with hookups.

For more information about the area's beach parks, contact the state parks office in Santa Cruz (600 Ocean St., 831/429-2850, www.santacruzstateparks.org). For state campground reservations, contact ReserveAmerica (800/444-7275, www.reserveamerica.com).

REDWOODS CAMPING

Big Basin Redwoods State Park (21600 Big Basin Hwy., Boulder Creek, 831/338-8860, www.bigbasin.org, family sites $20–24, tents-only trail sites $15–20; hiker/biker sites $3 per person) offers 146 family campsites, group camps, and horse camps. The park also boasts 41 year-round "tent cabins," each with two double beds, a camp lamp, and a woodstove. Tent cabins sleep four comfortably, but can house up to eight

Camping is allowed at New Brighton State Beach.

HOSTEL TERRITORY

Two spectacular lighthouse hostels, both affiliated with Hostelling International (HI-USA), are finds for travelers—including families—looking for cheap sleeps along the San Mateo coastline. And with online reservations available as of summer 2004, planning a stay in hostel territory is easier than ever.

Closest to Santa Cruz is the **Pigeon Point Lighthouse Hostel** (210 Pigeon Point Rd. at Hwy. 1, Pescadero, 650/879-0633 or 800/909-4776, #73, for phone-tree reservations, www.norcalhostels.org, bunk beds $18–25 adults and $13–18 children /youth, private rooms for up to two adults and two kids $47–57)—*the* inexpensive place to stay while visiting the elephant seals. Named after the clipper ship *Carrier Pigeon*, one of many notorious shipwrecks off the coastal shoals here, the 1872 lighthouse is now automated, but still impressive, with its Fresnel lens and distinctive 10-second flash pattern. Lighthouse tours (650/879-2120, 40 minutes, small fee) are offered by state park staff every weekend year-round, and also on Fridays in summer; rain cancels.

The hostel itself is made up of four former family residences for the U.S. Coast Guard—basic male or female bunk rooms, plus some spartan couples' and family rooms. The old Fog Signal Building is now a rec room; there's also a hot tub perched on rocky cliffs above surging surf. Fabulous sunset views, wonderful tidepools. There's an extra charge for linen rental (if you don't bring your own sleep sack or sleeping bag). Get groceries in Pescadero and prepare meals in the well-equipped communal kitchens, or ask for local restaurant suggestions. For information and/or to check in, the hostel office is open 7:30–10 A.M. and 4:30–11 P.M. only. Photo ID required. Very popular, so reserve well in advance.

Farther north, beyond Half Moon Bay between Montara and Moss Beach, is picturesque **Point Montara Lighthouse Hostel** (16th St. at Hwy. 1, Montara, 650/728-7177 or 800/909-4776, #64, for phone-tree reservations, www.norcalhostels.org, bunk beds $18–21 adults and $12 children, private rooms $51–78). Point Montara is popular with bicyclists, and it's also accessible via bus from the Bay Area. The 1875 lighthouse itself is no longer in operation, and the Fog Signal Building here is now a roomy, woodstove-heated community room. Hostel facilities include kitchens, dining rooms, laundry, bunkrooms, and five private rooms ideal for couples or families. Volleyball court, outdoor hot tub, and bicycle rentals are also available. Open to travelers of all ages. Popular, so reserve in advance.

(800/874-8368 for reservations, 1–6 P.M. Mon.–Fri., www.bigbasintentcabins.com, $50, two-night minimum on weekends, three-night minimum on holidays, add $10 for linen and blanket rental in lieu of sleeping bags). You can also arrange "hassle-free" tent camping—all you have to pack is kids and clothes.

Henry Cowell Redwoods State Park (831/335-4598 for administration or 831/438-2396 for campground, $20–24), just north of the UC campus on Highway 9 in Felton, offers 150 sites, 105 of them developed. Sites in the developed areas are quite civilized, with amenities including hot showers, flush toilets, tables, barbecues, and cupboards. Primitive hike-in and family backpacking campsites are available at **Castle Rock State Park** (15000 Skyline Blvd., Los Gatos, 408/867-2952 or 831/338-8861).

Family and group campsites at both Big Basin and Henry Cowell Redwoods State Park are sometimes available at the last minute, even in summer and on warm-season weekends. But make reservations—up to seven months in advance—to guarantee a space through ReserveAmerica (800/444-7275, www.reserveamerica.com).

HOSTELS

The **HI-USA Santa Cruz Hostel** (321 Main St. between Second and Third Sts., 831/423-8304, www.hi-santacruz.org, under $50), downtown on Beach Hill, occupies the historic 1870s Carmelita Cottages. The hostel is open year-round, is wheelchair-accessible, and features an onsite cyclery, fireplace, barbecue, lockers, and rose and herb gardens. Family rooms and limited parking available (extra fee for both). Reservations are strongly suggested.

In additional to the Hostelling International hostel in downtown Santa Cruz, the region boasts other exceptional budget choices—including the **Pigeon Point** and **Point Montara Lighthouse Hostels,** up the coast toward San Francisco, both unique and incredibly cheap for on-the-beach lodgings—if you don't mind bunk beds or spartan couples' rooms. (For details, see the sidebar *Hostel Territory* in this chapter.) Or try the **Sanborn Park** hostel (408/741-0166 or 408/741-9555, www.sanbornparkhostel.org), just over the hills in Saratoga. If you're heading south, another good bet is the new **Carpenter's Hall Hostel** in Monterey (see under *Hostels* in that chapter for details). Rates for all these options are under $50.

MOTELS AND HOTELS

As a general rule, motels closer to the freeway are cheaper, while those on the river are seedier. There are some fairly inexpensive motels near the beach (some with kitchens, whirlpool tubs, pools, cable TV, etc.). Off-season rates in Santa Cruz are usually quite reasonable, but prices can sometimes mysteriously increase in summer and on weekends and holidays—so, verify prices before you sign in.

$50–150

All of the following have rates starting at $50–100. The **Beachview Inn** (50 Front St., 831/426-3575 or 800/946-0614, $90 and up in high season), less than a block from the beach, features all the essentials, plus air-conditioning and direct-dial phones. The **Econo Lodge Santa Cruz** (550 Second St., 831/426-3626 or 800/553-2666, $75 and up) is just a block from the boardwalk and the wharf. Close to downtown is **Travelodge Santa Cruz** (525 Ocean St., 831/426-2300 or 800/578-7878, $89 and up).

Most rates at the following start at $100–150. Between Santa Cruz and Aptos, and quite close to the beach, is the renovated, 1930s-vintage **Ocean Echo Inn & Beach Cottages** (401 Johans Beach Dr., 831/462-4192, www.oceanecho.com). Cottages, including a two-story water

tower, accommodate two to six guests. Many have fully equipped kitchens or kitchenettes, and some offer ocean views. In the off season, some rates dip below $100. Endlessly convenient for boardwalkers is the boardwalk's own **Carousel Motel** (110 Riverside Ave., 831/425-7090 or 800/214-7400, www.santacruzmotels.com). Also a fine bet is the attractive **Best Inn & Suites** (600 Riverside Ave., 831/458-9660 or 800/527-3833, www.bestinnssantacruz.com), where standard rooms include two queen beds. Other options are available, including two-story suites and "evergreen" rooms with air, water, and shower filtration. The inn also features a heated pool and hot tubs, a pleasant garden courtyard, and a picnic area with barbecues, plus complimentary expanded continental breakfast. Some rooms at the pleasant **Sunset Inn** (2424 Mission St., 831/423-7500) close to UC Santa Cruz and Natural Bridges, also fit this price category. Amenities include microwaves, refrigerators, some in-room whirlpool tubs, free local phone calls, breakfast, a hot tub, and a sauna.

$150 and Up

Close to the wharf and overlooking the bay is the small but immensely popular **Sea & Sand Inn** (201 W. Cliff Dr., 831/427-3400, www.santacruzmotels.com, $150–250). All 20 rooms boast an ocean view; suites have abundant amenities. Off-season rates can go as low as $99.

All of the following have rates of $250 and up. Adjacent to the wharf and across from the Santa Cruz Beach Boardwalk, the imposing **Coast Santa Cruz Hotel** (175 W. Cliff Dr., 831/426-4330 or 800/716-6199, www.coasthotels.com) is right on the beach—the only beachfront hotel in Santa Cruz—and not far from the lighthouse. It features 163 rooms and suites with balconies and patios, in-room coffeemakers and refrigerators, modern extras, including terry robes and iron/ironing board, wireless high-speed Internet access, satellite TV and in-room movies, a Sony Playstation, a heated pool, and a whirlpool.

Even more romantic is the **Casa Blanca Inn** (Beach and Main, 831/423-1570 or 800/644-1570, www.casablanca-santacruz.com), at the beach and right across from the boardwalk. The historic Cerf Mansion has been remade into a stylish hotel with 39 rooms—some with fireplaces, terraces or balconies, and full kitchens—and all feature cable TV, phones with data ports, and in-room refrigerators, microwaves, coffeemakers, and safes. Elegant on-site restaurant, too.

For value and views, nothing beats **Chaminade at Santa Cruz** (1 Chaminade Lane, just off Paul Sweet Rd., 831/475-5600 or 800/283-6569, www.chaminade.com), up on the hill overlooking Monterey Bay. Occupying the old Chaminade Brothers Seminary and Monastery, this quiet resort and conference center offers a wealth of business amenities—but also personal perks, such as a health club (with massage and men's and women's therapy pools), jogging track, lighted tennis courts, heated pool, saunas, and whirlpools. There are full spa services, too. Rooms and suites are scattered around the 80-acre grounds in 11 "villas" that include shared parlors with refrigerators, wet bars, and conference tables. Rooms feature king or queen beds, in-room coffeemakers, irons and ironing boards, and two direct-line phones. Valet parking and airport transportation are available. Chaminade also boasts two good restaurants and a bar (with meal service), all open to the general public.

BED-AND-BREAKFASTS

One of the loveliest newer B&Bs in Santa Cruz is actually the nation's first "BB&B": Bed, Bud, and Breakfast. The **Compassion Flower Inn** (216 Laurel St., 831/466-0420, www.compassionflowerinn.com, $100–200, two-night minimum stay) opened in March 2000 with the express purpose of being a hemp- and medical marijuana–friendly bed-and-breakfast. The establishment is "named for both the beauty of the passionflower and the compassion of the medical marijuana movement" to which the owners have dedicated themselves. If you come, don't expect to find some tie-dyed, weed-happy scene reminiscent of San Francisco's Haight-Ashbury district during the Summer of Love. The proprietors have impeccably restored this gothic revival Victorian at a cost of half a million dollars. Tastefully and creatively decorated with antiques, hand-painted furniture, and custom tilework, the Compassion Flower Inn instead hearkens back to its historical roots as the one-time home of Judge Edgar Spalsbury, who made regular trips to a pharmacy downtown to buy opium as a pain medication for his tuberculosis. Rooms range from the fairly simple **Hemp Room** and **Passionflower Room,** "twin" accommodations tucked under the eaves (these two share a bath), to the first-floor, fully wheelchair-accessible **Canabliss Room** and the elegant **Lovers' Suite.** Particularly striking in the suite is its bathroom, where exquisite tiled hemp designs wrap the two-person sunken tub. Rates include full organic breakfast, with fair-trade coffee and fresh-baked bread.

Other Santa Cruz inns tend to cluster near the ocean. The stylishly renovated oceanfront **Pleasure Point Inn** (2-3665 E. Cliff Dr. at 37th Ave., 831/469-6161 for voicemail or 831/475-4657, www.pleasurepointinn.com, $200–250, second-story Coral Room $265) is indeed a pleasure. This adults-only inn offers four fresh, uniquely decorated rooms, each with abundant amenities—from in-room refrigerator, microwave, coffeemaker, and digital safe to gas-burning fireplace and private patio. Fresh fruit platter and continental breakfast every morning, and a "welcome basket" on arrival. And, oh, those views—especially from the hot tub and the rooftop deck. Ask about specials and packages.

Tastefully decorated is the **Cliff Crest Bed and Breakfast Inn** (407 Cliff St., 831/427-2609, www.cliffcrestinn.com, $200–250), a Queen Anne by the beach and boardwalk, just blocks from both downtown and Main Beach. Full breakfast is served in the solarium. The **Chateau Victorian** (118 First St., 831/458-9458, www.chateauvictorian.com, $100–155) offers seven rooms a bit more on the frilly side, with queen-sized beds, private tiled bathrooms, and wood-burning fireplaces. Local Santa Cruz Mountains wines are served, as are generous continental breakfasts.

For something more formal, the 1910 **Darling House** (314 W. Cliff Dr., 831/458-1958 or 800/458-1988, www.darlinghouse.com,

$100–300) is an elegant, 1910, Spanish Revival, seaside mansion designed by architect William Weeks. In addition to spectacular ocean views, Darling House offers eight rooms (two with private baths, two with fireplaces), telephones, and TV on request. There's a hot tub in the backyard; robes are provided. If you loved *The Ghost and Mrs. Muir,* you'll particularly enjoy the Pacific Ocean Room here—complete with telescope. Rates include breakfast and evening beverages.

Legendary is the been-there-forever local landmark, the 🅼 **Babbling Brook Inn** (1025 Laurel St., 831/427-2437 or 800/866-1131, www .babblingbrookinn.com, $150–300). Once a log cabin, this place was added to and otherwise spruced up by the Countess Florenzo de Chandler. All 13 rooms and suites are quite romantic, with private bathrooms, phones, and TVs. Most are decorated to suggest the works of Old World artists and poets, from Cézanne and Monet to Tennyson. Most also feature a fireplace, private deck, and outside entrance. Two have whirlpool bathtubs. Full breakfast and afternoon wine and cheese (or tea and cookies) are included. Also here: a babbling brook, waterfalls, and a garden gazebo.

For more bed-and-breakfast choices in the greater Santa Cruz area, see the listings below.

DAVENPORT

If you're heading up the coast from Santa Cruz, consider a meal stop or a room with a view at the **Davenport Bed and Breakfast Inn** (31 Davenport Ave./Hwy. 1, 831/425-1818 or 800/870-1817, www.davenportinn.com, $100–150), located in the midst of a vast coastal preserve. The 12 comfortable rooms are located in an adjacent cottage and upstairs, above the New Davenport Cash Store and Restaurant, where the food is very good at breakfast, lunch, and dinner. Rates include full breakfast at the restaurant. Some of the pastries served here are made just up the road at **Whale City Bakery Bar & Grill** (831/423-9803 or 831/429-6209), where the wide variety of homemade treats and very good coffee are always worth a stop.

BEN LOMOND AND FELTON

Nothing fancy, but fine for pine-paneled cabin ambience just five miles north of Santa Cruz, the **Fern River Resort Motel** (5250 Hwy. 9, Felton, 831/335-4412, www.fernriver.com, $50–150, $80 and up in summer) offers 14 cabins with kitchens or kitchenettes, fireplaces, cable TV, and a private beach on the river.

For a bed-and-breakfast stay in Ben Lomond, consider the lovely and woodsy **Fairview Manor** (245 Fairview Ave., 831/336-3355, www.fairview manor.com, $100–150), which features five rooms with private baths, as well as a big deck overlooking the San Lorenzo River. For a super-stylish (and expensive) stay, there's the elegant **Inn at Felton Crest** (780 El Solyo Heights Dr., Felton, tel./fax 831/335-4011 or tel. only 800/474-4011, www.feltoncrest.com, $400 and up), featuring just four guestrooms, each with in-room whirlpool tubs, cable TVs and VCRs, and private baths.

CAPITOLA

A long-standing Capitola jewel is the **Capitola Venetian Hotel** (1500 Wharf Rd., 831/476-6471 or 800/332-2780, www.capitolavenetian.com, $150–250 in high season), California's first condominium complex, built in the 1920s. These clustered, Mediterranean-style stucco apartments are relaxed and relaxing, and close to the beach. In various combinations, rooms have kitchens with stoves and refrigerators, in-room coffeemakers, color TV with cable, and telephones with voicemail and data ports; some have separate living rooms, balconies, ocean views, and fireplaces. Real deals are available in the off-season.

Almost legendary almost overnight, Capitola's 🅼 **Inn at Depot Hill** (250 Monterey Ave., 831/462-3376 or 800/572-2632, www.innatdepothill.com, $250 and up including taxes) is a luxurious bed-and-breakfast (essentially a small luxury hotel) housed in the onetime railroad depot. Each of the eight rooms features its own unique design motif, inspired by international locales (the Delft Room, Stratford-on-Avon, the

Paris Room, and Portofino, for example), as well as a private garden and entrance, fireplace, telephone with modem/fax capability, and state-of-the-art TV/VCR and stereo system. The private white-marble bathrooms feature bathrobes, hair dryers, and other little luxuries. Bathrooms have double showers, so two isn't necessarily a crowd. The pure linen bed sheets are hand-washed and hand-ironed daily. Rates include full breakfast, afternoon tea or wine, and after-dinner dessert. Off-street parking is provided. Inquire about specials and modest off-season discounts. A very special place for very special getaways.

APTOS

The apartment-style **Rio Sands Motel** (116 Aptos Beach Dr., 831/688-3207 or 800/826-2077, www.riosands.com, $150–250 in peak season, $70–150 in winter) has a heated pool, spa, and decent rooms not far from the beach. The "kitchen suites" feature full kitchens and a separate sitting room and sleep up to four. "Super rooms" sleep up to six and include a refrigerator and mi-

crowave. All rooms have two TVs. Extras include the large heated pool, spa, picnic area with barbecue pits, and expanded continental breakfast.

Also a pleasant surprise is the **Best Western Seacliff Inn** (7500 Old Dominion Court, 831/688-7300 or 800/367-2003, www.seacliffinn.com, $150–250), just off the highway. It's a cut or two above the usual motel and an easy stroll to the beach. Rooms are large and comfortable, with private balconies. They cluster village-style around a large outdoor pool and whirlpool tub area. Suites have in-room spas. But the best surprise of all is the restaurant, **Severino's** (831/688-8987), which serves good food both inside the dining room and outside by the koi pond. Great "sunset dinner" specials are served 5–6:30 P.M. Sunday–Thursday.

On the coast, just north of Manresa State Beach, is the luxurious condo-style **Seascape Resort Monterey Bay** (1 Seascape Resort Dr., 831/688-6800 or 800/929-7727,www.seascaperesort.com, $250 and up, two-night minimum late May–Sept.). Choices here include tasteful studios and one- and two-bedroom villas. You'll

Capitola, south of Santa Cruz

also find a restaurant, golf course, tennis courts, and onsite fitness and spa facilities.

For a bed-and-breakfast stay, the historic **N Sand Rock Farm** (6901 Freedom Blvd., 831/688-8005, www.sandrockfarm.com, $150–250) offers a huge, exquisitely restored, turn-of-the-20th-century, Craftsman-style home—complete with original push-button light switches. The 10-acre setting includes country gardens, walking trails, and the ruins of the old Liliencrantz family winery. Open since fall 2000, Sand Rock features five guestrooms and suites with in-room whirlpool tubs, cable TV, VCRs, and private baths, plus a lounge, fireplace, hot tub, and room service. Well-informed foodies will make a beeline to Sand Rock strictly for the wondrous breakfasts and winemaker dinners created by famed Chef Lynn Sheehan.

Historic Victoriana in Aptos includes the **Apple Lane Inn** (6265 Soquel Dr., 831/475-6868 or 800/649-8988, www.applelaneinn.com, $100–250). Also quite nice, and near Forest of Nisene Marks State Park, is the newly restored and redecorated **Bayview Hotel Bed and Breakfast Inn** (8041 Soquel Dr., 831/688-8654 or 800/422-9843, www.bayviewhotel.com, $100–150), an 1878 Italianate Victorian hotel with new owners and 12 elegant guestrooms, all with private baths and some with fireplaces and two-person tubs. Rooms also feature TVs, telephones, and modem hookups.

Food

FARM TRAILS AND MARKETS

To do Santa Cruz area farm trails, pick up a copy of the *Country Crossroads* map and brochure, a joint venture with Santa Clara County row-crop farmers and orchardists. It's the essential guide for hunting down strawberries, raspberries, apples, and homegrown veggies of all kinds. Or head for the local farmers markets. The **Santa Cruz Community Certified Farmers Market** (831/454-0566, 2:30–6:30 P.M. Wed.) is held downtown at Lincoln and Cedar. There are many other markets in the area; inquire at the visitors center for a current listing.

Everyone's favorite family-run grocery since 1938 is **Shopper's Corner** (622 Soquel Ave., 831/423-1398), where you can get regular and special grocery items, including fresh local produce (even organic fruits and vegetables), 150 kinds of cheeses, and locally baked breads and pastries. There's an old-time butcher shop, fresh fish and seafood, and a huge selection of wines, too, including just about every Santa Cruz Mountain wine you can imagine. For natural foods specifically, try **Staff of Life** (1305 Water St., 831/423-8632) or the **New Leaf Community Market** (1134 Pacific Ave., 831/425-1793).

VEGETARIAN

The **N Saturn Cafe** (downtown at 145 Laurel St., 831/429-8505, lunch and dinner daily) has inexpensive ($8 or less) and wonderful vegetarian and vegan meals for lunch, dinner, and beyond. If you're low on cash but really hungry, come midday (11:30 A.M.–5 P.M.) for the Cheap Eats Menu: lots of substantial, healthy choices for $5 or so. Open until late for desserts and coffee. Theme days here can be a scream. During Monday Madness, the decadent favorite, Chocolate Madness, sells at two for the price of one. Random Tuesdays (on random Tuesdays) showcase live local music. On Wig Out Wednesday, just wear a wig, and you'll get 20 percent off your tab. Such a deal. Also good for a quick vegetarian bite downtown is the Sri Lankan **Asian Rose Café** (1547 Pacific Ave., 831/458-3023); the main restaurant is on Soquel Avenue. **Erik's DeliCafe** (712 Front St.) is a local favorite for fresh, homemade soups and other good food—veggie choices, too—which explains why there are so many Erik's outlets in the greater Santa Cruz area.

But for "natural fast foods," and large portions you can savor guilt-free because it's healthy, don't miss **Dharma's Natural Foods Restaurant** (4250 Capitola Rd., Capitola, 831/462-

OUTSTANDING IN THE FIELD

Outstanding in the field of foodie tourism is **Outstanding in the Field** (877/886-7409, www.outstandinginthefield.com), a hugely popular food, wine, and farm experience originally served up by Chef Jim Denevan of the Gabriella Café in Santa Cruz. Local organic farmers and winemakers joyfully get together with visiting chefs—some of Northern and Central California's most honored—to create unique regional dining events that combine a personal farm tour with a spectacular multicourse meal.

The inviting, well-laden tables—yes, the tables are "outstanding": standing out in the farmer's field, that is—become the "meeting place between the sky and the soil." The family-style, four- to six-course meal, complete with a wine selected to accompany each course, salutes the land from which the bounty comes. Just for fun, dinner guests are encouraged to bring their own plates, especially plates that come with their own stories, as an icebreaker. All dinnerware is washed and returned by meal's end.

1717). You can feast on a Brahma Burger, Dharma Dog, or Nuclear Sub sandwich—baked tofu, guacamole, cheese, lettuce, olives, pickle, and secret sauce on a roll. Darma's has a wide selection of vegan dishes and a long list of organic ingredients.

INEXPENSIVE FARE DOWNTOWN

Unforgettable for breakfast or lunch is funky **Aldo's,** also Aldo's Bait & Tackle (616 Atlantic Ave., at the west end of the yacht harbor, 831/426-3736). The breakfast menu features various egg and omelette combinations. Best of all, though, is the raisin toast, made with Aldo's homemade focaccia bread. Eat outdoors on the old picnic tables covered with checkered plastic tablecloths and enjoy the sun, sea air, and seagulls. At lunch and dinner, look for homemade pastas and fresh fish. The place for the peoples' seafood is laid-back **Riva Fish House** (at the wharf, 831/429-1223).

Santa Cruz's classic **Jack's Hamburgers** (downtown at 202 Lincoln St., 831/423-4421, lunch and dinner daily) serves good 'n' juicy ones, not to mention great chocolate shakes and surprisingly good chocolate cake. A good late-night stop is the **Santa Cruz Diner** (909 Ocean St., 831/426-7151).

There are endless possibilities downtown. Absolutely wonderful is **Zoccoli's Delicatessen** (1534 Pacific Ave., 831/423-1711, 9 A.M.–5:30 P.M. Mon.–Sat.), where it's common to see people lining up for sandwiches, salads, fresh homemade pastas, and genuine "good deal" lunch specials, usually under $5 or $6. Legendary for breakfast, nearby **Zachary's** (819 Pacific Ave., 831/427-0646, breakfast and lunch daily) serves sourdough pancakes with real maple syrup, whole-grain cereals, and massive omelettes and scrambles. Mike's Mess will overwhelm even the heartiest of collegiate appetites. Weekend tip: Get here very early for breakfast, 7–8 A.M., or be prepared for a wait.

Another great local breakfast place is cozy, coffee shop–style **Walnut Avenue Café** (106 Walnut Ave. between Pacific and Cedar), 831/457-2307, breakfast and lunch daily), where you get a mountain of fresh, wholesome food for a reasonable price—everything from fluffy nine-grain pancakes to eggs Benedict, omelettes, and tofu scrambles. Grand lattes, too. Also particularly

Zoccoli's Delicatessen

great at breakfast is **Café Brasil** (116 Kalkar Dr., 831/429-1855), north of High Street and east of the university campus. They serve the real deal from way south of the border—from the Brazilian (chicken and creamed corn) omelette to the *feijoada* and *Orfeu negro*. Great chai, too. Try to bike it there if you can, since parking nearby is next to impossible.

A great choice for fast-food Mexican inside the UC Extension building is **Taqueria Vallarta** (1101 Pacific Ave., 831/471-2655, open until midnight), complete with neo-Aztec murals. It's all good, from the fresh snapper or roasted pork tacos to the red beans and burritos. Another great cheap-eats stop is **Tacos Moreno** (1053 Water St., 831/429-6095), a Santa Cruz favorite for two decades and counting for its *al pastor* barbecued pork and cabbage burritos, chile verde tacos, vegetarian favorites, quesadillas, and more. You can't miss it at lunchtime, what with the line of eager customers snaking down the street. **Planet Fresh Burritos** (1003 Cedar St., 831/423-9799) is another possibility.

The **Santa Cruz Coffee Roasting Company** (1330 Pacific Ave., 831/459-0100), at the Palomar Inn, serves excellent free-trade coffee and a bistro-style café lunch.

The Crepe Place (1134 Soquel Ave., west of Seabright, 831/429-6994, lunch and dinner daily, plus weekend brunch) offers inexpensive breakfasts, dessert crêpes (and every other kind), good but unpretentious lunches, and dinners into the wee hours—a great place for late-night dining. Great garden patio, too. The **Seabright Brewery** brewpub (519 Seabright Ave., Ste. 107, 831/426-2739) is popular for its Seabright Amber and Pelican Pale, not to mention casual dining out on the patio. If you're heading toward Boulder Creek, beer fans, stop by the **Boulder Creek Brewery and Cafe** (13040 Hwy. 9, 831/338-7882).

HIGH-END FARE DOWNTOWN

Downtown Santa Cruz is getting pretty uptown these days. ◪ **Gabriella Café** (910 Cedar St., 831/457-1677, lunch and dinner daily, plus weekend brunch), made famous by Chef Jim Denevan's Outstanding in the Field organic farm tours and dinners, is a long-running romantic

favorite. The seasonally changing menu is a cornucopia of dishes made from locally grown organic fruits and vegetables, other area farm products, and the freshest fish and seafood—from corn fritters with Nova smoked salmon crab cakes to the truffle gnocchi. Desserts are the stuff of local legend, too. Double chocolate torte, anyone? Great wine list.

Intimate **Oswald's** (1547 Pacific Ave. near Cedar, 831/423-7427) is another stylish local favorite, serving innovative California cuisine crafted from the freshest seafood, meats, and local produce. Fashionable yet eclectic is the fun **Pearl Alley Bistro** (110 Pearl Alley at Cedar, between Lincoln and Walnut, 831/429-8070, dinner daily), where the monthly changing menu might include zucchini parmigiana and Mongolian barbecue, with your choice of fresh meats and veggies, or corned beef pasties, chicken and buttermilk-biscuit pie, or Smithfield ham. Full bar. Everybody's favorite for sophisticated Chinese is **O'mei** (2316 Mission St. at King, 831/425-8458), whether it's the apricot-almond chicken, lychee pork, or gan pung chicken. And don't miss the toasted coconut ice cream. Sushi-lovers, locals say *the* place is **Mobo Sushi** (105 S. River St., east of Front, 831/429-8070).

El Palomar (1336 Pacific Ave., 831/425-7575, breakfast, lunch, and dinner daily), at the Pacific Garden Mall, is a winner for sit-down Mexican meals, and especially good for seafood. It's just about everybody's top choice for south-of-the-border fare, starting with oysters on the half shell topped with salsa fresca or the seafood appetizer plate, and continuing through entrées such as prawn burritos and enchiladas, charbroiled red snapper with guacamole and tomatillo salsa, and tostadas de ceviche. Full bar. At the yacht harbor, you'll find **Café El Palomar** (2222 E. Cliff Dr., 831/462-4248, 7 A.M.–5 P.M. daily).

Charming for patio dining, thanks to that three-story "Old World" mural, is **Ristorante Italiano** (555 Soquel Ave., 831/458-2321, lunch and dinner daily), in the Branciforte Plaza, everyone's favorite for both traditional and more innovative Italian selections. Surprises include *cacciuco,* or Italian seafood and fish stew in marinara sauce, and prawns Parma. "Light and early"

NEWMAN'S OWN SANTA CRUZ

Not Paul Newman, but the other one—**Nell Newman,** Cool Hand Luke's daughter—is the farm-loving Santa Cruz resident posing with the famed actor on all those tongue-in-cheek, stylized, *American Gothic* **Newman's Own Organics** (www.newmansownorganics.com) product labels. And how appropriate, since it was a father and daughter so stoically represented in the original *American Gothic*.

Formerly a biologist with the Ventana Wilderness Sanctuary Research and Education Center down the coast in Big Sur, Nell Newman is an accomplished cook, who, in 1993, was inspired by the Santa Cruz area's love affair with whole foods to add an organics division to her father's popular company, Newman's Own.

The point of Newman's Own Organics is pro-ducing "good-tasting food that just happens to be organic." Early on, the brand has focused on what might be considered the inessentials—snack foods, including chocolate bars, tortilla chips, pretzels, Pop's Corn, and several cookie varieties, from Fig Newmans to Oreo-like Newman-O's. Look for organic premium pet foods, too, and fair-trade coffee.

Like the first generation of Newman's Own, Newman's Own Organics—the second generation—donates 100 percent of after-tax profits to charitable causes. These have included the University of California Santa Cruz Farm and Garden Project, the Organic Farming Research Foundation, the Henry A. Wallace Institute for Alternative Agriculture, and the Western Environmental Law Center in Taos, New Mexico.

---

dinners are served 5–6:30 P.M. Everyone's favorite trattoria is **Caffè Bella Napoli** (503 Water St., 831/426-7401, lunch and dinner daily).

For romantic Bavarian cuisine, the place is **Casablanca Restaurant** (101 Main St. at Beach, 831/426-9063, dinner nightly, Sun. brunch). For fine dining farther afield: The historic 1929 **Hollins House** (20 Clubhouse Dr., 831/459-9177, dinner 5:30–8:30 P.M. Wed.–Sat.), at Pasatiempo Golf Club—where the renowned course was designed by Alister MacKenzie—is a destination in its own right, just the place for an exquisitely prepared dinner in a clubby atmosphere. For something simpler, consider breakfast or lunch at the **MacKenzie Bar & Grill** (next to the pro shop, 831/459-9162, dawn–dusk daily).

FELTON, BEN LOMOND, AND BOULDER CREEK

The **White Raven** bookshop (6253 Hwy. 9, Felton, 831/335-3611) is also a cool coffee and pastry stop. At the charmingly retro **La Bruschetta** Italian roadhouse, in the Felton Guild hall (5447 Hwy 9, 831/335-3337, breakfast, lunch, and dinner daily), specialty pastas, such as gnocchi in pomodoro sauce and agnolotti alla ragusana, are the stars. The been-there-forever **Trout Farm**

Inn (7701 E. Zayante Rd., 831/335-4317, lunch and dinner Tues.–Sun.) is serving good, solid surf and turf these days, such as trout almandine and sea scallops with artichoke heart. Your best bet for a wholesome, hearty, sit-down breakfast and lunch is the **Blue Sun Café** (13070 Hwy. 9, 831/338-2105), down the road in Boulder Creek. Ben Lomond's **Tyrolean Inn** (9600 Hwy. 9, 831/336-5188) serves good traditional German fare.

SOQUEL

Quite reasonable for impressive quantities of very good, very fresh fast food, kid-friendly **Carpo's** diner (2400 Porter St., 831/476-6260) is beloved for such things as shrimp and crab sandwiches, great burgers and fries (or onion rings), seafood and bell pepper kebabs, and broiled salmon. For dessert, try the ollallieberry pie. The way it works here: Place your order at the counter, and they'll give you a vibrating buzzer. When your food's up, you'll get the message. Carpo's is immensely popular, so come at off times if at all possible. Also a pretty good deal for families is **Little Tampico** (2605 Main St., 831/475-4700), which offers a daily lunch special and an all-you-can-eat taco and tostada bar at lunch for $5–6. A good value at dinner is the specialty Otila's Plate, a mini-taco, enchilada, tostada, and taquito, plus rice and beans, for just over $10. Another good choice: nachos with everything. If you miss this one, various Tampico restaurant relatives dot the county.

A tad fancier is lively **Café Cruz** rosticceria and bar (2621 41st Ave., 831/476-3801), which also emphasizes fresh food, including local produce. At lunch, sandwiches include such things as a grilled prawn club sandwich and the Cruz burger, made with Bradley Ranch natural beef. At dinner, expect the grilled gulf prawns, arugula, and strawberry salad, baby spinach and three-cheese ravioli, honey-cured smoked rotisserie chicken, and Harris Ranch New York steak. Children's menu, too.

Top of the food chain in these parts is **M Theo's** (3101 N. Main St., 831/462-3657, dinner from 5:30 P.M. Tues.–Sat.), where you might start with boar sausage–stuffed cabbage and sail on through Maine lobster pot pie, house-smoked wild salmon, or slow-roasted Sonoma duckling. Spectacular desserts, good wine list. Great winemakers' dinners, too.

CAPITOLA

Dharma's Natural Foods Restaurant (4250 Capitola Rd., 831/462-1717, breakfast, lunch, and dinner daily), a Santa Cruz institution, is purported to be the oldest completely vegetarian restaurant in the country. Also classic in Capitola is **Pizza-My-Heart** (209-A Esplanade, 831/475-5714).

Casual, in a more upscale style, and unbeatable for pastries and decadent desserts is **M Gayle's Bakery and Rosticceria** (504 Bay Ave., 831/462-1200, 7 A.M.–7 P.M. daily). The rosticceria has a wonderful selection of salads and homemade pastas, soups, sandwiches, pizza, spit-roasted meats—even dinners to go and heat-and-serve casseroles. But the aromas drifting in from Gayle's Bakery are the real draw. The bakery's breakfast pastries include various cheese danishes, croissants, chocolatine, lemon tea bread, muffins, pecan rolls, apple-nut turnovers, and such specialties as a schnecken ring smothered in walnuts. The apple crumb

and ollalieberry pies are unforgettable, not to mention the praline cheesecake and the two dozen other cakes: chocolate mousse, hazelnut, raspberry, poppy seed, mocha. . . . (All pies and cakes are also served by the slice.) For decadence to go, try Grand Marnier truffles, florentines, eclairs, or Napoleons. Gayle's also sells more than two dozen types of fresh-baked bread. The Capitola sourdough bread and sour baguette would be good for picnics, as would the two-pound loaf of the excellent Pain de Campagne. If you're heading toward the bay or San Jose the back way via Corralitos, stop by the **Corralitos Market and Sausage Co.** (569 Corralitos Rd., 831/722-2633) for homemade sausages, smoke-cured ham and turkey breast, or other specialty meats—all great with Gayle's breads.

Near the beach, on or near the Esplanade, you'll find an endless variety of eateries. **Margaritaville** (312 Esplanade, 831/476-2263, lunch and dinner daily, plus weekend brunch) serves appetizers and sandwiches and all kinds of Mexican fare, along with its margaritas. The **Paradise Beach Grill** (215 Esplanade, 831/476-4900, lunch and dinner daily) offers California cuisine, as well as a variety of international dishes. Great views. Also serving California cuisine is **Zelda's on the Beach** (203 Esplanade, 831/475-4900), which features an affordable lobster special on Thursday night.

The most famous restaurant in Capitola is the **Shadowbrook Restaurant** (1750 Wharf Rd. at Capitola Rd., 831/475-1511), known for its romantic garden setting—ferns, roses, ivy outside, a Monterey pine and plants inside—and the tram ride down the hill to Soquel Creek. The Shadowbrook is open for "continental-flavored American" dinners nightly. The wine list is extensive. Brunch, with choices like apple and cheddar omelettes, is served on weekends. Reservations recommended.

APTOS

For stylish and fresh Mexican food, the place is **Palapas** (at Seascape Village on Seascape Boulevard, 831/662-9000, lunch and dinner daily, plus Sun. brunch). For stylish, all-American comfort food—meat loaf, homemade chicken soup, boysenberry cobbler—the place is the **Bleu Spoon** bistro (207 Sea Ridge Rd., 831/685-8654). If you're out to dent your pocketbook, the  **Bittersweet Bistro** (787 Rio Del Mar Blvd., 831/662-9799) offers Mediterranean-inspired bistro fare, featuring fresh local and organic produce—everything from Greek pizzettas and seafood puttanesca to garlic chicken and grilled Monterey Bay king salmon.

Entertainment and Events

For an introduction to local galleries, go to the visitors council and request the self-guided **Gallery Walk** tour map of downtown Santa Cruz, which will also guide you to coffeehouses and unusual shops. (Come on the first Fri. of each month for the Gallery Walk as an evening event.)

FILM

Santa Cruz has more than its fair share of good movie theaters and film series. The historic 1936 **Del Mar Theatre** (1124 Pacific Ave., 831/469-3220) has been lovingly renovated and now shows great art house and independent films. Come to the Del Mar for the annual **Santa Cruz Film Festival** (www.santacruzfilmfestival.com), where Bernard Shakey—aka Neil Young—showed up for the benefit debut of his film *Greendale.* If it's not playing at the Del Mar, then it's probably at the associated **Nickelodeon Theatre** (210 Lincoln St., 831/426-7500). Pretty darned hip for flicks, too, is the **Rio Theatre for the Performing Arts** (1205 Soquel Ave., 831/423-8209, www.riotheatre.com), which also stages live performances. For what's playing where at a glance, scan local entertainment papers or see www.thenick.com.

NIGHTLIFE

If you're into big-band swing, check out **Cocoanut Grove** dances (831/423-5590, www.beachboardwalk.com, $15 and up). **The Kuumbwa Jazz Center** (320-2 Cedar St. #2, 831/427-2227, www.kuumbwajazz.com) is a no-booze, no-cigarettes, under-21-welcome place with great jazz (often big names), and it's rarely packed. Most shows are Monday and Friday at 8 P.M.; ticket prices vary and are often low. The **Catalyst** (1011 Pacific Ave., 831/423-1336) is legendary for its Friday afternoon happy hour in the Atrium—seems like *everybody's* here from 4:30 to 7 P.M., drinking beer, making the scene, and sometimes tapping their toes to the house band, Wally's Swing World, or groups like REO Haywagon. The 700-seat theater (massive dance floor) hosts good local bands or national acts nightly (cover charge). Wednesday is Dollar Night, and a buck will get you three new bands in the mainstage back room, plus DJed dancing in the Atrium out front. Other area clubs, hotspots for younger unknown bands, include the **Aptos**

MELISSA SHEROWSKI

the performing arts complex at UC Santa Cruz

Club (7941 Soquel Dr. in Aptos, 831/688-9888) and the **Mediterranean Club** (265 Center Ave., 831/688-9840), near Seacliff Beach. Local coffeehouses from Santa Cruz to Capitola also offer casual, relaxed, and sometimes highbrow entertainment (like poetry readings).

PERFORMING ARTS

On a smaller scale, local performing arts are always an adventure. The **Santa Cruz Chamber Players** (831/425-3149 for performance schedule) specialize in both traditional and modern chamber music, with an emphasis on the unusual. The **Santa Cruz County Symphony** (200 Seventh Ave., Ste. 225, 831/462-0553) schedules performances year-round at both the Santa Cruz Civic Auditorium and Watsonville's Mello Center.

The noted **Tandy Beal & Company** dance troupe (740 Front St., Ste. 300-B, 831/429-1324) performs locally when not touring internationally. The **Santa Cruz Ballet Theatre** (2800 S. Rodeo Gulch Rd., Soquel, 831/479-1600) is a good bet for a year-end production of *The Nutcracker.* **Santa Cruz County Actors' Theatre** (1001 Center St., 831/425-1003, www.sccat.org) schedules live stage productions year-round. In Capitola, the Quonset hut–housed Capitola Theater is now the **Bay Shore Lyric Opera Company and Theater for the Performing Arts** (120 Monterey Ave., 831/462-3131, www.bslopera.com).

For information on what's going on at UCSC, pick up a copy of the quarterly **UCSC Performing Arts Calendar** (http://arts.ucsc.edu), available around town, or call 831/459-2787 (459-ARTS). Other useful campus numbers include Arts and Lectures (831/459-2826), Theatre Arts (831/459-2974), and the Music Department (831/459-2292). To order tickets by phone for a small service charge, call the UCSC Ticket Office (831/459-2159).

EVENTS

For an up-to-date quarterly calendar of city and county events, contact the local visitors council (see *Information and Services,* below). Bike races have prominent local appeal, and professional volleyball competitions are also held year-round. Whale-watching in winter is another popular draw.

For wine-lovers, mid-January features the countywide **Wineries Passport Program** (www.scmwa.com), offering tours, tastings, and

SANTA CRUZ WINERIES

The coastal mountains near Santa Cruz are well known for their redwoods. But since the late 1800s, they have also been known for their vineyards. Regional winemaking is back, helped along since 1981 by the official federal recognition of the Santa Cruz Mountain appellation for wine grapes grown in the region defined by Half Moon Bay in the north and Mount Madonna in the south. More than 40 wineries now produce Santa Cruz Mountain wines.

North of Santa Cruz, the eclectic **Bonny Doon Vineyard** (10 Pine Flat Rd., 831/425-4518, www.bonnydoonvineyard.com, 11 A.M.–5 P.M. daily except holidays for tastings) specializes in Rhône and Italian varietals, though wine-lovers and critics are also smitten with the winery's worldly, witty, and wildly footnoted newsletter (also available online).

Nearby in Felton is the award-winning and historic **Hallcrest Vineyards** (379 Felton Empire Rd., 831/335-4441, 11 A.M.–5:30 P.M. daily), noted for its cabernet sauvignon, chardonnay, merlot, and zinfandel. Call for directions. Hallcrest is also home to **The Organic Wine Works** (800/699-9463), producing the nation's first certified organic wines. Using certified organically grown grapes, the winemaking process is also organic, without the use of sulfites. Also in Felton is the small **Zayante Vineyards** (420 Old Mount Rd., 831/335-7992, open by appointment only).

There are dozens more. For more information about area wineries, including a current wineries map and upcoming events, contact the **Santa Cruz Mountains Winegrowers Association** (7605 Old Dominion Ct., Ste. A, Aptos, 831/479-9463, www.wines.com/santa_cruz_mountains).

open houses at Santa Cruz Mountains wineries (also held in mid-April, mid-July, and mid-November). Mid-month, Santa Cruz celebrates its **Fungus Fair,** always fun for mushroom-lovers.

Cold and very cool in February is the **O'Neill Cold Water Classic** surfing competition, sponsored by Santa Cruz–based O'Neill, Inc., and its legendary founder, Jack O'Neill, inventor of the wetsuit. Also in February, the **Migration Festival** at Natural Bridges State Beach celebrates many migrants, from monarch butterflies and the gray whale to salmon, salamanders, elephant seals, and shorebirds. The decades-long tradition of the **Santa Cruz Baroque Festival** (831/457-9693, www.scbaroque.org) starts in February and continues until May, offering concerts of early music masterworks. Head for the boardwalk in late February for the annual **Clam Chowder Cook-Off.**

Come in March for the free annual **Jazz on the Wharf** festival, which serenades Monterey Bay from the Santa Cruz Municipal Wharf and its restaurants, and for the **Santa Cruz Kayak Surf Festival,** the world's largest. In mid- to late March, Felton holds its **Great Train Robberies** festival, followed by the **Amazing Egg Hunt,** usually in April. Memorial Day weekend brings the annual **Civil War Reenactment** at Roaring Camp.

May is big for art, wine, and music, starting with **Celebrate Santa Cruz Art, Wine & Jazz** in downtown Santa Cruz and continuing with the **Boulder Creek Art, Wine & Music Festival.** Also fun in May: **Bug Day** at Henry Cowell Redwoods State Park in Felton. Come in June for the **We Carnival Street Parade and World Music Festival,** and on July 4 for Aptos's **World's Shortest Parade.**

The acclaimed and innovative **Shakespeare Santa Cruz** festival (831/459-2121 for info, 831/459-2159 for tickets, www.shakespearesantacruz.org) runs mid-July through August in an outdoor theater in the redwoods at UCSC. The very fast **Santa Cruz to Capitola Wharf-to-Wharf Race** (831/475-2196, www.wharftowharf.com) in late July is a major event for runners,

with more than half the applicants turned away due to the event's immense popularity—a popularity fueled by the $12,000 total prize purse.

After 20-some years, the famed August **Cabrillo Music Festival** (831/426-6966 or 831/420-5260 for ticket reservations from late June, www.cabrillomusic.org)—described by *The New Yorker* as one of the most adventurous and attractive in America—is still going strong, with performances at UC Santa Cruz, Mission San Juan Bautista, and Watsonville. Make your plans well in advance. Another possibility in August is the **Musical Saw Festival** at Roaring Camp in Felton—not classical, but definitely a gas.

The first couple of weeks in September, Capitola's **Begonia Festival** (www.begoniafestival.com) includes several big events, including a sandcastle contest and a nautical parade. It's followed (and nearly overshadowed) in mid-September by the city's annual **Art & Wine Festival,** which has become incredibly popular. On three weekends in October, come for the countywide artists' **Open Studios,** with open-house art shows held everywhere, from private homes and studios to galleries and museums. It's wonderful exposure for artists and a great pleasure for aficionados. At last report, the first Open Studios weekend emphasized north-county artists; the second weekend, south-county artists; and the final weekend was an encore. For more information, contact the Cultural Council of Santa Cruz County (831/475-9600, www.ccscc.org/openstudios.htm). Each year's program/artist guide is available in September.

In late November, look for Felton's **Mountain Man Rendezvous** and the **Christmas Craft and Gift Festival** at the boardwalk's Cocoanut Grove. In December, Felton sponsors its **Holiday Lights Train** Christmas festivities.

For more information on many of the above festivals, contact the downtown **Santa Cruz County Conference and Visitors Council,** (1211 Ocean St., 831/425-1234 or 800/833-3494, www.santacruzca.org).

Santa Cruz

Shopping

For more shopping ideas, contact the **Downtown Association of Santa Cruz** (831/429-1512, www.downtownsantacruz.com) and the **Santa Cruz County Conference and Visitors Council** (1211 Ocean St., 831/425-1234 or 800/833-3494, www.santacruzca.org).

CLOTHES

Clothing shops abound along Pacific Avenue, including **The Vault** (1339 Pacific Ave., 831/426-3349), noted for unique jewelry and clothing, and **Eco Goods** (1130 Pacific Ave., 831/429-5758), "an alternative general store offering organic, recycled, and non-toxic products at affordable prices"—everything from organic cotton underwear and hemp backpacks to handcrafted maple bedroom sets. **Madame Sidecar** (907 Cedar St., 831/458-1606) offers distinctive style in quality women's clothing, lingerie, jewelry, and accessories inspired by flattering 1930s and 1940s fashions. Downtown also boasts thrift and vintage clothing shops. **Cognito Clothing** (821 Pacific, 831/426-5414) sells such things as swing dance fashions, two-toned panel shirts, and Hawaiian shirts. Another good bet is **The Wardrobe** (113 Locust St., 831/429-6363).

BOOKS AND MUSIC

There are plenty of bookstores, too, including the classic **Bookshop Santa Cruz** (1520 Pacific Ave., 831/423-0900, www.bookshopsantacruz.com), a community institution that offers a full calendar of author and reader events. Downtown also draws music fans, to **Rhythm Fusion** (1541 Pacific, 831/423-2048) and **Union Grove Music** (1003 Pacific, 831/427-0670).

HOUSEWARES

Santa Cruz County is marvelous for locally made wares—some almost affordable. Barbra Streisand and Oprah Winfrey are among the national fans of Santa Cruz's **Annieglass** (109 Cooper St., 831/427-4260, www.annieglass.com). Translucent sculptural glass dinnerware with fused metal rims, Annieglass comes in various styles, including Roman antique gold or platinum. For a large selection of strictly local wares, including **Strini Art Glass,** head for the Santa Cruz Wharf and **Made in Santa Cruz** (831/426-2257 or 800/982-2367, www.madeinsantacruz.com). Here you'll find everything from art glass, ceramics, and sculpture—check out the struttin' teapots—to soap, salsa, and jewelry.

For a truly unique housewarming gift, head for **West Coast Weather Vanes** in Bonny Doon (831/425-5505 or 800/762-8736 in U.S. only), a company where artisans carefully craft—without molds—copper and brass weather vanes in the Victorian tradition. Visitors are welcome by appointment.

MADE IN SANTA CRUZ

It should surprise no one that the Santa Cruz area's creativity is also expressed in fine arts and crafts. **Lundberg Studios** in Davenport is noted for its luminescent blue "worldweights"—globe-styled paperweights that have been presented to various luminaries. Another star is **Annieglass**, featuring handcrafted sculptural glass dinnerware designed by artist Ann Morhauser: everyday, dishwasher-safe "art for the table" sought out by celebrities, including Barbra Streisand and Oprah Winfrey. **West Coast Weather Vanes** is famed for its custom handcrafted American folk art copper and brass weather vanes. The **Santa Cruz Guitar Co.** is at the forefront of modern guitar-making, famous for its acoustic guitars.

Santa Cruz

Information and Services

The best all-around source for city and county information is the **Santa Cruz County Conference and Visitors Council** (1211 Ocean St., 831/425-1234 or 800/833-3494, www.santacruzca.org, 9 A.M.–5 P.M. Mon.–Sat., 10 A.M.–4 P.M. Sun.). Definitely request the current accommodations, dining, and visitor guides. If you've got time to roam farther afield, also pick up a current copy of the *County Crossroads* farm trails map and ask about area wineries. Cyclists, request the *Santa Cruz County Bikeway Map.* Antiquers, ask for the current *Antiques, Arts, & Collectibles* directory for Santa Cruz and Monterey Counties, published every June—not a complete listing, by far, but certainly a good start. If you once were familiar with Santa Cruz and now find yourself lost (post–1989 earthquake), pick up the *Downtown Santa Cruz Directory* brochure.

PUBLICATIONS

A valuable source of performing arts information, focused on the university, is the *UCSC Performing Arts Calendar,* published quarterly and available all around town. The excellent UC Santa Cruz paper, *City on a Hill* (http://slugwire.ucsc.edu), is published only during the regular school year. *Metroactive Santa Cruz* (www.metroactive.com/cruz) is the noteworthy local alternative newspaper, and a good source for local goings-on. *Santa Cruz Good Times* (www.gdtimes.com) is a good, long-running free weekly with an entertainment guide and sometimes entertaining political features. The free *Student Guide* comes out seasonally, offering lots of ads and some entertaining reading about Santa Cruz. The *Santa Cruz County Sentinel* (www.santacruzsentinel.com) and the *Watsonville Register-Pajaronian* (www.register-pajaronian.com) are the traditional area papers. The **Santa Cruz Parks and Recreation Department** (831/420-5270) usually publishes a *Summer Activity Guide,* especially useful for advance planning.

Other useful stops in Santa Cruz include the post office (850 Front St., 831/426-5200, 8 A.M.–5 P.M. Mon.–Fri.) and the **Santa Cruz Public Library** (224 Church St., 831/420-5700). If you want to hobnob with the people on the hill, visit the **Dean McHenry Library** (831/459-4000) on campus.

ROARING CAMP AND BIG TREES RAILROAD

F. Norman Clark, the self-described "professional at oddities" who also owns the narrow-gauge railroad in Felton, bought the Southern Pacific rails connecting Santa Cruz and nearby Olympia to make it possible for visitors to get to Henry Cowell Redwoods State Park and Felton (*almost* to Big Basin) by train. During logging's commercial heyday here in the 1900s, 20 or more trains passed over these tracks every day.

Today, you can still visit Roaring Camp and ride the rails on one of two different trips. Hop aboard a 100-year-old steam engine and make an hour-and-fifteen-minute loop around a virgin redwood forest ($18 general, $12 kids age 3–12), or take a 1940s-vintage passenger train from Felton down to Santa Cruz (round-trip fare $20 general, $15 kids age 3–12). Parking is $6. The year-round calendar of special events includes October's **Harvest Faire** and the **Halloween Ghost Train,** the **Mountain Man Rendezvous** living history encampment in November, and December's **Holiday Lights Train.**

The railroad offers daily runs (usually just one train a day on non-summer weekdays) from spring through November, and operates only on weekends and major holidays in winter. For more information, contact Roaring Camp and Big Trees Narrow-Gauge Railroad (831/335-4484, www.roaringcamp.com). For advance tickets to the popular Ghost Train and the Holiday Lights Train, call the Blue & Gold Fleet's TeleSails (415/705-5555 or 888/253-83687).

GETTING AROUND

Bicyclists will be in hog heaven in Santa Cruz, with everything from excellent bike lanes to locking bike racks at bus stops. But drivers, be warned: Parking can be impossible, especially in summer, and especially at the beach. There's a charge for parking at the boardwalk (in lots with attendants) and metered parking elsewhere. Best bet: Park elsewhere and take the shuttle. Second best: Drive to the beach, unload passengers and beach paraphernalia, then park a mile or so away. By the time you walk back, your companions should be done battling for beach towel space. You can usually find free parking on weekends in the public garage at the county government center (701 Ocean St.).

The **Santa Cruz Metro** (230 Walnut Ave., 831/425-8600, www.scmtd.com) provides superb public transit throughout the northern Monterey Bay area, including bus service to the beach, mission, lighthouse, university, and even nearby burgs, including Bonny Doon. The Metro has a "bike and ride" service for bicyclists who want to hitch a bus ride partway (bike racks on board). Call for current route information or pick up a free copy of the excellent *Headways* (which includes Spanish translations). Buses will get you anywhere you want to go in town and considerably beyond for $1.50 ($4.50 for an all-day pass)—exact change only.

Metro buses can get you to Boulder Creek, Big Basin State Park, Ben Lomond, Felton, north coast beaches, *almost* all the way to Año Nuevo State Reserve (just across the San Mateo County line), and to south coast beaches and towns. (**Monterey-Salinas Transit** from Watsonville provides good service in Monterey County.)

You can rent a car from **Enterprise Rent-A-Car** (1025-B Water St., 831/426-7799 or 800/325-8007); **Avis** (630 Ocean St., 831/423-1244 or 800/831-2847); or **Budget** (919 Ocean St., 831/429-6612 or 800/527-0700). **Yellow Cab** is at 131 Front St., 831/423-1234, also home to the **Santa Cruz Airporter,** 831/423-1214 or in California 800/497-4997, which provides shuttle van service to both the San Francisco and San Jose Airports, as well as to *Caltrain* and the Amtrak station in San Jose.

North of Santa Cruz

Travelers heading north toward San Francisco via Highway 1 will discover Año Nuevo State Reserve, breeding ground for the northern elephant seal—it's quite popular, so don't expect to just drop by—and two delightful hostels housed in former lighthouses. Not far from Año Nuevo, as the crow flies, is spectacular Big Basin Redwoods State Park, California's first state park, and other spectacular redwood parks.

AÑO NUEVO STATE RESERVE

About 20 miles north of Santa Cruz and just across the county line is the 4,000-acre Año Nuevo State Reserve, breeding ground and rookery for sea lions and seals—particularly the unusual (and once nearly extinct) northern elephant seal. The pendulous proboscis of a "smiling" two- to three-ton alpha bull dangles down like a fire hose, so the name is apt.

At first glance, the windswept and cold seaward stretch of Año Nuevo seems almost desolate and inhospitable to life. This is far from the truth, however. Año Nuevo is the only place in the world where people can get off their bikes or the bus or get out of their cars and walk out among aggressive, wild northern elephant seals in their natural habitat. Especially impressive is that first glimpse of hundreds of these huge seals nestled like World War II torpedoes among the sand dunes. A large number of other animal and plant species also consider this area home; to better appreciate the ecologically fascinating animal and plant life of the entire area, read *The Natural History of Año Nuevo,* by Burney J. Le Boeuf and Stephanie Kaza.

California poppies explode in bloom on the hillsides of Año Nuevo State Reserve.

Northern Elephants Seals

Hunted almost to extinction for their oil-rich blubber, northern elephant seals numbered only 20 to 100 at the turn of the 20th century. All these survivors lived on Isla de Guadalupe, off the west coast of Baja California. Their descendants eventually began migrating north to California. In the 1950s, a few arrived at Año Nuevo Island, attracted to its rocky safety. The first pup was born on the island in the 1960s. By 1975, the mainland dunes had been colonized by seals crowded off the island rookery, and the first pup was born onshore. By 1988, 800 northern elephant seals had been born on the mainland, part of a total known population of more than 80,000 and an apparent ecological success story. (Only time will tell, though, since the species' genetic diversity has been eliminated by the swim at the brink of extinction.) Though Año Nuevo was the first northern elephant seal rookery established on the California mainland, northern elephant

seals are now establishing colonies elsewhere along the state coastline.

Mating Season

Male northern elephant seals start arriving in December. Who arrives first and who remains dominant among the males during the long mating season is important, because the alpha bull gets to breed with most of the females. Since the males are biologically committed to conserving their energy for sex, they spend much of their time lying about as if dead, in or out of the water, often not even breathing for stretches of up to a half hour. Not too exciting for spectators. But when two males battle each other for the "alpha" title, the loud, often bloody, nose-to-nose battles are something to see. Arching up with heads back and canine teeth ready to tear flesh, the males bellow and bark and bang their chests together.

In January, the females start to arrive, ready to bear offspring conceived the previous year. They give birth to their pups within the first few days of their arrival. The males continue to wage war, the successful alpha bull now frantically trying to protect his harem of 50 or so females from marauders. For every two pounds in body weight a pup gains, its mother loses a pound. Within 28 days, she loses about half her weight, then, almost shriveled, she leaves. Her pup, about 60 pounds at birth, weighs 300 to 500 pounds a month later. Although inseminated by the bull before leaving the rookery, the emaciated female is in no condition for another pregnancy, so conception is delayed for several months, allowing the female to feed and regain her strength. Then, after an eight-month gestation period, the cycle starts all over again.

Etiquette

The Marine Mammal Act of 1972 prohibits people from harassing or otherwise disturbing these magnificent sea mammals, so be respectful. While walking among the elephant seals, remember that the seemingly sluglike creatures *are* wild beasts and can move as fast as any human across the sand, though for shorter distances. For this reason, keeping a 20-foot minimum distance

Santa Cruz

between you and the seals (especially during the macho mating season) is important. No food or drinks are allowed on the reserve, and nothing in the reserve may be disturbed. The first males often begin to arrive in November, before the official docent-led tours begin, so it's possible to tour the area unsupervised. You can also visit the dunes without a tour guide in spring and summer, when many elephant seals return here to molt.

The reserve's "equal access boardwalk" across the sand makes it possible for wheelchair users to see the seals.

Information and Tours

No pets are allowed, not even if left in your vehicle. Official 2.5-hour guided tours of Año Nuevo begin in mid-December and continue through March, rain or shine, though January and February are the prime months, and reservations are necessary. The reserve is open 8 A.M.–sunset; the day-use parking fee is $6 (hike-ins and bike-ins are free, but you still must pick up a free day-use permit). Tour tickets ($4–8, plus surcharge for credit-card reservations) are available only through ReserveAmerica's Año Nuevo and Hearst Castle reservations line (800/444-4445 or 916/638-5883 for international reservations). Reservations cannot be made before November 1. To take a chance on no-shows, arrive at Año Nuevo before scheduled tours and get on the waiting list. The reserve offers a 1,700-foot-long wheelchair-accessible boardwalk for seal-viewing. There's also a van equipped with a wheelchair lift to transport visitors from the parking lot to the boardwalk; accessible restrooms; and guided walks offered in American Sign Language (by advance reservation). For wheelchair-access reservations (available Dec. 15–Mar. 15), call 650/879-2033, 1–4 P.M. only on Monday, Wednesday, and Friday.

Organized bus excursions, which include walking tour tickets, are available through **San Mateo County Transit** (800/660-4287 or 650/508-6441, www.samtrans.com, call after Nov. 1 for reservations) and **Santa Cruz Metro.** The HI-USA Pigeon Point Hostel, near Año Nuevo, sometimes has extra tickets for hostelers. For more information, contact the Año Nuevo State Reserve office (New Year's Creek Rd., Pescadero, 650/879-0227 for recorded info or 650/879-2025).

ℕ BIG BASIN REDWOODS STATE PARK

California's first state park was established here, about 24 miles up canyon from Santa Cruz on Highway 9. To save Big Basin's towering *Sequoia sempervirens* coast redwoods from loggers, 60-some conservationists, led by Andrew P. Hill, camped at the base of Slippery Rock on May 15, 1900, and formed the Sempervirens Club. Just two years later, in September 1902, 3,800 acres of primeval forest were deeded to the state, the beginning of California's state park system.

Flora and Fauna

Today, Big Basin Redwoods State Park includes more than 18,000 acres on the ocean-facing slopes of the Santa Cruz Mountains, and efforts to protect (and expand) the park still continue under the auspices of the Sempervirens Fund and the Save-the-Redwoods League. (Donations are always welcome.) Tall coast redwoods and Douglas fir predominate. Wild ginger, violets, and milkmaids are common in spring, also a few rare orchids grow here. Native azaleas bloom in early summer, and by late summer, huckleberries are ready for picking. In the fall and winter rainy season, mushrooms and other forest fungi "blossom."

At one time, the coast grizzly (one of seven bear species that roamed the state's lower regions) thrived between San Francisco and San Luis Obispo. The last grizzly was spotted here in 1878. Common are black-tailed deer, raccoons, skunks, and gray squirrels. Rare are mountain lions, bobcats, coyotes, foxes, and opossums. Among the fascinating reptiles in Big Basin is the endangered western skink. Predictably, rattlers are fairly common in chaparral areas, but other snakes are shy. Squawking Steller's jays are ever-present, and acorn woodpeckers, dark-eyed juncos, owls, and hummingbirds—about 250 bird species altogether—also haunt Big Basin. Spotting marbled murrelets (shorebirds that nest 200 feet up in the redwoods) is a birding challenge.

Sights and Recreation

The best time to be in Big Basin is in the fall, when the weather is perfect and most tourists have gone home. Winter and spring are also prime times, though usually rainier. Road cuts into the park offer a peek into local geology—tilted, folded, twisted layers of thick marine sediments. Big Basin's **Nature Lodge** museum features good natural history exhibits and many fine books, including *Short Historic Tours of Big Basin,* by Jennie and Denzil Verado. The carved-log seating and covered stage at the amphitheater attract impromptu human performances (harmonica concerts, freestyle soft-shoe, joke routines) when no park campfires or other official events are scheduled.

Also here: miles and miles of hiking trails. (Get oriented in the Sempervirens Room, adjacent to park headquarters.) Take the half-mile **Redwood Trail** loop to stretch your legs and see one of the park's most impressive stands of virgin redwoods. Or hike the more ambitious **Skyline-to-the-Sea** trail, at least an overnight trip. It's 11 miles from the basin rim to the seabird haven of Waddell Beach and adjacent **Theodore J. Hoover Natural Preserve,** a freshwater marsh.

There are trail camps along the way (camping and fires allowed only in designated areas). Hikers, bring food and water, as Waddell Creek flows with reclaimed wastewater. Another popular route is the **Pine Mountain Trail.** Thanks to recent land acquisitions along the coast north of Santa Cruz, the new 1.5-mile **Whitehouse Ridge Trail** now joins Big Basin with Año Nuevo State Reserve; call ahead or inquire at either park for directions. Also ask about hiking in other new area park lands.

Most dramatic in Big Basin are the waterfalls. **Berry Creek Falls** is a particularly pleasant destination, with rushing water, redwood mists, and glistening rocks fringed with delicate ferns. Nearby are both **Silver Falls** and the **Golden Falls Cascade.**

Information

For reasonably current area hiking information, pick up a copy of *The Santa Cruz Mountains Trail Book* by Tom Taber (Oak Valley Press), which also offers coastal access details. For park information, contact Big Basin Redwoods State Park (21600 Big Basin Way, Boulder Creek, 831/338-8860, www.bigbasin.org)

Highway 1 entrance to Big Basin Redwoods State Park

MELISSA SHEROWSKI

WILDER RANCH STATE PARK

Open to the public since mid-1989, Wilder Ranch State Park (1401 Coast Rd., 831/423-9703 or 831/426-0505, www.santacruzstateparks.org or www.scparkfriends.org,, day-use fee $6) is best summed up as "a California coastal dairy-farm museum," a remnant of the days when dairies were more important to the local economy than tourists. Before it was a dairy farm, this was the main rancho supplying Mission Santa Cruz. Though damaged by the 1989 earthquake, the old Victorian ranch house is open again, decked out in period furnishings. The grounds also include an elaborate 1890s stable, a dairy barn, and a bunkhouse/workshop with water-driven machinery. Seasoned vehicles and farm equipment, from a 1916 Dodge touring sedan to seed spreaders and road graders, are scattered throughout the grounds.

Almost more appealing, though, are the park's miles of coastline and thousands of acres of forest, creeks, and canyons (not to mention the Brussels sprouts). To help visitors take in the landscape, 7,000-acre Wilder Ranch features 34 miles of hiking, biking, and equestrian trails. Restoration of these coastal wetlands is ongoing.

General ranch tours, led by docents dressed in period attire, are offered every Saturday and Sunday, usually at 1 P.M. Historical games are played on the lawn—hoop 'n' stick, bubbles, stilts—on weekends as well. A variety of other history- and natural history–oriented events are sponsored throughout the year, from demonstrations on making cornhusk dolls or quilts to mastering cowboy-style roping, plus guided hikes and bird walks. Usually on the first Saturday in May is the park's annual open house, a full day of old-fashioned family fun (and fundraising, for future park restoration work).

The main entrance to Wilder Ranch is two miles north of Santa Cruz on the west side of Highway 1, about a mile past the stoplight at Western Drive. The ranch is open for equestrian camping (call for details). No dogs are allowed. The park's new interpretive center is open daily in summer, but at last report, only 10 A.M.–4 P.M. Friday–Saturday in winter. To get here by bus, take Santa Cruz Metro No. 40 and ask the driver to drop you at the ranch.

and the **Mountain Parks Foundation** (525 North Big Trees Park Rd., Felton, 831/335-3174, www.mountainparks.org), which offers educational and interpretive activities at Big Basin and also at Henry Cowell State Park, including the Fall Creek area. To get oriented to the town, pick up a copy of the Boulder Creek Historical Walking Tour, available at most area merchants and at the **San Lorenzo Valley Historical Museum** (12547 Hwy. 9, 831/338-8382, open afternoons Wed., Sat., and Sun.), now at home in a onetime church built with local old-growth redwood. Call for current details. To get oriented to the coastal side of Big Basin Redwoods, head for Rancho Del Oso State Park near Davenport and contact the **Rancho Del Oso Nature and History Center** (831/427-2288, 831/338-8861 for backpackers' trail camps, or 831/425-1218 for equestrian trail camps), some 16 miles north of Santra Cruz via Highway 1.

Big Basin has reservable family campsites, plus five group camps. Make reservations through ReserveAmerica (800/444-7275, www.reserveamerica.com, $20–24) up to seven months in advance. An unusual "outdoor" option: the park's tent cabins. (For details, see *Camping* under *Accommodations*, above.) To reserve backpacker campsites at the park's six trail camps, contact park headquarters. Hiker-biker campsites are $3. Big Basin's day-use fee is $6 per vehicle (walk-ins and bike-ins are free), and a small fee is charged for the map/brochure showing all trails and major park features.

HENRY COWELL REDWOODS STATE PARK

The redwood grove in the dark San Lorenzo Canyon here is the hub of Henry Cowell Redwoods State Park (Hwy. 9, Felton, 831/335-4598 or 831/438-2396 for the campground) and one of the most impressive redwood groves along the central coast, with the Neckbreaker, the Giant, and the Fremont Tree all standouts; the self-guided nature path is wheelchair- and stroller-accessible. And check out the state-of-the-art nature center. You can camp at Graham Hill, picnic near the grove, or head out on the vast web of hiking and horseback trails. The park's northern **Fall Creek** section takes in most of the creek's watershed, known for its limestone deposits; ruins of lime kilns are scattered among the more natural trailside attractions. New in summer 1999 was the **U-Con Trail** connecting Henry Cowell to Wilder Ranch State Park on the coast—making it possible to hike, bike, or horseback ride from the redwoods to the ocean on an established trail.

The fine family campground at Henry Cowell was recently named one of the nation's top 100 by ReserveAmerica. 150 campsites are available; reserve through ReserveAmerica (800/444-7275, www.reserveamerica.com).

OTHER PARKS OFF HIGHWAY 9

Between Big Basin and Saratoga is **Castle Rock State Park** (15300 Skyline Blvd., Los Gatos, 408/867-2952), an essentially undeveloped park and a hiker's paradise offering some primitive camping. **Highlands County Park** (8500 Hwy. 9, Ben Lomond, 9 A.M.–dusk daily) is another option. This old estate, transformed into a park with picnic tables and nature trails, also has a sandy beach along the river. Another swimming spot is at **Ben Lomond County Park** (Mill St., open daily in summer, free), which also offers shaded picnic tables and barbecue facilities. Closer to Big Basin is **Boulder Creek Park** (Middleton Ave., east of Hwy. 9, Boulder Creek, also free). The swimming hole here has both shallows and deeps, plus there's a sandy beach. Other facilities include shaded picnic tables and barbecue pits.

South of Santa Cruz

MOSS LANDING AND VICINITY

Near the mouth of Elkhorn Slough on the coast, Moss Landing is a crazy quilt of weird shops and roadside knickknack stands, watched over by both a towering steam power plant—built circa 1948, the second largest in the world, formerly under PG&E Pacific Gas & Electric) control and now owned and recently expanded by Duke Energy—and a Kaiser firebrick-making plant. All of which makes for an odd-looking community. First a Salinas Valley produce port, then a whaling harbor until 1930, Moss Landing is now surrounded by artichoke and broccoli fields. The busy fishing harbor and adjoining slough are home to hundreds of bird and plant species, making this an important center for marine-life studies.

These days, the area is also noted for its indoor recreational opportunities, with more than two dozen antique and junk shops along Moss Landing Road. Show up on the last Sunday in July for the annual **Antique Street Fair,** which draws

more than 350 antiques dealers and at least 12,000 civilian antiquers.

For more information about the area, contact the **Moss Landing Chamber of Commerce** (831/633-4501, www.monterey-bay.net/ml).

Moss Landing Marine Laboratories

The laboratories here (895 Blanco Circle, 831/755-8650) are operated by San Jose State University and shared by other researchers, including the Monterey Bay Aquarium Research Institute. Students and faculty study local marine life, birds, and tidepools, but particularly Monterey Bay's spectacular underwater submarine canyons, which start where Elkhorn Slough enters the bay at Moss Landing. Stop for a visit and quick look around, but don't disturb classes or research projects. Better yet, come in spring—usually the first Sunday after Easter—for the big open house, when you can take a complete tour; explore the "touch tank" full of starfish, sea cucumbers, sponges, snails, and anemones; and see slide shows, movies, and marine-life dioramas.

Moss Landing State Beach

New at the marine lab, expected to be completed by the end of 2005, is a $4 million, 500-foot-long concrete **research pier,** which replaces the 1870s-vintage wooden pier damaged in the 1989 Loma Prieta earthquake and later demolished. The new pier will allow scientists studying everything from global warming to whales to more efficiently load research ships, and also allow large research ships—like the 209-foot *Melville*—to tie up at Moss Landing. Though locals would have liked pier access, including the chance to fish, public access is limited to a small, informational public viewing area at the foot of the pier. Guided pier tours are also offered.

▶ Elkhorn Slough Reserve

Most people come here to hike and bird-watch, but the fish life in this coastal estuary, the second largest in California, is also phenomenal. No wonder the Ohlone people built villages here some 5,000 years ago. Wetlands like these, oozing with life and nourished by rich bay sediments, are among those natural environments most threat-

ened by "progress." Thanks to the Nature Conservancy, the Elkhorn Slough (originally the mouth of the Salinas River until a 1908 diversion) is now protected as a federal and state estuarine sanctuary and recognized as a National Estuarine Research Reserve—California's first. Elkhorn Slough is managed by the California Department of Fish and Game.

These meandering channels along a seven-mile river are thick with marshy grasses and wildflowers beneath a plateau of oaks and eucalyptus. In winter, an incredible variety of shorebirds (not counting migrating waterfowl) call this area home. Endangered and threatened birds, including the brown pelican, the California clapper rail, and the California least tern, also thrive here at Elkhorn, designated a Globally Important Bird Area by the American Bird Conservancy. The tule elk once hunted by the Ohlone are long gone, but harbor seals bask on the mudflats, and bobcats, gray foxes, muskrats, otters, and black-tailed deer are still here.

Though this is a private nature sanctuary, not a

park, the public can visit. Some 4.5 miles of trails pass by tidal mudflats, salt marshes, and an old abandoned dairy. The visitors center (same hours as reserve, 9 A.M.–5 P.M. Wed.–Sun.) offers a bird-watchers' map/guide to the Pajaro Valley. There's a small day-use fee to use the trails. Docent-led walks are offered year-round on Saturday and Sunday at 10 A.M. and 1 P.M. On the first Saturday of the month, there's also an Early Bird Walk at 8:30 A.M. Still, there's no better way to see the slough than from the seat of a kayak. Stop by the visitors center at the entrance to arrange a guided tour, or contact the **Elkhorn Slough Foundation** (1700 Elkhorn Rd., Moss Landing, 831/728-2822 or 831/728-5939, www.elkhornslough.org). Arrange kayak tours through **Monterey Bay Kayaks** (693 Del Monte Ave., Monterey, 831/373-5357 or 800/649-5357, www.montereybaykayaks.com) or **Kayak Connection** (831/724-5692, www.kayakconnection.com). For a guided tour aboard a 27-foot pontoon boat, contact **Elkhorn Slough Safari** in Moss Landing (831/633-5555, www.elkhornslough.com).

Practicalities

A big plus in Moss Landing is the 1906 vintage **⋈ Captain's Inn B&B** (831/633-5550, www.captainsinn.com, $100–200 in main building, $150–250 in boathouse), once home to the Pacific Coast Steamship Company, and now meticulously, creatively, nautically restored and expanded—from the cozy library and game area in the historic building to the classic "boat beds" in the newer boathouse. A stay here offers style as well as a terrific location and good value. All rooms have private baths, antiques or creative furnishings, and refreshing decor; many have fireplaces and "romance showers" or two-person tubs. Boathouse rooms face the river, with large windows for wildlife-watching. The boat beds are the real deal, be they fishing boats or catamarans. Rates include big breakfasts and other goodies included. Go ahead—sail away. Determined landlubbers, at last report "en route camping" for self-contained RVs was still possible at **Moss Landing State Beach** (Jetty Rd., 831/649-2836), a beach area popular for picnics and bird-watching.

Time-honored people's eateries abound in Moss Landing, particularly near the harbor. Most serve chowders and seafood and/or ethnic specials. Quite good, right on the highway, is **The Whole Enchilada** (831/633-3038, lunch and dinner daily), specializing in Mexican seafood entrées. (The "whole enchilada," by the way, is filet of red snapper wrapped in a corn tortilla and smothered in enchilada sauce and melted cheese.) The Enchilada's associated **Moss Landing Inn and Jazz Club** (adjacent, 831/633-9990) is a bar featuring live jazz 4:30–8:30 P.M. on Sunday. Hit **Haute Enchilada Art Cafe** (7902-A Sandholdt Rd., 831/633-5843) for some folk art along with your food. Everyone's favorite for fish is **⋈ Phil's Fresh Fish Market and Eatery** (Sandholdt Rd., 831/633-2152, www.philsfishmarket.com). Monday and Thursday are bluegrass nights. (To get there from Moss Landing Road, take the first and only right-hand turn and cross the one-lane bridge; it's the wooden warehouse just past the research institute.) Stop for fresh fruit smoothies and generous deli sandwiches at the associated **Phil's Snack Shack & Deli** (7921 Moss Landing Rd., 831/633-1775). Head for the shack in mid-May for the annual **Bluegrass on the Slough** festival.

CASTROVILLE

The heart of Castroville is Swiss-Italian, which hardly explains the artichokes all over the place. Calling itself "Artichoke Center of the World," Castroville grows 75 percent of California's artichokes—real artichokes, the globe variety—though that delicious leathery thistle grows throughout Santa Cruz and Monterey Counties. Come for the annual **Artichoke Festival** and parade (831/633-6545, www.artichoke-festival.org) every May. It's some party, too, replete with artichokes: fried, baked, mashed, boiled, and added as colorful ingredients to cookies and cakes. Nibble on artichoke nut cake and french-fried artichokes with mayo dip, sip artichoke soup, and sample steamed artichokes. Sometimes Hollywood gets in on the action: In 1947, Marilyn Monroe reigned as California's Artichoke Queen. If

FOREST OF NISENE MARKS STATE PARK

Forest of Nisene Marks (Aptos Creek Rd. at Soquel Dr., Aptos, 831/763-7062 for recorded info or 831/763-7063 for campsite reservations, www.santacruzstateparks.org, 6 A.M.–sunset daily, day-use fee $6) is definitely a hiker's park. Named for the Danish immigrant who hiked here until the age of 96 and whose family donated the land for public use, Nisene Marks is an oasis of solitude. (This was also the epicenter of the 1989 earthquake that brought down much of Santa Cruz.) You'll have lots to see here, but less to hear—little more than birdsong, rustling leaves, and babbling brooks. The park encompasses 10,000 acres of hefty second-growth redwoods on the steep southern range of the Santa Cruz Mountains, six creeks, lovely Maple Falls, alders, maples, and more

rugged trails than anyone can hike in a day. Also here are an old mill site, abandoned trestles and railroad tracks, and logging cabins.

To get here from the coast, take the Aptos-Seacliff exit north from Highway 1 and turn right on Soquel Drive. At the first left after the stop sign, drive north on Aptos Creek Road and across the railroad tracks. Bring water and food for day trips. No fires are allowed. Dogs, on short leashes, are allowed only on fire roads. Call to reserve the trailside campsites at least one week in advance. For $3 per person per night, you get glorious solitude, but not much else—a six-mile one-way hike, just six primitive sites to choose from, no water (BYO), no fires allowed, and pit toilet only.

you miss the festival, there are other artichoke options, including **Giant Artichoke Fruits and Vegetables** (11241 Merritt St., 831/633-2778831/633-3501)—wine and cheese shop adjacent—and the **Thistle Hut** (2047 Watsonville Rd. at Cooper-Molera Rd., 831/633-4888), just off Highway 1. The best place around for barbecue is Castroville's **The Central Texan BBQ** (10500 Merritt St., 831/633-2285). The Italian **Ristorante La Scuola** (10700 Merritt St., 831/633-3200) is housed in Castroville's first schoolhouse.

WATSONVILLE AND VICINITY

Watsonville, an agriculturally rich city of about 50,000, is the mushroom capital of the United States, though the town calls this lovely section of the Pajaro Valley the Strawberry Capital of the World and Apple City of the Ives. Farming got off to a brisk, clod-busting start during the gold rush, when produce grown here was in great demand. Among the early settlers were Chinese, Germans, Yugoslavs, and immigrants from the Sandwich Islands and the Azores. None gained as much notoriety as Watsonville stagedriver Charley Parkhurst, one of the roughest, toughest, most daring muleskinners in the

state—a "man" later unveiled as a woman, the first ever to vote in California.

Watsonville made history still earlier. Nothing remains today to commemorate the site of the 1820s Casa Materna, or "Mother House," of California's Vallejo clan, yet the **House of Glass** once stood about 2.5 miles southeast of Watsonville near Highway 1. (The precise location was at the edge of the bluff, 1, 000 feet north of the intersection of Hillcrest and Salinas Roads.) General Mariano Guadalupe Vallejo was one of five sons and eight daughters born to his parents there, in a house with 20-inch-thick walls and hand-hewn redwood window frames and joists. It was called the House of Glass for its completely glassed-in second-story veranda. Legend has it the veranda got its unique fishbowl design when Don Ignacio Vincente Ferrer Vallejo mistakenly received a shipment of 12 dozen windows instead of one dozen. It was from the Vallejo ranch that Jose Castro, Juan Bautista Alvarado, and their rebel troops launched their 1835 attack on Monterey to create the free state of Alta California. The victorious single shot (fired by a lawyer who consulted a book to figure out how to work the cannon) hit the governor's house, and he surrendered immediately.

Sights

Watsonville itself is mushrooming these days, with plans for a new, four-story, downtown civic center and higher density downtown residential development saving space for mushrooms and other agricultural production. Other outposts of the new Watsonville include the **Green Valley Grill** (upstairs at 40 Penny Ln. at Green Valley Rd., 831/728-0644, lunch Mon.–Fri., dinner Mon.–Sat.). It's all here: tortilla lime soup, tender green salads and local produce in many other guises, oakwood-grilled duck breast and prawns wrapped in pancetta, even Gizdich Ranch olallieberry pie for dessert. For the local *Country Crossroads* farm trails map and other visitor information, contact the **Pajaro Valley Chamber of Commerce** (444 Main St., Watsonville, 831/724-3900, www.pajarovalleychamber.com) or stop by Country Crossroads headquarters at the farm bureau office (141 Monte Vista Ave., 831/724-1356). Get up to speed on local agricultural history at the **Agricultural History Project** (2601 E. Lake Ave., 831/724-5898, noon–4 P.M. Fri.–Sat.) at the Santa Cruz County Fairgrounds. From May through January, an almost mandatory stop is **Gizdich Ranch** (55 Peckham Rd., 831/722-1056, www.gizdichranch.com), fabulous for its fresh apples, homemade apple pies, and fresh-squeezed natural apple juices. Earlier in the season, this is a "Pik-Yor-Self" berry farm, with raspberries, olallieberries, and strawberries (usually also available in pies, fritters, and pastries). Another fine bet is **Emile Agaccio Farms** (4 Casserly Rd., 831/728-2009), known for its pick-you-own raspberries and chesterberries (a blackberry variety). Also worth seeking in Watsonville are Mexican and Filipino eateries, many quite good, most inexpensive. Watsonville has its share of motels, too, in addition to camping at Pinto Lake (see below) and at the Santa Cruz KOA.

Beaches

At **Manresa State Beach** (400 San Andreas Rd., 831/724-3750, day-use fee $6, campsites $20–35), stairways lead to the surf from the main parking lot and Sand Dollar Drive; there are restrooms and an outdoor shower. No camping here, but walk-in camping is available one mile south at Manresa Uplands Campground ($20). Rural San Andreas Road also takes you to **Sunset State Beach** (201 Sunset Beach Rd., 831/763-7062 or 831/763-7063, day-use fee $6, campsites $20–35), four miles west of Watsonville in the Pajaro Dunes (take Bus No. 54B from Santa Cruz). Sunset offers 3.5 miles of nice sandy beaches and tall dunes, with the historic Van Laanan farm as backdrop. Sunset also features a wooded campground with 90 campsites (tents and RVs, but way too many RVs and not much privacy), group campsites, and 60 picnic sites. After sunset, the beach is open only to campers. For more on area state parks, see www.santacruzstateparks.org and www.scparkfriends.org. To reserve family campsites at all state beaches and parks, contact ReserveAmerica (800/444-7275, www.reserveamerica.com).

Parking for pretty **Palm Beach,** near Pajaro Dunes—a great place to find sand dollars—is near the end of Beach Street. Also here are picnic facilities, a par course, and restrooms. **Zmudowski State Beach** is near where the Pajaro River reaches the sea. You'll find good hiking and surf fishing. The beach is rarely crowded. Next, near Moss Landing, are **Salinas River State Beach** (Potrero Rd., 831/384-7695) and **Jetty State Beach.**

Recreation

Just a few miles northwest of Watsonville is tiny **Pinto Lake City Park** (451 Green Valley Rd., 831/722-8129, www.pintolake.com), where you can go swimming, sailing, pedal-boating, sailboarding, fishing, or RV camping (28 sites with full hookups, $25, tent trailers OK).

The **Ellicott Slough National Wildlife Refuge** (510/792-0222) a 180-acre ecological reserve of coastal uplands for the Santa Cruz long-toed salamander, is four miles west along San Andreas Road and generally closed to the public. To get there, turn west off Highway 1 at the Larkin Valley Road exit and continue west on San Andreas Road to the refuge, next to the Santa Cruz KOA.

Events

The Watsonville area also offers unusual diversions. The biggest event here is the annual **West Coast Fly In & Air Show** in May (Memorial Day weekend), when more than 50,000 people show up to appreciate hundreds of classic, antique, and home-built airplanes on the ground and in the air. Originally held over Memorial Day weekend, but now usually scheduled for early August, is the annual **Monterey Bay Strawberry Festival** (www.mbsf.com). Come in mid-September for the **Santa Cruz County Fair.**

Know
Monterey
& Carmel

The Land

Much of the redwood country from San Francisco to Big Sur resembles the boulder-strewn, rough-and-tumble coast of far Northern California. Here the Pacific Ocean is far from peaceful; posted warnings about dangerous swimming conditions and undertows are no joke. Back on dry land, the San Andreas Fault menaces, veering inland from the eastern side of the Coast Ranges through the Salinas Valley and on to the San Francisco Bay Area.

GEOGRAPHY

The Monterey Peninsula

Steinbeck captured the mood of the Monterey Peninsula in *Tortilla Flat:* "The wind . . . drove the fog across the pale moon like a thin wash of watercolor. . . . The treetops in the wind talked huskily, told fortunes and foretold deaths." The peninsula juts into the ocean 115 miles south of San Francisco and forms the southern border of Monterey Bay. The north shore sweeps in a crescent toward Santa Cruz and the Santa Cruz Mountains; east is the oak- and pine-covered Santa Lucia Range, rising in front of the barren Gabilan ("Sparrow Hawk") Mountains beloved by Steinbeck. Northward are the ecologically delicate Monterey Bay Dunes, now threatened by off-road vehicles and development. To the south, the piney hills near Point Piños and Asilomar overlook rocky crags and coves dotted with wind-sculpted trees; farther south, beyond Carmel and the Pebble Beach golf mecca, is Point Lobos, said to be Robert Louis Stevenson's inspiration for Spyglass Hill in *Treasure Island.*

Monterey "Canyon"

Discovered in 1890 by George Davidson, Monterey Bay's submerged valley teems with sea life: bioluminescent fish glowing vivid blue to red, squid, tiny rare octopi, tentacle-shedding jellyfish, and myriad microscopic plants and animals. This is one of the most biologically prolific spots on the planet. Swaying with the ocean's motion, dense kelp thickets are home to sea lions, seals, sea otters, and giant Garibaldi "goldfish." Opal-eyed perch in schools of hundreds swim by leopard sharks and bottom fish. In the understory near the rocky ocean floor live abalones, anemones, crabs, sea urchins, and starfish.

Students of Monterey Canyon geology quibble over the origins of this unusual underwater valley. Computer-generated models of canyon creation suggest that the land used to be near Bakersfield and was carved out by the Colorado River; later, it shifted westward due to plate tectonics. More conventional speculation focuses on the creative forces of both the Sacramento and San Joaquin Rivers, which perhaps once emptied at Elkhorn Slough, Monterey Canyon's principal "head."

However Monterey Canyon came to be, it is now centerpiece of the 5,312-square-mile **Monterey Bay National Marine Sanctuary,** which extends some 400 miles along the coast, from San Francisco's Golden Gate in the north to San Simeon in the south. Established in 1992 after a 15-year political struggle, this federally sanctioned preserve is now protected from offshore oil drilling, dumping of hazardous materials, the killing of marine mammals or birds, personal watercraft, and aircraft flying lower than 1,000 feet. As an indirect result of its federal protection, Monterey Bay now boasts a total of 18 marine research facilities.

Big Sur

Farther south, the land itself is unfriendly, at least from the human perspective. The indomitable, unstable terrain—with its habit of sliding out from under whole hillsides, houses, highways, and hiking trails during winter rains and at the slightest provocation—has made the area hard to inhabit. But despite its contrariness, the central coast, that unmistakable pivotal point between California's north and south, successfully blends both.

Though the collective Coast Ranges continue south through the region, here the terrain takes on a new look. Northern California's redwoods begin to thin out, limiting themselves to a few large groves in Big Sur country and otherwise straggling south a short distance beyond San Simeon, tucked into hidden folds in the rounded coastal mountains. Where redwood country ends, either the grasslands of the dominant coastal oak woodlands begin or the chaparral takes over, in places almost impenetrable. Even the coastline reflects the transition—the rocky, rough-and-tumble shores along the Big Sur coast transform into tamer beaches and bluffs near San Simeon and points south.

Los Padres National Forest, inland from the coast, is similarly divided into two distinct sections. The northernmost (and largest) Monterey County section includes most of the rugged, 100-mile-long Santa Lucia Range and its Ventana Wilderness. The southern stretch of Los Padres, essentially the San Luis Obispo and Santa Barbara backcountry, is often closed to hikers and backpackers during the summer due to high fire danger.

Another clue that the north–south transition occurs here is water or, moving southward, the increasingly obvious lack of it. Though both the North and South Forks of the Little Sur River, the Big Sur River a few miles to the south, and other northern waterways flow to the sea throughout the year, as does the Cuyama River in the south (known as the Santa Maria River as it nears the ocean), most of the area's streams are seasonal. But off-season hikers, beware: even inland streams with a six-month flow are not to be dismissed during winter and spring, when deceptively dinky creek beds can become death-dealing torrents overnight.

Major lakes throughout California's central coast region are actually water-capturing reservoirs, including Lake San Antonio, known for its winter bald eagle population; Lake Nacimiento, on the other side of the mountains from San Simeon; and Santa Margarita Lake, east of San Luis Obispo near the headwaters of the Salinas River.

CLIMATE

The legendary California beach scene is almost a fantasy here—almost, but not quite. Surfers can be seen year-round, though often in wetsuits. Sunshine warms the sands (between storms) from fall to early spring, but count on fog from late spring well into summer. Throughout the Monterey Bay area, it's often foggy and damp, though clear summer afternoons can get hot; the warmest months along the coast are August, September, and October. (Sunglasses, suntan lotion, and hats are prudent, but always bring a sweater.) Inland, expect hotter weather in summer, colder in winter. Rain is possible as early as October, though big storms don't usually roll in until December.

Flora and Fauna

FLORA

California's central coast region, particularly near Monterey, exhibits tremendous botanic diversity. Among the varied vascular plant species found regionally is the unusually fast-growing Monterey pine, an endemic tree surviving in native groves only on hills and slopes near Monterey, Cambria, and Año Nuevo, as well as on Guadalupe and Cedros Islands off the coast of Baja, Mexico. It's now a common landscaping tree—and the world's most widely cultivated tree, grown commercially for its wood and pulp. The unusual Monterey cypress is a relict, a specialized tree that can't survive beyond the Monterey Peninsula. The soft, green Sargent cypress is more common, ranging south to Santa Barbara along the coast and inland. The Macnab cypress is found only on poor serpentine soil, as are Bishop pines, which favor swamps and the slopes from "Huckleberry Hill," near Monterey, south to the San Luis Range near Point Buchon and Santa Barbara County.

Coastal redwoods thrive near Santa Cruz and south through Big Sur. Not as lusty as those on

A spectacular variety of aquatic life thrives just off shore of Monterey Bay.

the north coast, these redwoods often keep company with Douglas fir, pines, and a dense understory of shade-loving shrubs. Other central coast trees include the Sitka spruce and beach pines. A fairly common inland tree is the chaparral-loving knobcone pine, with its tenaciously closed "fire-climax" cones. Other regional trees include the California wax myrtle, the aromatic California laurel, or "bay," tree, the California nutmeg, and the tan oak (and many other oaks), plus alders, big-leaf maples, and occasional madrones. Eucalyptus trees thrive in the coastal locales where they've been introduced.

FAUNA
Whales and Sharks
The annual migration of the California gray whale, the state's official mammal, is big news all along the coast. From late October to January, these magnificent 20- to 40-ton creatures head south from the Arctic seas toward Baja (pregnant females first). Once the mating season ends, males, newly pregnant females, and juveniles start their northward journey from February to

June. Females with calves, often traveling close to shore, return later in the year, between March and July. Once in a blue moon, when the krill population mushrooms in winter, rare blue whales will feed in and around Monterey Bay and north to the Farallon Islands.

A wide variety of harmless sharks is common in Monterey Bay. Occasionally, 20-foot-long great white sharks congregate here to feed on sea otters, seals, and sea lions. Unprovoked attacks on humans do occur (to surfers more often than to scuba divers), but are very rare. The best protection is avoiding ocean areas where great whites are common, such as Año Nuevo Island at the north end of the bay; don't go into the water alone, and never where these sharks have been recently sighted.

Seals and Sea Lions
Common in these parts is the California sea lion; the females are the barking "seals" popular in aquatic amusement parks. True seals don't have external ears, and the gregarious, fearless creatures swimming in shallow ocean waters or lolling on rocky jetties and docks usually do. Also here

are northern, or Steller's, sea lions, which roar instead of bark and are usually lighter in color. Chunky harbor seals (no ear flaps, usually with spotted coats) more commonly haul out on sandy beaches, since they're awkward on land. Less common, but rapidly increasing in numbers along the California coast—viewable at the Año Nuevo rookery during the winter mating and birthing season—are the massive northern elephant seals, the largest pinnipeds (fin-footed mammals) in the Western Hemisphere. One look at the two- or three-ton, 18-foot-long males explains the creatures' common name: their long, trunklike noses serve no real purpose beyond sexual identification, as far as humans can tell.

Pelicans and Other Seabirds

The ungainly-looking, web-footed brown pelicans—most noticeable perched on pilings or near piers in and around harbors—are actually incredibly graceful when diving for their dinners. A squadron of 25 or more pelicans "gone fishin'" first glide above the water, then, one by one, plunge dramatically to the sea. Brown pelicans are another back-from-the-brink success story, their numbers increasing dramatically since DDT (highly concentrated in fish) was banned. California's pelican platoons are often accompanied by greedy gulls, somehow convinced they can snatch fish from the fleshy pelican pouches if they just try harder.

Seabirds are the most obvious seashore fauna; besides brown pelicans, you'll see long-billed curlews, ashy petrels nesting on cliffs, surf divers like grebes and scooters, and various gulls. Pure white California gulls are seen only in winter here (they nest inland), but yellow-billed western gulls and the scarlet-billed, white-headed Heermann's gulls are common seaside scavengers. Look for the hyperactive, self-important sandpipers along the shore, along with dowitchers, plovers, godwits, and avocets. Killdeers—so named for their "ki-dee" cry—lure people and other potential

CALIFORNIA GRAYS

A close-up view of the California gray whale, the state's official (and largest) mammal, is a life-changing experience. As those dark, massive, white-barnacled heads shoot up out of the ocean to suck air, spray with the force of a firehose blasts skyward from blowholes. Watch the annual migration of the gray whale all along the California coast—from "whale vistas" on land or by boat.

Despite the fascination they hold for Californians, little is yet known about the gray whale. Once endangered by whaling—as so many whale species still are—the grays are now swimming steadily along the comeback trail. Categorized as baleen whales—which dine on plankton and other small aquatic animals sifted through hundreds of fringed, hornlike baleen plates—gray whales were once land mammals that went back to sea. In the process of evolution, they traded their fore and hind legs for fins and tail flukes. Despite their fish-like appearance, these are true mammals: warm-blooded, air-breathing creatures who nourish their young with milk.

Adult gray whales weigh 20–40 tons, not counting a few hundred pounds of parasitic barnacles. Calves weigh in at a hefty 1,500 pounds at birth and can expect to live for 30–60 years. They feed almost endlessly from April to October in the arctic seas between Alaska and Siberia, sucking up sediment and edible creatures on the bottom of shallow seas, then squeezing the excess water and silt out their baleen filters. Fat and sassy with an extra 6–12 inches of blubber on board, early in October they head south on their 6,000-mile journey to the warmer waters of Baja in Mexico.

Pregnant females leave first, traveling alone or in small groups. Larger groups make up the rear guard, with the older males and nonpregnant females engaging in highly competitive courtship and mating rituals along the way—quite a show for human voyeurs. The rear guard becomes the frontline on the way home: males, newly pregnant females, and young gray whales head north from February to June. Cows and calves migrate later, between March and July.

Know Monterey & Carmel

predators away from their clutches of eggs by feigning serious injury.

Tidepool Life
The twice-daily ebb of ocean tides reveals an otherwise hidden world. Tidepools below rocky headlands are nature's aquariums, sheltering abalone, anemones, barnacles, mussels, hermit crabs, starfish, sea snails, sea slugs, and tiny fish. Distinct zones of marine life are defined by the tides. The highest, or "splash," zone is friendly to creatures naturally protected by shells from desiccation, including black turban snails and hermit crabs. The intertidal zones (high and low) protect spiny sea urchins and the harmless sea anemone. The "minus tide" or surf zone—farthest from shore and almost always underwater—is home to hazardous-to-human-health stingrays (particularly in late summer, watch where you step) and jellyfish.

History

Cabrillo spotted Point Piños and Monterey Bay in 1542. Sixty years later, Vizcaíno sailed into the bay and named it for the viceroy of Mexico, the count of Monte-Rey. A century further along came Portolá and Father Crespi, who later, together with Father Junípero Serra, founded both Monterey's presidio and mission at Carmel.

The quiet redwood groves near Santa Cruz remained undisturbed by civilization until the arrival of Portolá's expedition in 1769. The sickly Spaniards made camp in the Rancho de Osos section of what is now Big Basin, experiencing an almost miraculous recovery in the valley they called Cañada de Salud (Canyon of Health). A Spanish garrison and mission were soon established on the north end of Monterey Bay.

By the end of the 1700s, the entire central California coast was solidly Spanish, with missions, pueblos, and military bases or presidios holding the territory for the king of Spain. With the Mexican revolution, Californio loyalty went with the new administration closer to home. But the people here carried on their Spanish cultural heritage despite the secularization of the missions, the increasing influence of cattle ranches, and the foreign flood (primarily American) that threatened existing California tradition. Along the rugged central coast, just south of the boisterous and booming gold rush port of San Francisco, the influence of this new wave of "outsiders" was felt only later and locally, primarily near Monterey and Salinas.

MONTEREY

In addition to being the main port city for both Alta and Baja California, from 1775 to 1845, Monterey was the capital of Alta California—and naturally enough, the center of much political intrigue and scheming. Spared the devastating earthquakes that plagued other areas, Monterey had its own bad times, which included being burned and ransacked by the Argentinean revolutionary privateer Hippolyte Bouchard in 1818. In 1822, Spanish rule ended in California, and

Father Junípero Serra

RESCUE MISSIONS

California's 21 adobe missions, the legacy of Spanish territorial settlement dating to 1769, are the state's most recognizable cultural and historic symbols. That history is not universally celebrated, particularly among native California peoples, yet mission architectural features, from whitewashed walls to red tile roofs, still influence California style. But the original California icons, attracting 5.5 million visitors each year, are fading fast. Cracking and crumbling adobe, earthquake and termite damage, water leaks, structural failures, art and artifacts in need of restoration—the list of needed repairs is so long and so significant that the U.S. Congress has finally taken action, allocating $10 million in federal funds to match state funds and private contributions.

For current information about the current rescue of California's missions—and to contribute much-needed cash—contact the California Missions Foundation, 4129 Main Street, Suite 207, Riverside, 909/369-0440 or 877/632-3623, www.missionsofcalifornia.org.

the 1797 establishment of Branciforte—a "model colony" financed by the Spanish government just across the San Lorenzo River—made life hard for the mission fathers. The rowdy, quasi-criminal culture of Branciforte so intrigued the native peoples that Santa Cruz men of the cloth had to use leg irons to keep the Ohlone home. And things just got worse. In 1818, the threat of pirates at nearby Monterey sent the mission folk into the hills, with the understanding that Branciforte's bad boys would pack up the mission's valuables and cart them inland for safekeeping. Instead, they looted the place and drank all the sacramental wine. The mission was eventually abandoned, then demolished by an earthquake in 1857. A small port city grew up around the plaza and borrowed the mission's name—Santa Cruz—while Branciforte, a smuggler's haven, continued to flourish until the late 1800s.

CARMEL

Carmel-by-the-Sea was established in 1903 by real estate developers who vowed to create a cultured community along the sandy beaches of Carmel Bay. To do this, they offered "creative people" such incentives as building lots for as little as $50. As the result of such irresistible inducements, Carmel was soon alive with an assortment of tents and shacks, which eventually gave way to cottages and mansions.

Tourism grew right along with the art colony; the public had a passion for travel during the early days of automobile adventuring. Quaint Carmel, home to "real Bohemians," also offered tourists the chance to view (and buy) artworks—a prospect cheered by the artists themselves. Carmel's commitment to the arts and artists was formalized by the establishment of the Carmel Art Association in 1927. Still going strong, with strict jury selection, this artists' cooperative is a cultural focal point in contemporary Carmel.

Mexico took over. In 1845, Monterey lost part of its political prestige when Los Angeles temporarily became the territory's capital city. When the rancheros surrendered to Commodore Sloat in July 1846, the area became officially American, though the town's distinctive Spanish tranquility remained relatively undisturbed until the arrival of farmers, fishing fleets, fish canneries, and whalers. California's first constitution was drawn up in Monterey's Colton Hall in 1849, during the state's Constitutional Convention.

SANTA CRUZ

Santa Cruz, the site of Misión Exaltación de la Santa Cruz and a military garrison on the north end of Monterey Bay, got its start in 1791. But

Getting There

BY CAR

If you're driving from the San Francisco Bay Area, the preferred local route to Santa Cruz (and the only main alternative to Hwy. 1) is to take I-280 or I-880 south to San Jose, then hop over the hills on the congested and treacherously twisting Highway 17. If you're driving to Monterey and environs, you can come the same way, skirting Monterey Bay on the way south from Santa Cruz, or—from either north or south—taking Highway 101 instead.

BY BUS

Look for the **Greyhound** bus terminals in Santa Cruz (425 Front St., 831/423-1800); Monterey (1042 Del Monte Ave., 831/373-4735); and Salinas (19 W. Gabilan St., 831/424-4973). Greyhound provides service from San Francisco to Santa Cruz, Fort Ord, and Monterey, as well as connections south to L.A. via Salinas or San Jose.

For current route details and current fares, call the company's toll-free line (800/229-9424, 800/752-4841 to request assistance for travelers with disabilities, or 800/345-3109 TDD) or visit www.greyhound.com; the online "Fare Finder" is easy and handy. Bus connections also serve Amtrak and the Bay Area's Caltrain system; for details, see *By Train,* below.

BY TRAIN

Amtrak's Coast Starlight runs from Los Angeles to Seattle with central coast stops in Oxnard, Santa Barbara, San Luis Obispo, Salinas, and Oakland. Monterey-Salinas Transit buses can get you to and from the **Amtrak** station in Salinas (11 Station Place, 831/422-7458 for depot or 800/872-7245, www.amtrak.com). Check the website for reservations and schedule information, including details on Amtrak's bus connections from Monterey. If you'll be heading to the San Francisco Bay Area from the Monterey Penin-

Highway 1 is California's first scenic highway.

sula—or vice versa—keep in mind that Amtrak also connects in San Jose with the San Francisco-San Jose **Caltrain** (650/817-1717 or 800/660-4287 in the service area, www.caltrain.com). For help in figuring out the way to San Jose—and how to get around the entire Bay Area by rapid transit—see www.transit.511.org.

Another way to get out of town is via Santa Cruz Metro's **Highway 17 Express** buses (831/425-8600, www.scmtd.com) to the San Jose train station, which connect directly with **Caltrain** (to San Francisco; 650/508-6200 or 800/660-4287 in the service area, www.caltrain.com) and **Amtrak** (to Oakland, Berkeley, and Sacramento; 831/422-7458 for depot or 800/872-7245, www.amtrak.com). The fare is just $4 one way, $8 for an all-day pass.

BY AIR

Not far from Santa Cruz, **San Jose International Airport** (408/501-7600, www.sjc.org) is the closest major airport served by commuter and major airlines. Airport shuttle service to and from San Jose or SFO is available through the **Santa Cruz Airporter** (131 Front St., 831/423-1214 or 800/497-4997). To get to Monterey from the airports in San Jose or San Francisco—or vice versa—you can take **Monterey-Salinas Airbus** (791 Neeson Rd., Marina, 831/883-2871) based at Marina Municipal Airport. The buses shuttle back and forth up to 10 times daily.

You can fly directly into the Monterey Peninsula area. The **Monterey Peninsula Airport** (200 Fred Kane Dr. #200, 831/648-7000, www.montereyairport.com) offers direct and connecting flights from all domestic and foreign locales—primarily connecting flights, because this is a fairly small airport. **United Airlines/United Express** (800/241-6522); **American/American Eagle Airlines** (800/433-7300), and **America West Airlines/America West Express** (800/235-9292) are all allied with major domestic and/or international carriers. You can fly directly into Monterey from San Francisco, Los Angeles, or Phoenix.

The newest peninsula airport is the **Marina Municipal Airport** (831/582-0102, www.air-nav.com/airport/oar), north of Monterey proper on Neeson Road in Marina. Another possibility is the **Salinas Municipal Airport** (831/758-7214, www.salinasairport.com), a mecca for private pilots and charters, helicopter tours, and flight training companies.

Suggested Reading

The virtual "publisher of record" for all things Californian is the **University of California Press** (510/642-4247 or 800/777-4726, www.ucpress.edu), which publishes hundreds of titles on the subject—all excellent. Other publishers offering California titles include **Chronicle Books** (415/537-3730 or 800/722-6657, www.chronbooks.com) and notable **Heyday Books** (510/549-3564, www.heydaybooks.com). California's own **Avalon Travel Publishing** (510/595-3664, www.travelmatters.com) offers **Moon Handbooks** to California (including this one), **The Dog Lover's Companion** titles, and numerous **Foghorn Outdoors** California recreation guides, including camping, fishing, hiking, biking, and "getaways" guides. Contact these and other publishers mentioned below for a complete list of current titles relating to California.

The following listings represent a fairly basic but useful introduction to relevant area books. The interested reader can find many other titles by visiting good local bookstores and/or state and national park visitors centers.

GENERAL TRAVEL

Brautigan, Richard. *A Confederate General from Big Sur, Dreaming of Babylon, and the Hawkline Monster.* New York: Mariner Books, reissue edition, 1991. Did you miss the sixties? If so, you probably also missed Richard Brautigan, whose literary star flamed out too quickly.

Bright, William O. *1,500 California Place Names: Their Origin and Meaning.* Berkeley: University of California Press, 1998. A revised version of the classic *1,000 California Place Names,* by Erwin G. Gudde, first published in 1949. Though you can also get the revised edition of Gudde's original masterpiece (see below for details), this convenient, alphabetically arranged pocketbook—now in an expanded and updated edition—is perfect for travelers, explaining the names of mountains, rivers, and towns throughout California.

Clark, Donald Thomas. *Monterey County Place Names: A Geographical Dictionary.* Carmel Valley, CA: Kestrel Press, 1991. This marvelous resource, meticulously researched and guaranteed to enlighten all who dip into it, is a gift from the UC Santa Cruz University Librarian, Emeritus. Also well worth searching for, though out of print at last report, is the same author's *Santa Cruz County Place Names* (1986).

de la Pérouse, Jean François, with commentary by Malcolm Margolin. *Monterey in 1786: The Journals of Jean François de la Pérouse.* Berkeley: Heyday Books, 1989. On September 14, 1786, two ships sailed out of the fog and into Monterey Bay. The ships were French, *L'Astrolabe* and *La Boussole,* the first foreign vessels to visit the Spanish colonies in California. Onboard, as Malcolm Margolin tells us in his introduction, "was a party of eminent scientists, navigators, cartographers, illustrators, and physicians," sent by King Louis XVI to explore the western coast of North America, look for sea otters (for the fur trade), and report on Spain's colonies. Leader of the expedition was Jean François de la Pérouse, whose journal describes the presidio at Monterey, the mission at Carmel, Indian customs, and the land and its abundant plant and animal life. Reading his journals, as Margolin points out, allows to unfold before us "not a tale of a distant fantasy land, but the far more gripping story of our place, of our times, the story of 'us.'" The journals are greatly enhanced by Margolin's historical introduction and careful annotations.

Gudde, Erwin G. Edited by William O. Bright. *California Place Names: The Origin and Etymology of Current Geographical Names.* Berkeley: University of California Press, 1998. Did you know that *Siskiyou* was the Chinook word for "bobtailed horse," as borrowed from the Cree language? More such complex truths await every time you dip into this fascinating volume— the ultimate guide to California place names (and how to pronounce them). A revised and expanded fourth edition, building upon the masterwork of Gudde, who died in 1969.

Jeffers, Robinson. *Selected Poems.* New York: Random House, 1965. The poet Robinson Jeffers died in 1961 at the age of 75, on a rare day when it actually snowed in Carmel. One of California's finest poets, classically sophisticated yet accessible, Jeffers composed many poems that paid homage to the beauty of his beloved Big Sur coast. Pieces collected here are selections from some of his major works, including *Be Angry at the Sun, The Beginning and the End, Hungerfield,* and *Tamar and Other Poems.*

Jeffers, Robinson, with an introduction by James Karman, photography by Morley Baer. *Stones of the Sur.* Stanford, CA: Stanford University Press, 2001. A coffee-table book for people who don't even have coffee tables, this stunning work is crafted from the words of the Carmel poet Robinson Jeffers and the brilliant black-and-white photos of Morley Baer. As a general introduction to the significance of Jeffers's work and his connection to Carmel, scholar James Karman's contribution is invaluable.

Karman, James. *Robinson Jeffers: Poet of California.* Brownsville, OR: Story Line Press, Inc., revised second edition, 1995. This marvelous critical biography details the life and times of the reticent poet Robinson Jeffers, for whom the Big Sur coast was once named. "It is not possible to be quite sane here," Jeffers wisely observed. Karman also sympathetically introduces us to Jeffers's wife, Una; of additional interest to Jeffers fans is Story Line's *Of Una Jeffers,* by Edith Greenan.

Kerouac, Jack. *Big Sur.* New York: Penguin USA, reprint edition, 1992. Here is Kerouac's hellish Big Sur hike into the dark side of manic depression, paranoia, and alcoholism, as experienced by his alter ego Jack Dulouz, now a writer experiencing fame. A sobering follow-up to Kerouac's more optimistic *On The Road* and *The Dharma Bums.*

Miller, Henry. *Big Sur and the Oranges of Hieronymus Bosch.* New York: W.W. Norton & Co., 1978. First published in 1958, this volume includes the famed writer's impressions of art and writing, along with his view of life as seen from the Big Sur coastline—the center of his personal universe in his later years, and the first real home he had ever found.

Paddison, Joshua, ed. *A World Transformed: Firsthand Accounts of California Before the Gold Rush.* Berkeley: Heyday Books, 1999. According to popular California mythology, the Golden State was "born" with the onrushing change that accompanied the gold rush of 1848. But this collection of earlier California writings gathers together some intriguing precedent observations—from European explorers and visitors, missionaries, and sea captains—that reveal pre–gold rush California.

Stegner, Wallace Earle. *Where the Bluebird Sings to the Lemonade Springs: Living and Writing in the West.* New York: Penguin USA, reprint edition, 1993. It's certainly understandable that, at the end of his days, Wallace Stegner wasn't entirely optimistic about the future of the West, bedeviled as it still is by development pressures and insane political decisions. In these 16 thoughtful essays, he spells out his concerns—and again pays poetic homage to the West's big sky and bigger landscapes. In

the end, he remains hopeful that a new spirit of place is emerging in the West—and that within a generation or two, we will "work out some sort of compromise between what must be done to earn a living and what must be done to restore health to the earth, air, and water."

Steinbeck, John. *Cannery Row.* New York: Penguin USA, reprint edition, 1993. Here it is: A poem, a stink, a grating noise, told in the days when sardines still ruled the boardwalk on Monterey's Cannery Row. Also worth an imaginative side-trip on a tour of the California coast is Steinbeck's *East of Eden,* first published in 1952, the Salinas Valley version of the Cain and Abel story. Steinbeck's classic California work, though, is still *The Grapes of Wrath.*

Stevenson, Robert Louis. *The Complete Short Stories of Robert Louis Stevension: With a Selection of the Best Short Novels.* New York: Da Capo Press, 1998. It's hard to know where to start with Stevenson, whose California journeys served to launch his literary career. Da Capo's collection is as good a place as any.

WPA Guide to the Monterey Peninsula. Introduced by Page Stegner (son of Wallace Stegner). Tucson: University of Arizona Press, 1990. Another Federal Writers Project guide, long out of print in its original version. This more recent paperback version is also out of print, but finding a used copy would be well worth it.

HISTORY AND PEOPLE

Gutiérrez, Ramon A., and Richard J. Orsi, eds. *Contested Eden: California Before the Gold Rush.* Berkeley: University of California Press, 1998. In this first volume of a projected four-part series, essays explore California before the gold rush.

Harlow, Neal. *California Conquered: The Annexation of a Mexican Province, 1846–1850.* Berkeley: University of California Press, 1982.

Know Monterey & Carmel

Heizer, Robert F. *The Destruction of the California Indians.* Utah: Gibbs Smith Publishing, 1974.

Heizer, Robert F., and Albert B. Elsasser. *The Natural World of the California Indians.* Berkeley: University of California Press, 1980. As an adjunct to the rest of Heizer's work, this fact-packed volume provides the setting—the natural environment, the village environment—for California's native peoples.

Heizer, Robert F., and M. A. Whipple. *The California Indians.* Berkeley: University of California Press, 1971. A worthwhile collection of essays about California's native peoples, covering general, regional, and specific topics—a good supplement to the work of A. L. Kroeber (who also contributed to this volume).

Holiday, James. *The World Rushed In: The California Gold Rush Experience: An Eyewitness Account of a Nation Heading West.* New York: Simon and Schuster, 1981. Reprint of a classic history made while new Californians were busy creating American California—and ending the Spanish-Mexican era over which Monterey presided.

Kroeber, Alfred L. *Handbook of the Indians of California.* New York: Dover Publications, 1976 (unabridged facsimile version of the original work, *Bulletin 78* of the Bureau of American Ethnology of the Smithsonian Institution, published by the U.S. Government Printing Office). The classic compendium of observed facts about California's native peoples by the noted UC Berkeley anthropologist who befriended Ishi—but also betrayed him, posthumously, by allowing his body to be autopsied (in violation of Ishi's beliefs) and his brain to be shipped to the Smithsonian Institution.

Margolin, Malcolm. *The Way We Lived.* Berkeley: Heyday Books, 1981. A wonderful collection of California native peoples' reminiscences, stories, and songs. Also by Margolin: *The Ohlone Way,*

about the life of California's first residents of the San Francisco–Monterey Bay Area.

McCaffery, Jerry. *Lighthouse: Point Piños.* Pacific Grove, CA: Jerry McCaffery, 2001. This gem of a book tells the story of the lighthouse at Point Piños, starting in 1855 and continuing to the present. The story is particularly strong on Emily Fish, principal keeper from 1893 to 1914, sometimes known as the "socialite lightkeeper." Yet Emily, in the author's view, was the lighthouse's hero—"not a heroine in the fainting but persistent Scarlett O'Hara fashion" but a straight-on heroine, who battled on behalf of the lighthouse for 21 years. Great black and white photos, lighthouse plans, timeline, and map of nearby shipwreck locations are included, along with select lightkeeper log entries.

McDonald, Linda, and Carol Cullen. *California Historical Landmarks.* Sacramento, CA: California Department of Parks and Recreation, 1997. Revised edition. Originally compiled in response to the National Historic Preservation Act of 1966, directing all states to identify all properties "possessing historical, architectural, archaeological, and cultural value," this updated edition covers more than 1,000 California Registered Historical Landmarks, organized by category—sites of aboriginal, economic, or government interest, for example—and indexed by county.

Monroy, Douglas. *Thrown Among Strangers: The Making of Mexican Culture in Frontier California.* Berkeley: University of California Press, 1990.

Nasaw, David. *The Chief: The Life of William Randolph Hearst.* New York: Mariner Books, 2001. *The Chief* draws on papers and interviews that were previously unavailable, as well as on newly released documentation of Hearst's interactions with such figures as Hitler, Mussolini, Churchill, every president from Grover Cleveland to Franklin Roosevelt, and movie giants Louis B. Mayer, Jack Warner, and Irving

Thalberg. David Nasaw completes the picture of this colossal American "engagingly, lucidly and fair-mindedly," according to Arthur Schlesinger, Jr.

Pitt, Leonard. *Decline of the Californios: A Social History of the Spanish-Speaking Californians, 1846–1890.* Berkeley: University of California Press, 1966.

Robinson, W.W. *Land in California: The Story of Mission Lands, Ranchos, Squatters, Mining Claims, Railroad Grants, Land Scrip, Homesteads.* Berkeley: University of California Press, 1979.

Rowland, Leon. *Santa Cruz: The Early Years.* Santa Cruz, CA: Otter B Books (out of print). A great little history if you can find it, originally privately published as four separate tracts in the 1940s by Santa Cruz newspaper reporter Leon Rowland.

Royce, Josiah. *California: A Study of American Character: From the Conquest in 1846 to the Second Vigilance Committee in San Francisco.* New York: AMS Press. Originally published in Boston, 1886.

St. Pierre, Brian. *John Steinbeck: The California Years.* San Francisco: Chronicle Books, 1983 (out of print).

Starr, Kevin. *Americans and the California Dream: 1850–1915.* New York: Oxford University Press, 1973. A cultural history, written by a native San Franciscan, former newspaper columnist, onetime head of the city's library system, professor, historian, and California State Librarian. The focus on Northern California taps an impressively varied body of sources as it seeks to "suggest the poetry and the moral drama of social experience" from California's first days of statehood through the Panama-Pacific Exposition of 1915, when, in the author's opinion, "California came of age."

Stevenson, Robert Louis. *From Scotland to Silverado.* Cambridge, MA: The Belknap Press of Harvard University Press, 1966. An annotated collection of the sickly and lovelorn young Stevenson's travel essays, including his first impressions of Monterey and San Francisco, and the works that have come to be known as *The Silverado Squatters.* Contains considerable text—marked therein—that the author's family and friends had removed from previous editions. A useful introduction by James D. Hart details the journeys and relationships behind the essays.

NATURE AND NATURAL HISTORY

Bakker, Elna. *An Island Called California: An Ecological Introduction to Its Natural Communities.* Berkeley: University of California Press, 1985. Expanded, revised edition. An excellent, time-honored introduction to the characteristics of, and relationships between, California's natural communities.

Barbour, Michael, Bruce Pavlik, Susan Lindstrom, and Frank Drysdale, with a foreword by Pulitzer Prize–winning California poet Gary Snyder. *California's Changing Landscapes: Diversity and Conservation of California Vegetation.* Sacramento: California Native Plant Society Press, 1993. This well-illustrated, well-indexed lay guide to California's astonishing botanical variety is an excellent introduction. For more in-depth personal study, the society also publishes excellent regional floras and plant keys.

California Coastal Commission, State of California. *California Coastal Resource Guide.* Berkeley: University of California Press, 1997. This is the revised and expanded fifth edition of the California coast–lover's bible, the indispensable guide to the Pacific coast and its wonders—the land, marine geology, biology—as well as parks, landmarks, and amusements. But for practical travel purposes, get the commission's *The California Coastal Access Guide,* listed below under *Enjoying the Outdoors.*

Collier, Michael. *A Land in Motion: California's San Andreas Fault.* Berkeley: University of California Press, 1999. An intriguing geologic tour of the world's most famous fault, which runs the entire length of western California—and right through the San Francisco Bay Area. Wonderful photographs.

Duremberger, Robert. *Elements of California Geography.* Out of print, but worth searching for. This is the classic work on California geography.

Farrand, John Jr. *Western Birds: An Audubon Handbook.* New York: McGraw-Hill Book Co., 1988. This birding guide includes color photographs instead of artwork for illustrations; conveniently included along with descriptive listings. Though the book contains no range maps, the "Similar Species" listing helps eliminate birds with similar features.

Fitch, John. *Tidepool and Nearshore Fishes of California.* Berkeley: University of California Press, 1975.

Fix, David, and Andy Bezener. *Birds of Northern California.* Renton, WA: Lone Pine Publishing, 2000. This great birding guide includes detailed, full-color illustrations of 328 birds found in Northern California, along with other visual identification aids, range maps, complete bird descriptions, and lesser-known facts about each bird.

Henson, Paul, Donald J. Usner, and Valerie Kells (illustrator). *The Natural History of Big Sur.* Berkeley: University of California Press, 1996. Both a useful guide to Big Sur's public lands and a fascinating natural—geology, climate, flora, and fauna—and human history, this user-friendly book includes color photographs, drawings, maps, species lists, and a bibliography.

Kaufman, Kenn. *Lives of North American Birds.* New York: Houghton Mifflin Co., 1997. Sponsored by the Roger Tory Peterson Institute. A bit bulky for a field guide, but already considered a classic, this 674-page hardbound tome focuses less on identifying features and names and more on observing and understanding birds within the contexts of their own lives. Now *there's* a concept.

Langstroth, Lowell, Libby Langstroth, and Todd Newberry. *A Living Bay: The Underwater World of Monterey Bay.* Berkeley: University of California Press (Monterey Bay Aquarium Series in Marine Conservation), 2000. A stunning introduction to the complexity of life in Monterey Bay, organized by habitat, complete with 200 color photos.

Le Boeuf, Burney J., and Stephanie Kaza. *The Natural History of Año Nuevo.* Santa Cruz, CA: Otter B Books, 1985. Reprint edition, though out of print at last report. An excellent, very comprehensive guide to the natural features of the Año Nuevo area just north of Santa Cruz.

Orr, Robert T., and Roger Helm. *Marine Mammals of California.* Berkeley: University of California Press, 1989. Revised edition. A handy guide for identifying marine mammals along the California coast, with practical tips on the best places to observe them.

Pavlik, Bruce, Pamela Muick, Sharon Johnson, and Marjorie Popper. *Oaks of California.* Santa Barbara: Cachuma Press, 1991. In ancient European times, oaks were considered spiritual beings, the sacred inspiration of artists, healers, and writers, since these particular trees were thought to court the lightning flash. Time spent with this stunning book will soon convince anyone that this truth lives on. Packed with photos and lovely watercolor illustrations, maps, and even an oak-lover's travel guide, this book celebrates the many species of California oaks.

Peterson, Roger Tory. *A Field Guide to Western Birds.* Boston: Houghton Mifflin Co., 1998. The third edition of this birding classic has striking new features, including full-color illustrations (including juveniles, females, and in-flight birds) facing the written descriptions. The only thing you'll have to flip around for are the range maps, tucked away in the back. Among other intriguing titles in the Peterson Field Guide series: *A Field Guide to Western Birds' Nests,* by Hal Harrison.

Raven, Peter H. *Native Shrubs of California.* Berkeley: University of California Press, 1966.

Rigsby, Michael A. (ed.), and Lawrence Ormsby (illus.). *The Natural History of Monterey Bay.* Boulder, CO: Roberts Rinehart Publishers, 1997. Here's a look-see beneath the waters of the nation's largest marine sanctuary, the first complete natural history of one of the most popular dive and tourist meccas in this country.

Robbins, Chandler, et al. *Birds of North America.* New York: Golden Books Publishing Co., 2001. Revised and updated edition. A good field guide for California bird-watching.

Roos-Collins, Margit. *The Flavors of Home: A Guide to the Wild Edible Plants of the San Francisco Bay Area.* Berkeley: Heyday Books, 1990. Just the thing to help you whip up a fresh trailside salad, it's a botanical essay, field guide, and cookbook all in one.

Schmitz, Marjorie. *Growing California Native Plants.* Berkeley: University of California Press, 1980. A handy guide for those interested in planting, growing, and otherwise supporting the success of California's beleaguered native plants.

Schoenherr, Allan A. *A Natural History of California.* Berkeley: University of California Press, 1992. With introductory chapters on ecology and geology, *A Natural History* covers California's climate, geology, soil, plant life, and animals based on distinct bioregions, with almost 300 photographs and numerous illustrations and tables. An exceptionally readable and well-illustrated introduction to California's astounding natural diversity and drama written by an ecology professor from CSU Fullerton, this 700-some-page reference belongs on any Californiac's library shelf.

Schoenherr, Allan A. and C. Robert Feldmeth. *A Natural History of the Islands of California.* Berkeley: University of California Press, 1999. A comprehensive introduction to California's Año Nuevo Island, Channel Islands, Farallon Islands, and the islands of San Francisco Bay—living evolutionary laboratories with unique species and ecological niches.

Starker, Leopold A. *The California Quail.* Berkeley: University of California Press, 1985. This is the definitive book on the California quail, its history, and its biology.

RECREATION

California Coastal Commission, State of California. *The California Coastal Access Guide.* Berkeley: University of California Press, 2003. Sixth revised edition. According to the *Oakland Tribune,* this is "no doubt the most comprehensive look at California's coastline published to date."

Emory, Jerry. *The Monterey Bay Shoreline Guide.* Berkeley: University of California Press (Monterey Bay Aquarium Series in Marine Conservation), 1999. A great guide to what to see and do.

Jeneid, Michael. *Adventure Kayaking: Trips from the Russian River to Monterey.* Berkeley: Wilderness Press, 1998. Tired of fighting that freeway traffic? Try a kayak. Under decent weather conditions—and with an experienced kayaker to clue you in—you can get just about everywhere. If you'll be shoving off a bit farther south, try *Adventure Kayaking: Trips from Big Sur to San Diego,* by Robert Mohle (1998).

Kirkendall, Tom, and Vicky Springs. *Bicycling the Pacific Coast.* Seattle: The Mountaineers, 1998. Third edition. A very good, very practical, mile-by-mile guide to the tricky business of cycling along the California coast (and north).

Lorentzen, Bob, and Richard Nichols. *Hiking the California Coastal Trail, Volume One: Oregon to Monterey.* Mendocino, CA: Bored Feet Publications, 2002. Second edition. The first comprehensive guide to the work-in-progress California Coastal Trail, America's newest and most diverse long-distance trail. Published in conjunction with Coastwalk—which receives a hefty percentage of the proceeds to support its efforts to complete the trail—this accessible guide describes 85 sections of the California Coastal Trail's northern reach. Keep an eye out, too, for *Hiking the California Coastal Trail, Volume Two: Monterey to Mexico.*

National Register of Historic Places. *Early History of the California Coast.* Washington, D.C.: National Conference of State Historic Preservation Officers, 1997. Map. This fold-out introduction to the California coast serves as a travel itinerary, with 45 stops illustrating the coast's earliest settlement and culture.

Schaffer, Jeffrey. *Hiking the Big Sur Country: The Ventana Wilderness.* Berkeley: Wilderness Press, 1988.

Soares, Marc J. *Best Coast Hikes of Northern California: A Guide to the Top Trails from Big Sur to the Oregon Border.* San Francisco: Sierra Club Books, 1998. There's something for everyone here: 75 scenic trails, organized north to south, suited for all skill levels (including mention of those that allow dogs). Also well worth it from Soares: *75 Year-Round Hikes in Northern California* and *100 Classic Hikes in Northern California,* the latter coauthored with John R. Soares.

Stevens, Barbara, and Nancy Conner. *Where on Earth: A Guide to Specialty Nurseries and Other Resources for California Gardeners.* Berkeley: Heyday Books, 1999. Fourth edition. Ever wondered where to get that unusual color of iris or that exotic azalea, or where to find the state's best native plant nurseries? Wonder no more. California gardeners won't be able to live for long without *this* essential resource.

Stienstra, Tom. *Foghorn Outdoors California Camping.* Emeryville, CA: Avalon Travel Publishing, 2005. 14th edition. This is undoubtedly the ultimate reference to California camping and campgrounds, public and private. Every single one is in here. In addition to a thorough practical introduction to the basics of California camping—and reviews of the latest high-tech gear for hiking and camping comfort and safety—this guidebook is meticulously organized by area, starting with the general subdivisions of Northern, Central, and Southern California. Even accidental outdoorspeople should carry this one along at all times.

Taber, Tom. *The Santa Cruz Mountains Trail Book.* Oak Valley Press, 2002. Ninth edition. Hey, trail-lovers—beachcombers, off-road bicyclists, equestrians, and hikers—this book will keep you busy, with more than 1,000 miles of trails weaving through some 153,000 acres of mountains, forests, and coastline. The most popular coastal access guide to the Santa Cruz County coast and area parks and trails.

Thomas Bros. (eds.) *Thomas Guide, Metropolitan Monterey Bay: Including Monterey, Santa Cruz & San Benito Counties (Metropolitan Monterey Bay Street Guide).* Irvine, CA: Thomas Bros. Maps. Issued annually. This is it, the definitive spiral-bound map book to the area—probably essential only if you plan to stay awhile.

Index

A

accommodations: Big Sur 94–96; Carmel 71–74; Marina 35, 36; Monterey 36–41; Moss Landing 157; Pacific Grove 56–58; Salinas 110–111; San Juan Bautista 115–116; Santa Cruz area 134–140; Seaside 35
Agricultural History Project: 159
agriculture: 11–12
agriculture-related art: 107, 111
airports/airlines: 169
Andrew Molera State Park: 14, 82, 86–87
antiques: 46, 79–80, 155
Aptos: 122, 139–140, 144–145
arboretums: *see* botanic gardens
architecture: 15–16, 26–29, 107
Arroyo Seco: 110
art, agricultural: 107, 111
art galleries: 80, 88
artichokes: 11–12, 157–158
Asilomar: 50, 53, 56
astronomical observatory: 116
AT&T Pebble Beach National Pro Am Golf Tournament: 55

B

ballet: 146
banana slugs: 130

beachcombing: 33
bed-and-breakfasts: Carmel 71–72; Monterey 40–41; Moss Landing 157; Pacific Grove 57–58; Salinas 111; Santa Cruz 137–138
Ben Lomond: 138, 143
Ben Lomond County Park: 155
Berry Creek Falls: 153
Big Basin Redwoods State Park: 6, 14, 120, 134–135, 152–154
Big Sur: 10, 81–98, 162–163
Big Sur International Marathon (BSIM): 83
biking: 32–33, 47, 98, 150
Bird Rock: 54
birds/birdwatching: general information 8; Big Sur 90; Carmel 63, 69; Moss Landing 156–157; Pacific Grove 53; Santa Cruz 152
Bixby Creek Bridge: 86
boardwalks: 14, 120, 123–124
boating: 33, 133
Bonfante Gardens: 14, 106, 118
bookstores: 46, 148
Boronda Adobe: 107
Boston Store: 28–29, 46
botanic gardens: 14, 63, 103, 106, 118
Boulder Creek: 143
Boulder Creek Park: 155
brown pelicans: 8, 69, 165

Beaches

Asilomar State Beach: 32, 53
Bonny Doon Beach: 132
Carmel River State Beach: 32, 63
Cowell Beach: 131
Davenport Beach: 132
Del Monte Beach: 36
Fanshell Beach: 54
Jetty State Beach: 159
Lighthouse Field State Beach: 128, 131
Manresa State Beach: 159
Middle Beach: 63, 65
Monastery Beach: 63, 65, 69
Monterey Beach: 32
Moss Landing State Beach: 157
Natural Bridges State Beach: 7, 131

New Brighton State Beach: 132, 134
Palm Beach: 159
Pebble Beach: 54–55
Pfeiffer Beach: 87–88, 93
Red White and Blue Beach: 132
Rio del Mar State Beach: 132
Salinas River State Beach: 159
Santa Cruz Beach: 131
Santa Cruz Beach Boardwalk: 14, 120, 123–124
Seacliff State Beach: 132, 134
Sunset State Beach: 159
26th Street Beach: 132
Twin Creek Beach: 101
Twin Lakes State Beach: 132
Zmudowski State Beach: 159

Nature Reserves

U.S.~Metric Conversion

1 inch	=	2.54 centimeters (cm)
1 foot	=	.304 meters (m)
1 yard	=	0.914 meters
1 mile	=	1.6093 kilometers (km)
1 km	=	.6214 miles
1 fathom	=	1.8288 m
1 chain	=	20.1168 m
1 furlong	=	201.168 m
1 acre	=	.4047 hectares
1 sq km	=	100 hectares
1 sq mile	=	2.59 square km
1 ounce	=	28.35 grams
1 pound	=	.4536 kilograms
1 short ton	=	.90718 metric ton
1 short ton	=	2000 pounds
1 long ton	=	1.016 metric tons
1 long ton	=	2240 pounds
1 metric ton	=	1000 kilograms
1 quart	=	.94635 liters
1 US gallon	=	3.7854 liters
1 Imperial gallon	=	4.5459 liters
1 nautical mile	=	1.852 km

To compute Celsius temperatures, subtract 32 from Fahrenheit and divide by 1.8. To go the other way, multiply Celsius by 1.8 and add 32.

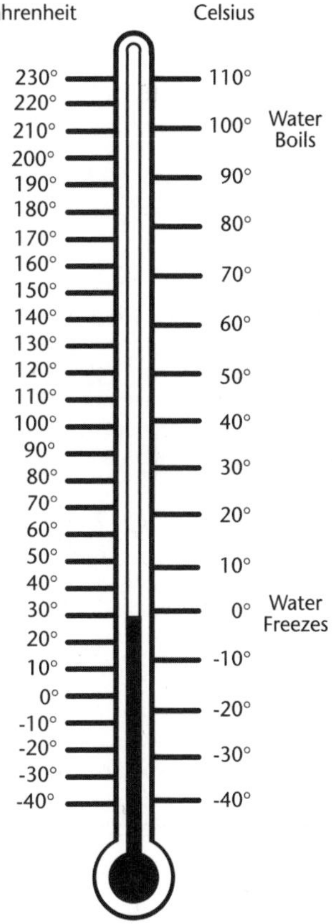

Fahrenheit   Celsius

230° — 110°
220°
210° — 100° Water Boils
200°
190° — 90°
180°
170° — 80°
160°
150° — 70°
140°
130° — 60°
120°
110° — 50°
100° — 40°
90°
80° — 30°
70°
60° — 20°
50°
40° — 10°
30°
20° — 0° Water Freezes
10°
0° — -10°
-10°
-20° — -20°
-30°
-40° — -30°
         -40°

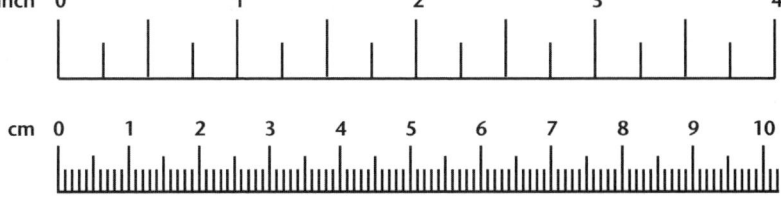

inch 0   1   2   3   4

cm 0 1 2 3 4 5 6 7 8 9 10

Keeping Current

Although we strive to produce the most up-to-date guidebook humanly possible, change is unavoidable. Between the time this book goes to print and the moment you read it, a handful of the businesses noted in these pages will undoubtedly change prices, move, or even close their doors forever. Other worthy attractions will open for the first time. If you have a favorite gem you'd like to see included in the next edition, or see anything that needs updating, clarification, or correction, please drop us a line. Send your comments via email to atpfeedback@avalonpub.com, or use the address below.

Moon Handbooks Monterey & Carmel
Avalon Travel Publishing
1400 65th Street, Suite 250
Emeryville, CA 94608, USA
www.moon.com

Editor: Ellen Cavalli
Series Manager: Kevin McLain
Acquisitions Manager: Rebecca K. Browning
Copy Editor: Mia Lipman
Graphics and Production Coordinator: Justin Marler
Cover Designer: Kari Gim
Interior Designer: Amber Pirker
Map Editors: Kevin Anglin, Olivia Solís
Cartographers: Kat Smith, Kat Kalamaras, Mike Morgenfeld, Annett Olson, Bart Wright
Proofreader: Sabrina Young
Indexer: Judy Hunt

ISBN: 1-56691-903-7
ISSN: 1539-9656

Printing History
1st Edition—2002
2nd Edition—May 2005
5 4 3 2 1

Avalon Travel Publishing is a division of Avalon Publishing Group, Inc.